Case Studies in Special Education and Additional Learning Needs

SPECIAL EDUCATION LAW, POLICY, AND PRACTICE

Series Editors
Mitchell L. Yell, PhD, University of South Carolina
David F. Bateman, PhD, Special Education Consultant

The *Special Education Law, Policy, and Practice* series highlights current trends and legal issues in the education of students with disabilities. The books in this series link legal requirements, evidence-based instruction, and practical applications for working with students with disabilities. The titles are designed to be textbooks for general education and special education preservice education programs and also for practicing teachers, administrators, principals, school counselors, school psychologists, parents, and others interested in improving the lives of students. The series is committed to research-based practices to provide appropriate and meaningful educational programming for students with disabilities and their families.

Titles in Series

Sexuality Education for Students with Disabilities by T. C. Gibbon, E. A. Harkins Monaco, and D. F. Bateman

Developing Educationally Meaningful and Legally Sound IEPs by M. L. Yell, D. F. Bateman, and J. G. Shriner

Creating Positive Elementary Classrooms: Preventing Behavior Challenges to Promote Learning by S. Smith and M. L. Yell

Service Animals in Schools: Legal, Educational, Administrative, and Strategic Handling Aspects by A. O. Papalia, K. B. Ewoldt, and D. F. Bateman

Evidence-Based Practices for Supporting Individuals with Autism Spectrum Disorder edited by L. C. Chezan, K. Wolfe, and E. Drasgow

Special Education Law Annual Review 2021 by D. F. Bateman, M. L. Yell, and K. P. Brady

Dispute Resolution Under the IDEA: Understanding, Avoiding, and Managing Special Education Disputes by D. F. Bateman, M. L. Yell, and J. S Dorego

Advocating for the Common Good: People, Politics, Process, and Policy on Capitol Hill by J. E. West

Related Services in Special Education: Working Together as a Team
by L. Goran and D. F. Bateman

The Essentials of Special Education Advocacy by A. M. Markelz,
S. A. Nagro, K. Monnin, and D. F. Bateman

Disability and Motor Behavior: A Handbook of Research
by A. S. Brian and P. S. Haibach-Beach

Supporting and Accommodating Students with Special Health Care Needs
by A. D. S. Angelov and M. Rattermann

*You're Hired! Practical Strategies for Guiding Individuals with
Autism Spectrum Disorder to Competitive Employment*
by P. S. Arter, T. B. H. Brown, and J. Barna

Unraveling Dyslexia: A Guide for Teachers and Families by K. L. Sayeski

*Disability, Intersectionality, and Belonging in Special Education:
Socioculturally Sustaining Practices* by E. A. Harkins Monaco, L. L.
Stansberry Brusnahan, M. C. Fuller, and M. Odima Jr.

*The Educator's Guide to Action Research: Practical Connections for
Implementation of Data-Driven Decision-Making*
by M. E. Little, D. D. Slanda, and E. Cramer

The Essentials of Special Education Research by A. M. Markelz and B. Riden

*The Classroom Teacher's Guide to Special Education: Essential Knowledge,
Skills, and Dispositions* by D. D. Slanda, L. Pike, and M. E. Little

The Essentials of Special Education Law, Second Edition
by A. M. Markelz and D. F. Bateman

Disability and Motor Behavior: Practical Applications
by A. S. Brian and P. S. Haibach-Beach

Case Studies in Special Education and Additional Learning Needs
by M. A. Houser, T. S. Guerriero and C. E. Commisso

For a full list of books in this series, visit https://www.bloomsbury.com/us/series/special-education-law-policy-and-practice

Case Studies in Special Education and Additional Learning Needs

Mary A. Houser
Tara S. Guerriero
Colleen E. Commisso

BLOOMSBURY ACADEMIC
NEW YORK • LONDON • OXFORD • NEW DELHI • SYDNEY

BLOOMSBURY ACADEMIC
Bloomsbury Publishing Inc, 1359 Broadway, New York, NY 10018, USA
Bloomsbury Publishing Plc, 50 Bedford Square, London, WC1B 3DP, UK
Bloomsbury Publishing Ireland, 29 Earlsfort Terrace, Dublin 2, D02 AY28, Ireland

BLOOMSBURY, BLOOMSBURY ACADEMIC and the Diana logo are
trademarks of Bloomsbury Publishing Plc

First published in the United States of America 2026

Copyright © Mary A. Houser, Tara S. Guerriero, and Colleen E. Commisso, 2026

Cover design by Sally Rinehart
Cover image © iStock.com/majivecka

All rights reserved. No part of this publication may be: i) reproduced or transmitted in any form, electronic or mechanical, including photocopying, recording or by means of any information storage or retrieval system without prior permission in writing from the publishers; or ii) used or reproduced in any way for the training, development or operation of artificial intelligence (AI) technologies, including generative AI technologies. The rights holders expressly reserve this publication from the text and data mining exception as per Article 4(3) of the Digital Single Market Directive (EU) 2019/790.

Bloomsbury Publishing Inc does not have any control over, or responsibility for, any third-party websites referred to or in this book. All internet addresses given in this book were correct at the time of going to press. The author and publisher regret any inconvenience caused if addresses have changed or sites have ceased to exist, but can accept no responsibility for any such changes.

Library of Congress Cataloging-in-Publication Data is available

ISBN:	HB:	979-8-216-39689-5
	PB:	979-8-216-39688-8
	ePDF:	979-8-216-39691-8
	eBook:	979-8-216-39690-1

Typeset by Integra Software Services Pvt. Ltd.
Printed and bound in the United States of America

For product safety related questions contact productsafety@bloomsbury.com.

To find out more about our authors and books visit www.bloomsbury.com
and sign up for our newsletters.

Contents

Preface xi
Acknowledgment of Additional Contributors xiv
General Acknowledgments xv
Characteristics Matrix xvii
Crosswalk Table xxi

Part I Case Studies by Disability and Additional Learning Need Categories

Introduction to Part I 1

1 Assistive Technology 3
Assistive Technology #1 4
Assistive Technology #2 9

2 Attention Deficit Hyperactivity Disorder 15

3 Autism Spectrum Disorder 21
Autism Spectrum Disorder #1 22
Autism Spectrum Disorder #2 25

4 Culturally and Linguistically Diverse Exceptional Learners 31

5 Developmental Delay 37

6 Emotional Disturbance 45
Emotional Disturbance #1 46
Emotional Disturbance #2 50

7 Gifted and Talented 53

8 Intellectual Disability 59

9 Learning Disability 65

10 Multiple Disabilities 71
Multiple Disabilities #1 72
Multiple Disabilities #2 75

11 Other Health Impairment: Epilepsy 81

12 Orthopedic Impairment: Cerebral Palsy 87

13 Sensory Impairments 93
Sensory Impairments: Deafness 94
Sensory Impairments: Deaf-Blindness 98
Sensory Impairments: Hearing Impairment 104
Sensory Impairments: Visual Impairment 107

14 Speech or Language Impairment 115

15 Trauma-Informed Practice 121
Trauma-Informed Practice #1 122
Trauma-Informed Practice #2 127

16 Traumatic Brain Injury 131

Part II Case Studies by Special Education Topic

Introduction to Part II 139

17 Laws 141
Introduction to Laws Related to Disability and Additional Learning Needs 141
Every Student Succeeds Act (ESSA) and State Testing Requirements 142
Family Educational Rights and Privacy Act (FERPA) 145
Individuals with Disabilities Education Act (IDEA) 149
    Addressing Procedural Safeguards and Manifestation Determination 149
    Dispute Resolution: Mediation and Due Process 155
    Least Restrictive Environment and Team Decision Making 169
Section 504 of the Rehabilitation Act of 1973 173

18 Individualized Education Programs (IEPs) 181
Annual Goals, Present Levels, and Progress Monitoring 183
Case Management 186
IEP Meetings 191
    IEP Meeting #1: First-Year Teacher 191
    IEP Meeting #2: Veteran Teacher 197
Specially Designed Instruction (SDI) 203
    Specially Designed Instruction #1 203
    Specially Designed Instruction #2 210
Transition (Secondary) 216

19 Early Intervention (EI) and Individualized Family Service Plans (IFSPs) 223
Diagnostic Process 224
Early Childhood Special Education Service Delivery 231
Family Response to a Disability Diagnosis 237

20 Collaboration and Inclusive Practices 245
    Co-Teaching and Consultation 246
    Home-School Collaboration 255
    Paraprofessionals 261
    Teaching Across Student Populations 267

Index 274
About the Authors 286

Preface

Case Studies in Special Education and Additional Learning Needs is a practitioner- and learner-friendly supplemental book written to assist in the understanding of foundational/introductory topics in special education and other learning needs. The purpose of this book is to provide case studies depicting real-world situations and examples to highlight some of the most critical aspects of educating students with exceptional learning needs, which will assist in developing the knowledge and skills required of a highly effective educator. There are forty-four case studies that allow the reader to gain a deeper understanding of disability, other learning needs, and significant foundational theory and concepts in special education. The case studies also examine best practices in education while, at times, reflect challenges that might be encountered in the classroom or in the life of a student with special learning needs. This book benefits teacher preparation faculty (special education and general education) in their instruction of undergraduate and graduate students. It helps to expand undergraduate and graduate students' knowledge base of introductory topics in special education. Additionally, PK–12 school administrators, teachers, and specialists might benefit from using this book as part of their professional development.

There are two parts in this book: Part I: "Case Studies by Disability and Additional Learning Need Categories" and Part II: "Case Studies by Special Education Topic." Part I is comprised of case studies showcasing various disability categories recognized in the United States in children who receive special education services under the Individuals with Disabilities Education Act (IDEA) and/or Section 504. Further, it includes case studies that reflect additional learning needs that children might encounter. Examples of disabilities include autism spectrum disorder, developmental delay, emotional disturbance, intellectual disability, learning disability, multiple disabilities, orthopedic impairment, other health impairments, sensory impairments, and traumatic brain injury. Students who have experienced trauma, students with language differences, students who use assistive technology, and gifted and talented students are also featured in this part of the book. The case studies in part I cover a range of topics related to exceptional learning needs (e.g., the possible causes of their disability, family involvement and home life, and their school life as a student with a particular disability). Part II of this book consists of case studies depicting different processes and procedures related to core special education topics. They include scenarios related to law, Individualized Education Program (IEP) development and meetings, early intervention, and communication and collaboration. These are relevant because current teachers and future teachers must be cognizant of issues related to legal compliance, students' and parents' rights, obtaining appropriate services, and accountability and documentation. The case studies in part I and part II may be used independently of each other or in conjunction with each other. In some instances, the case studies in part II feature a specific student described in part I or refer to students(s) in part I through the part II comprehension questions.

The case studies in this book are written from a variety of perspectives and voices (e.g., narrator, child, parent, teacher). The names and the scenarios in this book are fictional, and the case studies are not intended to be representative of all situations or scenarios related to their topic.

In addition to a detailed table of contents, this book includes the following two resources that will assist in navigating the book and its contents:

- **Characteristics Matrix:** The Characteristics Matrix (located following the "General Acknowledgments") allows the reader to easily locate a desired case study by disability/additional learning need category, gender, grade band, educational placement, geographic location (urban, suburban, or rural), and parental structure.
- **Crosswalk Table:** The Crosswalk Table (located following the Characteristics Matrix) indicates which students from part I are included in part II, as well as in which part II case studies they are included. The purpose of this table is to provide continuity between parts I and II as well as to assist with the connections between disability and special education concept. Additionally, it could help with planning and preparation when teaching these concepts.

Each case study in *Case Studies in Special Education and Additional Learning Needs* includes comprehension questions that address the content of each case study to assess the learner's understanding. *Some questions may require additional knowledge (not provided in the case study) that is typical of the scope of a foundational/introductory special education class; therefore, outside investigation might be required for some of the questions.* They also feature challenge question(s) to evaluate students' critical thinking skills and extend their learning on a topic related to the case study.

Teacher preparation faculty (special education and general education) can closely align the content they are teaching to the case studies in this book. Additionally, they could use this book as a supplement to enrich student learning through learning activities. To illustrate, an instructor could assign a project in which students select several case studies of interest and respond to the questions that follow each case study.

Acknowledgment of Additional Contributors

One of the unique aspects of this book is the collective body of special education professionals from West Chester University who contributed their time and knowledge through the creation of some of these valuable case studies. Their individual perspectives provide the reader with different viewpoints from which to learn about those with disabilities, additional learning needs, and topics related to special education. We want to acknowledge the following contributing authors of *Case Studies in Special Education and Additional Learning Needs*:

Alyssa Blasko, PhD, BCBA
Ashlee M. Brown, PhD, BCBA, LBS
Dawn R. Patterson, EdD
Lesley N. Siegel, PhD
Brittany Severino, EdD

General Acknowledgments

Writing a book can involve the contributions of many people in various ways. We are truly thankful to those who participated in this endeavor by making it possible. First and foremost, we would like to thank our families. Because of your support, we were able to take the necessary time and effort to complete this book. We recognize the sacrifices you made for us along the way and are indebted to you. You mean everything to us.

To our individual mentors, of which there are several, thank you for your wisdom, guidance, and expertise in making us the professionals we are today. Without you, we would not be able to accurately and effectively take this deep dive into the important content we share throughout this book.

To West Chester University, thank you for being an outstanding place to work and for always putting our students first. We are appreciative that by working together as special education professionals, we have had the opportunity to share our thoughts and write together about what is truly important for teacher preparation students to know about disabilities and additional learning needs.

Lastly, thank you to those who use this book as a supplemental text or guide for your teacher preparation students (special education or regular education) or staff. It is through our shared knowledge and experiences that we continue to support individuals with disabilities and additional learning needs to help them to reach their potential.

Characteristics Matrix

The **Characteristics Matrix** provides the demographics of the individuals depicted in the part I case studies. The demographics include disability/additional learning need category, gender, grade band, educational placement, geographic location (urban, suburban, or rural), and parental structure. The purpose for including this matrix is to give the reader an understanding of the variety of demographics that they might encounter in an educational setting.

Table The Characteristics Matrix

Disability or Additional Learning Need	Gender	Grade Band			Educational Placement			Geographic Location			Family Structure			
											Parents/Guardians			
		EI/PK-5th	6th-8th	9th-12th+	Inclusive Classroom Full/Partial	Special Ed. Classroom Full-Time	Separate School Full-Time	Urban	Suburban	Rural	One Parent	Two Parents	Three+ Parents	Siblings
Assistive Technology (#1)	M			X		X		X				X		X
Assistive Technology (#2)	F	X			X				X			X		X
Attention Deficit Hyperactivity Disorder	M		X		X				X			X		
Autism Spectrum Disorder (#1)	M			X	X				X			X		X
Autism Spectrum Disorder (#2)	M	X				X				X	X			
Culturally and Linguistically Diverse Exceptional Learners	M	X			X				X			X		
Developmental Delay	M	X			X					X		X		
Emotional Disturbance (#1)	M	X			X				X			X		X
Emotional Disturbance (#2)	F		X			X		X			X			X
Gifted and Talented	F	X			X				X			X		X

Category	Sex													
Intellectual Disability	M		X		X		X				X			X
Learning Disability	F		X		X						X			X
Multiple Disabilities (#1)	M	X							X					X
Multiple Disabilities (#2)	F			X		X		X	X		X			X
Other Health Impairment	F	X		X			X				X			X
Orthopedic Impairment	M		X		X		X				X			
Sensory Impairments: Deafness	M			X	X					X				
Sensory Impairments: Deaf-Blindness	F		X			X	X		X				X	
Sensory Impairments: Hearing impairment	F		X		X			X			X		X	X
Sensory Impairments: Visual Impairment	M				X	X					X			X
Speech or Language Impairment	F		X		X		X	X			X			X
Trauma Informed (#1)	M		X		X		X						X	X
Trauma Informed (#2)	F			X		X							X	X
Traumatic Brain Injury	F		X		X			X			X			

Crosswalk Table

The **Crosswalk Table** indicates which students from part I are included in part II, as well as in which part II case studies they are included. The purpose of this table is to provide continuity between parts I and II as well as to assist with the connections between disability and special education concept. Additionally, it could help with planning and preparation when teaching these concepts. The students' appearance in part II has been categorized by whether they are included as the subject of the case study or within a question at the end of the case study.

Table The Crosswalk Table

Disability or Additional Learning Need	Student's Name	Appears in Part II	How the Student Appears in Part II		Part II Case Study
			Subject of Case Study	Appears in Questions	
Assistive Technology (#1)	Darius	X		X	Least Restrictive Environment and Team Decision Making
Assistive Technology (#2)	Chaya	X			
Attention Deficit Hyperactivity Disorder	Aaron	X		X	Every Student Succeeds Act (ESSA) and State Testing
Autism Spectrum Disorder (#1)	Rahul	X	X	X	IEP Meeting #2: Veteran Teacher Transition (Secondary) Home-School Collaboration
Autism Spectrum Disorder (#2)	Trevor	X	X		Addressing Procedural Safeguards and Manifestation Determination
Culturally and Linguistically Diverse Exceptional Learners	Mateo	X	X		Teaching Across Student Populations
Developmental Delay	Hao	X		X	Family Response to a Disability Diagnosis
Emotional Disturbance (#1)	Matthew (Matt)	X	X		Specially Designed Instruction (SDI) #2
Emotional Disturbance (#2)	Sarah Johnson	X	X		Paraprofessionals
Gifted and Talented	Gabriella	X			
Intellectual Disability	Tyrese	X	X		Diagnostic Process
Learning Disability	Anna	X	X		Specially Designed Instruction (SDI) #1
Multiple Disabilities (#1)	Markeith	X	X		IEP Meeting #1: First-Year Teacher

Multiple Disabilities (#2)	Mahsumah	X	Every Student Succeeds Act (ESSA) and State Testing
Other Health Impairment	Alexandra (Alex)	X	Transition (Secondary) Home-School Collaboration
Orthopedic Impairment	Michael	X	Early Childhood Special Education Service Delivery Family Response to a Disability Diagnosis
Sensory Impairments: Deafness	Jackson		
Sensory Impairments: Deaf-Blindness	Allie	X	Least Restrictive Environment and Team Decision Making
Sensory Impairments: Hearing Impairment	Gia	X	Section 504 Plans/Service Agreements
Sensory Impairments: Visual Impairment	Max	X	Section 504 Plans/Service Agreements
Speech or Language Impairment	Sara Reader	X	Every Student Succeeds Act (ESSA) and State Testing
Trauma Informed (#1)	Jonathan	X	Family Education Rights and Privacy Act (FERPA)
Trauma Informed (#2)	Eva		
Traumatic Brain Injury	Lauren	X	Least Restrictive Environment and Team Decision Making

Part I

Case Studies by Disability and Additional Learning Need Categories

Introduction to Part I

Would it help you to better understand disabilities and additional learning needs if you could envision it through real-life scenarios of students in the classroom and/or in their home lives? Part I of this book gives insight into students who possess a disability or additional learning need that is present in today's schools. Each disability or other learning need covered begins with a brief description or overview and is followed by one or more case studies depicting an authentic narrative as well as student demographic information.

The following are the disabilities and additional learning needs featured in this section of the book:

Table Part I.1 Disabilities and Additional Learning Needs

Assistive Technology	Developmental Delay
Attention Deficit Hyperactivity Disorder	Emotional Disturbance
Autism Spectrum Disorder	Gifted and Talented
Culturally and Linguistically Diverse Exceptional Learners	Intellectual Disability
	Learning Disability

Multiple Disabilities	Sensory Impairments: Visual Impairment
Other Health Impairment: Epilepsy	
Orthopedic Impairment: Cerebral Palsy	Speech or Language Impairments
Sensory Impairments: Deaf-Blindness	Trauma-Informed Practice
Sensory Impairments: Deafness	Traumatic Brain Injury

Why are case studies depicting disability categories and additional learning needs important and helpful? All too often, when teacher preparation students are learning about these various disabilities and related learning needs in their university coursework, it might be hard to visualize all the content in reality, particularly at the foundational/introductory level. As such, this can leave the teacher preparation students wanting more tangible knowledge and engagement with these topics. A priority of this part of the book is to provide extra knowledge and engagement with this subject matter and allow a more personal view of how students with these specific learning needs can appear in a school setting or at home.

As mentioned in the preface, the case studies are written from a variety of perspectives and voices (e.g., narrator, child, parent, teacher). Please note that the language used in some of the case studies that are written from the perspective of the child may not fully reflect the language capabilities of the child in the case study. The language that was used was chosen so that the reader could fully understand the child's thoughts and characteristics.

Part I lays the groundwork and helps develop an understanding of exceptional populations for the processes and procedures discussed in part II of this book. By better understanding the various disabilities and additional learning needs PK–12 students might have, the reader will have the necessary context from which to refer and interpret the case studies more fully.

1

Assistive Technology

Mary A. Houser, EdD

Assistive technology (AT) is defined as "products, equipment, and systems that enhance learning, working, and daily living for persons with disabilities" (ATIA, 2025, para. 2). Students with disabilities benefit from AT in a wide variety of ways. One of the greatest benefits of AT is that it allows students with disabilities to be included in a wide variety of functional, educational, and social opportunities they might not have previously been able to without it. In essence, AT helps to remove many of the barriers caused by their disabilities that inhibit their participation.

AT is classified based on the level of technology incorporated into the tool. AT can be no-tech (e.g., body language and gestures); low-tech (e.g., picture exchange communication systems [traveling binder that accompanies a student], writing implements), mid-tech (e.g., screen magnifier), or high-tech (e.g., voice output devices). Devices that are no-tech and low-tech do not include electronics or electricity. Currently, low-tech AT is the most used type of AT in schools, followed by high-tech AT (Autism Adventures, 2025). Low-tech AT devices do not require a lot of training and are easily accessible. Devices that are mid-tech and high-tech are often battery-operated and/or include software. Other examples of AT include visual schedules, pencil grips, slant boards, braille translation software, adapted switches, voice amplification, electric wheelchairs, augmentative and alternative communication (AAC) devices, Smartboards, and speech-to-text devices. There are different ways AT can be funded for school-age students. These funding sources include school systems, government, and private health insurance (ATIA, 2025).

If the IEP (individualized education program) team deems it is necessary, a child may have their AT device with them at all times, including both at home and at school.

Assistive Technology (AT) #1

Table 1.1 Student Demographics

Student Name	Darius Walker
Gender	Male
Grade	9
Educational Placement	Full-time multiple disabilities support (MDS) special education classroom
Geographic Location	Urban
Parent/Siblings	**Parents:** Two parents (Mr. and Mrs. Walker) **Siblings:** Two sisters
School	East City High School
LEA	Brooklyn Area School District
Academic Profile	**Reading:** Well below grade level **Writing:** Well below grade level **Mathematics:** Well below grade level

Who Is Darius?

Darius is a friendly fifteen-year-old boy who lives in an urban setting with both of his parents and his two younger sisters. They are a close-knit family who enjoy spending free time together at a local park, attending sporting events, and going to church on Sundays. Darius also has grandparents who live down the street from him, with whom he spends time regularly. Darius enjoys NASCAR, hip-hop music, and paralympic sports. His best friend is Naomi. She is his next-door neighbor.

Medical and Health-Related History

Darius has been experiencing medical problems from an early age. By the time he turned two years old, Darius was diagnosed with spastic cerebral palsy (CP). Doctors noticed that his muscle tone was not typical; he had difficulties sitting and rolling over; and he was not able to grasp objects easily, indicating fine motor challenges. He drooled a lot and had stiff joints. Darius also failed his newborn hearing screening, and follow-up tests were performed, including the ABR (auditory brainstem response) test and the OAE (otoacoustic emissions) test. Results indicated that Darius had a severe hearing loss. Darius struggles with understanding speech, engaging in conversations, and is always asking others to repeat themselves due to his hearing loss. Darius tries to lip-read or use visual cues to better understand, but he is often unsuccessful. He has the most difficulty understanding speech when the environment is loud or overstimulating. Furthermore, Darius has cognitive impairments resulting from his CP and has been diagnosed with a moderate intellectual disability (ID). His cognitive deficits have caused difficulties with problem-solving, expressing emotions, and delayed motor skills. All of these challenges have impacted Darius's educational performance and growth at school.

At School

Darius began receiving early intervention services when he was a toddler and has continued to receive special education services since this time. He is now in the ninth grade and receives special education services at a local urban high school due to his multiple disabilities. East City High School serves grades 9–12 and has an enrollment of approximately three thousand students. Roughly 92 percent of the students are minority students, and 85 percent of the students are considered economically disadvantaged. The school includes children from many single-parent families. The administration has challenges with hiring quality teachers. There is a high rate of student absenteeism and student pregnancy. East City High School also has significant problems with classroom management and discipline. Although there are dedicated special education teachers, the school lacks resources such as updated textbooks and technology, which would strengthen their programs and enhance their students' learning.

Darius attends an MDS (multiple disabilities support) self-contained classroom with seven other students with significant support needs for most of his school day. His learning activities center around acquiring daily living skills he will need to be as independent as possible when he gets older. Darius and his classmates are learning things such as performing personal hygiene, cooking small meals, taking transportation, and budgeting money. Darius also participates in inclusive general education classrooms for music and art and attends lunch with his neurotypical peers. Darius receives specific therapies that are helping with his development. He currently receives speech and language therapy, physical therapy, and occupational therapy in addition to his specially designed instruction.

Strengths and Challenges

As a result of Darius's CP, hearing impairment, and ID, his strengths and challenges are vast. As indicated, Darius loves being around other students his age and has a strong desire to make friends. His desire to make friends, however, has been impacted by his hearing loss. Sometimes, he cannot hear what others are saying to him. This has been particularly upsetting to him. His teacher is aware of the negative impact of his hearing loss and how much this bothers him. Recently, when Darius stepped out of the classroom for a few minutes, she let the other students in the class know that they should be speaking more loudly when conversing with him and to be sure that he can see their faces when they are talking to him to help him lip-read, as needed.

Darius's academic skills fall well below grade level. He is several years behind in all his academic subjects, which is often indicative of someone who has an intellectual disability. To illustrate, he has difficulty sounding out words, has deficits in reading comprehension skills, and is a weak speller. In addition, Darius has a hard time remembering math facts or applying mathematical reasoning when asked to do so.

As a teenager, Darius wants to be active and participate in all the physical activities his classmates are doing. He loves the idea of being on a team! His CP significantly impacts his mobility, however, as he experiences jerky movements and has an awkward gait as he walks. This affects his balance and ability to physically engage with others. In class, Darius has demonstrated some recent strengths in creative writing, and his teachers are excited about his interest in expressing himself. His fine motor skills are weak, though, and he often complains that his hand gets tired when completing his written assignments. His teacher is concerned this will affect his desire to complete his work and express himself.

Darius's Support Needs and the Benefits of AT

Due to his CP, severe hearing loss, and ID, Darius has high support needs. Having high support needs means that he requires significantly more assistance to achieve activities of daily living than the average person. Because of this, Darius uses several types of AT to support his learning. The purpose of Darius's AT is to help him improve his functional capabilities both in and out of school. Although Darius requires AT, because he attends a school in a low-income school district, it has been a struggle for his school to obtain the necessary supports for him. Depending on the level of technology involved, AT devices and supports can be costly. As a result, Darius's district had to participate in a state-level AT loan program as well as seek assistance from a few nonprofit organizations to meet his needs.

AT has been a game changer for Darius. Without it, his life would not be nearly as enjoyable or active as it is. When he was in elementary school, Darius received an initial assistive technology assessment to determine the different types of AT he could benefit from. The assistive technology team consisted of Darius, his parents, a special education classroom teacher, a school psychologist, a speech and language pathologist, an occupational therapist, a physical therapist, and a family physician. The SETT (student, environment, tasks, tools) framework was completed to determine what AT would be best for him. This framework examines the *student*, his *environment*, the *tasks* he needs to complete, and the *tools* that he can effectively use to complete his tasks. Darius's needs are reassessed regularly to ensure his AT is appropriate for him as he continues to build skills and outgrow some of his AT.

Darius's AT Devices/Tools

The following are examples of AT Darius currently uses both at home and at school:

1 **Hearing:** *Cochlear Implant: high-tech*
    As stated, Darius's hearing loss was identified during his infancy. At the age of two, Darius's audiologist recommended he get a cochlear

implant. The goal of a cochlear implant is to improve his hearing. It also helps with Darius's ability to both listen and talk. The cochlear implant is composed of two distinct parts: (1) the external sound processor and (2) an implant that is placed under the skin and attached to an electrode array in the inner ear. These parts work together, bypassing the ineffective part of the ear and sending sound directly to the hearing nerve.

2 **Communication:** *Augmentative and Alternative Communication (AAC) device: high-tech*

Darius has an iPad and has become quite adept at using it over the past few years. Currently, his iPad is loaded with the Voice4U app. Voice4U is a picture-based communication app that comes with 180 preprogrammed images and allows him to add pictures and voice. Having this communication app allows him to both lead and participate in conversations with his peers and adults. This has truly helped him be more social both in and out of school. Darius also uses this AAC device when he participates in activities in the community, such as going grocery shopping, going out to eat, and riding the city bus.

3 **Mobility:** *Posterior Walker: low-tech*

Due to his limited mobility, Darius uses a posterior walker to help him get around. A posterior walker is an AT device that helps improve ambulation. Posterior walkers are generally three-sided, and the back of the frame is behind the person. The open front allows the user to pull the walker by grasping the sides. This makes it particularly effective for balance support and walking support.

4 **Adaptive Writing:** *Pencil Grips and Slant Boards: low-tech*

The AT team also wanted to address the issues Darius was having concerning his fine motor issues associated with finger movement and strength. As such, the team determined that he would benefit from a pencil grip and a slanted writing board. A pencil grip is designed to strengthen students' fine motor skills and hand strength. This will help improve Darius's handwriting. The slanted writing board helps to align the hand and the forearm, which reduces strain and aids in proper hand posture. This helps to keep his muscles relaxed and properly aligned when writing.

Questions:

1. Define assistive technology (AT).
2. How would you describe Darius as a person?
3. What disabilities does Darius have? What type of special education classroom does he currently attend? Is he included with his neurotypical peers? If so, in what capacity?
4. Discuss Darius's strengths and challenges.
5. What is the purpose of an AT assessment? Who are the members of Darius's AT assessment team?
6. What is the SETT framework? What does the acronym SETT stand for? Why do you think this type of assessment is important?
7. Discuss the different types of AT that Darius is currently using. Are they low-tech, mid-tech, or high-tech? Explain.

Challenge: Select one of the Individuals with Disabilities Education Act (IDEA) disability categories (e.g., autism, specific learning disabilities, emotional and behavioral disorders, etc.). Lead a class discussion about the various types of AT that students with this disability might benefit from and why.

Assistive Technology (AT) #2

Table 1.2 Student Demographics

Student Name	Chaya Williams
Gender	Female
Grade	Kindergarten
Educational Placement	Inclusive general education classroom
Geographic Location	Suburban
Parent/Siblings	**Parents:** Two parents (Charlotte and James Williams)
	Siblings: Terrell (age 7); and Laticia (age 2)
School	Morris Elementary School
LEA	Miller Area School District
Academic Profile	**Reading:** Below grade level
	Writing: Below grade level
	Mathematics: On grade level

Who Is Chaya?

Chaya is a bright, six-year-old, African American girl with an autism spectrum disorder (ASD) who is starting kindergarten in Mr. Simmons's and Mrs. Reynold's inclusive general education classroom this year. This means she will be in a general education classroom that serves both general education students and students with disabilities. Chaya made significant progress in her early intervention (EI) program before coming to Morris Elementary School, a suburban school, and was recommended to attend an inclusive general education class for kindergarten. The focus of her EI program was on speech and language therapy, social skills instruction, family training, and behavioral and emotional regulation.

Caseload Description and Teamwork

Mr. Simmons and Mrs. Reynolds have a vibrant kindergarten class at Morris Elementary School. Mr. Simmons is a general education teacher, and Mrs. Reynolds is a special education teacher. Together, they have a caseload of twenty-two students in their classroom. There are seventeen students without disabilities and five students who have disabilities in the class. The students with disabilities have varying disabilities such as learning disabilities, attention deficit hyperactivity disorder (ADHD), and autism spectrum disorder (ASD). Each of them requires different modifications and accommodations to be successful in an inclusive general education classroom. The students with learning disabilities benefit from extra time to complete activities and visual aids. The student with ADHD has special seating, scheduled movement breaks, and structured routines. Chaya and the other students with ASD have visual schedules, sensory activities, different types of assistive technology, positive reinforcement, and social skills training.

Together, Mr. Simmons and Mrs. Reynolds share many of the classroom responsibilities, such as co-teaching, co-planning, and developing classroom management strategies that benefit all their students. They are also able to effectively communicate with each other, which is paramount for their type of collaboration. Mr. Simmons and Mrs. Reynolds do not hesitate to discuss concerns they have about their students with each other, whether they be academic, behavioral, or social in nature. Similarly, both teachers love to share the successes of their students with each other. Mr.

Grant is a new special education, one-on-one paraprofessional who will be providing direct support to Chaya this school year. His job will center around facilitating and supporting Chaya's communication, assisting her in social situations, and helping her with transitions from activity to activity during the school day. Mr. Grant is assigned only to Chaya, and his role is to ensure she receives the personal attention she needs to be successful in an inclusive environment.

Chaya's AT Assessment

In preparation for Chaya's transition to an inclusive general education setting, an assistive technology (AT) assessment was conducted before she completed her EI program. The intention of this evaluation was to determine what forms of AT will help Chaya improve her functional skills moving forward. Because she will be included with her typical peers in an inclusive general education classroom, her teachers want to be sure she will be able to fully interact and participate with them. Due to Chaya's ASD, she possesses expressive and receptive language difficulties, and the IEP team determined she will benefit from some different forms of assistive technology (AT). Chaya's receptive language skills (understanding language) are stronger than her expressive language skills (using language). Currently, she speaks in single words (e.g., cat, dog, car). This differs from how her typically developing classmates are conversing as most of them are speaking in complete sentences. Chaya does understand quite a bit of what is spoken to her if the messages are in short, simple sentences. For example, if one of her teachers wants her to sit down in her seat, he should turn to her and say, "Please sit," as opposed to saying, "Chaya, please go to your seat and sit down in your chair." This language is simpler and more direct, and results in a better response from Chaya. The IEP team concluded that Chaya would begin learning the Picture Exchange Communication System (PECS) to increase her communication skills. PECS is an alternative/augmentative communication system (AAC) that is used to teach functional communication skills. It is also a low-tech form of AT that is commonly used in schools. PECS is picture-based and consists of six phases of language development, beginning with making simple requests advancing to more complex skills such as answering questions and commenting. Learning to use PECS will be important for Chaya in her inclusive general education classroom because it will provide her with a way to communicate with the other students. Mr. Simmons and Mrs. Reynolds have already planned to set aside time to explain how PECS works to the other students so they will know how to interact and play with Chaya using this method. Both teachers agreed that having the other students in class learn how to use PECS will be a unique and beneficial experience for them. After all, a primary goal for including Chaya in an inclusive general education class is to teach her how to socialize with other students as much as possible.

Chaya's Picture Schedule

Mr. Simmons and Mrs. Reynolds also considered the daily class schedule Chaya will be following while at school. Typically, Mr. Simmons posts the daily class schedule at the front of the classroom for the students to follow. Mrs. Reynolds stated that because that is a language-based schedule, Chaya will not be able to easily follow it. Mrs. Reynolds suggested that Chaya follow a picture schedule for her class schedule. Picture schedules are a common form of AT for students with ASD since most children on the autism spectrum are visual learners. Simply put, this means they learn concepts faster when they can see a picture/photo of it, rather than just words. A picture schedule consists of individual picture icons representing a school activity (e.g., a paint brush for art or a book for reading). The picture icons are put in the order that the subjects/activities occur each day. When Chaya completes a subject/activity, she will remove the picture icon from the schedule and place it in an "all done" envelope, signifying that the subject/activity has been completed. Visuals help students with ASD and developmental disabilities to understand language, communicate, and help to reduce anxiety. Mrs. Reynolds suggested they post Chaya's schedule on the side of her desk, so she has easy access to it.

Sensory Considerations for Chaya

The IEP team made some additional AT suggestions for Chaya based on her needs. As determined by the results of Chaya's sensory profile (an assessment of sensory processing patterns and their effect on functional performance), it was determined that she will benefit from using a weighted vest that she can wear periodically throughout the school day. Weighted vests are advantageous because they provide a calming sensation that will help Chaya relax and be able to complete various school activities. To illustrate, the weighted vest will assist Chaya in sitting on the carpet at circle time with her many classmates and attending to instruction more easily while wearing it.

Improving Transitions

Mr. Simmons asked Mrs. Reynolds how she thought Chaya would do during transitions throughout the school day. He wondered how Chaya would be able to transition from one subject to the next or even come back inside from the playground when recess is over. Transitions can be challenging for many students, and with twenty students in class, transitions need to run as smoothly as possible! Mrs. Reynolds stated that Chaya's EI teacher mentioned transitions had been challenging for her because of the noise and the commotion that occurs. She also said that Chaya resists changing from a preferred activity (e.g., art) to a more challenging one (e.g., English language arts [ELA]), and this has led to some lost instructional time. After some discussion, Mr. Simmons and Mrs. Reynolds decided they would try using a visual timer to show Chaya how much time she has left before she needs to transition to the next activity. This will give Chaya the needed "heads-up" to successfully make that change from one activity to the next. A visual timer shows the passage of time by using visual cues such as a disappearing dial or sand. Mr. Simmons and Mrs. Reynolds also created a procedure for how all students in the class will line up when it is time to go to lunch or recess to reduce potential commotion. They also created procedures for how students should enter the classroom when they arrive in the morning and how they should behave when it is time to pack up at the end of the school day.

Mr. Simmons and Mrs. Reynolds felt they made a good start at integrating Chaya into her new inclusive classroom. Including Chaya in a large classroom with many students will be a big change for her from her smaller, EI classroom, but they are confident that the AT choices the IEP team selected for her will contribute to her success. They also talked about the role of Mr. Grant, her one-on-one aide, and how he will help her thrive. He will play a significant role in facilitating her AT use from creating her PECS notebook, to managing her picture schedule, to setting her timer, and most importantly, to helping her interact with her classmates and participate in all the classroom activities.

Questions:

1. Describe Chaya's characteristics.
2. List some of the other disabilities which students in Mr. Simmons's and Mrs. Reynolds's classroom possess and identify the adaptations that are provided to these students.
3. What is the role of Mr. Kind, Chaya's paraprofessional, in supporting her?
4. Do you think that Mr. Simmons and Mrs. Reynolds are a good match as co-teachers? Why or why not?
5. List the different types of AT Chaya will be using in her inclusive general education kindergarten class. Indicate how each one of them would be beneficial in this type of educational setting.

Challenge: Create a one-page fact sheet about the Picture Exchange Communication System (PECS). Be sure to include what it is, who benefits from using it, what it is composed of, and the six phases of PECS.

References

ATIA (2025). *What Is AT?* https://www.atia.org/home/at-resources/what-is-at/#how-do-you-choose-the-right-assistive-technology

Autism Adventures (2025). *Low-Tech, Mid-Tech, and High-Tech Assistive Technology: Augmentative and Alternative Communication Uncategorized.* https://www.autismadventures.com/low-tech-mid-tech-and-high-tech/

2

Attention Deficit Hyperactivity Disorder

Tara S. Guerriero, PhD

Attention deficit hyperactivity disorder (ADHD) is a neurodevelopmental disorder in which individuals demonstrate characteristics of inattention, and/or hyperactivity and impulsivity. Individuals with ADHD may have three different types of ADHD (CDC, 2024) including the following:

- **The predominantly inattentive type**, in which individuals may have difficulties maintaining attention and listening for long periods of time when someone is speaking to them; they may be easily distracted, forgetful, and/or lose things easily.
- **The predominantly hyperactive-impulsive type**, in which individuals may fidget or move around a lot, have difficulty sitting for long periods of time, talk excessively, call out without raising their hand, and interrupt when others are talking.
- **The combined type**, in which there is evidence of both inattention and hyperactivity and impulsivity.

Individuals with ADHD demonstrate characteristics of ADHD in more than one setting; it often impacts children and adolescents in their personal lives as well as in school settings.

Table 2.1 Student Demographics

Student Name	Aaron Hunt
Gender	Male
Grade	6
Educational Placement	Inclusive general education with learning support services in the learning support room
Geographic Location	Suburban
Parent/Siblings	**Parents:** Two parents (Mr. and Mrs. Hunt) **Siblings:** None
School	North Stratton Elementary School
LEA	Evansville School District
Elementary Academic Profile	**Reading:** Above grade level **Writing:** On grade level **Mathematics:** Above grade level
Middle School Academic Profile (Prior to Receiving Services)	**Reading:** Receiving a low B in honors class **Writing:** Receiving a B in grade-level class **Mathematics:** Receiving a C in honors class
Middle School Academic Profile (at the End of Sixth Grade)	**Reading:** Receiving an A- in honors class **Writing:** Receiving a B+ in grade-level class **Mathematics:** Receiving a B+ in honors class

Who Is Aaron?

Aaron is a sixth grader who was recently diagnosed with ADHD (the combined type) by his family doctor. Aaron is an only child who lives with his mom and dad in a townhouse community in a large suburban town. Mr. Hunt is a middle school history teacher, and Mrs. Hunt is a high school English teacher. Aaron has always been a very active child; throughout his childhood, he has played many sports including baseball, soccer, and tennis. As a young child, he would spend most of his summers running around (e.g., playing sports, playing at the park, going from house to house) or riding his bike in his neighborhood with neighborhood friends and swimming in the community pool. In addition to being active, he loves playing video games and watching movies with his friends. His parents and teachers would describe him as a funny, intelligent, and kind child. He has had a strong group of friends from his neighborhood since he was young, and they have been a constant in his life. As an only child, his parents have really made an effort to help him to maintain good friendships over the years.

The Elementary Years

In elementary school, his parents and teachers described him as a good student with a lot of energy. From kindergarten through third grade, he generally did really well in school. He didn't get homework, so he didn't have to worry about bringing a lot of things back and forth from school, but he often accidentally left his jacket or water bottle on the bus. As he got into fourth and fifth grade, he started getting homework, but he often forgot to bring it home. He also started having difficulties with organization and keeping track of his things. In addition, he often said that it was hard to focus on what his teachers said (especially when they were giving directions) and he had to ask the teachers to repeat things that had just been said. As he got older, they spent longer periods of time sitting in the classroom working, and he noticed that he was really having difficulties sitting still all day. He asked his teachers if he could stand up and move around a little during the day, and he was such a good kid that they typically let him because it didn't seem to bother the other kids. Whenever the teachers asked a question, he was always the first to call out an answer, but he often had to be reminded to raise his hand or let others answer questions, as well.

Beginning Middle School

Aaron was so excited to start middle school; he had eight periods a day and got to switch classes every period. He also played soccer on the school soccer team. By the end of September, his parents noticed that he was losing some of his excitement for school. Even though he had always been a good student, he was starting to fall behind in his classes. His teachers were concerned that he frequently called out in class, and it was starting to disrupt the flow of the class. He couldn't keep track of the papers in his backpack, and he was missing many homework assignments. Mr. and Mrs. Hunt worked with him to organize his folders for each class; further, each day after school, they would look at the learning management system on the computer and help him to make a list of the assignments that he had.

His performance in his sports was also beginning to suffer. For example, in soccer, when he was subbed out of a game and waiting on the bench, he couldn't sit there and kept asking his coach when he would go back in the game. He also got easily distracted during games because the field was much more spread out than it was when he was younger, and he had a hard time staying in position without trying to run to the ball. The Hunts also noticed at home that he was being more impulsive when riding his bike (e.g., riding too fast down a hill, crossing the street without fully looking), which concerned them because they wanted him to be safe. Aaron also was having difficulties getting to sleep at night because he said that he couldn't stop his thoughts from racing.

Diagnosing Aaron's ADHD

At his next well-child check-up, he and his parents talked with the doctor about what Aaron was experiencing, and after several questionnaires and an observation, his doctor diagnosed him with ADHD (the combined type). After a long conversation about possible pros (e.g., more focus, less impulsivity) and cons (e.g., difficulties sleeping, stomach problems) of medication with his doctor, he and his family decided that he wasn't going to take medication for his ADHD. Instead, they were going to try different types of strategies (e.g., develop organizational checklists/systems, come up with more specific rules for riding his bike) to help Aaron at home. In addition, Mr. and Mrs. Hunt shared his diagnosis with his school, and with the Hunts' written permission, the school completed a comprehensive evaluation to determine whether he was eligible for special education services under the Individuals with Disabilities Education Act (IDEA). He was found to be eligible for special education services under the category of Other Health Impairment (OHI).

Supports for Aaron

The multidisciplinary team (which included his sixth-grade teachers, a special education teacher, the principal, the school psychologist, and his parents) developed an individualized education program (IEP) for him that provided for learning support services to help with his organization and study skills; he is also learning strategies for how to decrease his impulsive behavior (e.g., every time he wants to answer a question in class, he would count to five in his head and then raise his hand without calling out).

In addition, since he has fallen behind in his English and math classes, his learning support services also focus on helping him in the areas of math and written language. In math, there have been several concepts that he hasn't mastered from fifth and sixth grade, and it is making it difficult for him to move forward in math without those foundational skills. The learning support teacher is breaking down several earlier concepts so that Aaron can become more proficient with those skills and start to catch up in his general education math class. In written language, a lot of focus has been placed on prewriting strategies to help him to gather and organize his thoughts before writing. Additionally, after writing, he is learning to use a revising and editing checklist. These supports are helping him to focus and maintain attention during the writing process.

Aaron also has had many accommodations built into his services that included allowing breaks when he needs to take them during class, allowing him to use a small fidget toy in his pocket to help him concentrate during class, and providing him with an extra five minutes at the end of each class to organize his belongings before moving to the next class. He has also been provided with a homework list for each class at the beginning of each week. The homework list is a physical list that he carries with him, and it is also emailed to his school so that he can access it throughout the week. At home, Aaron's parents have helped him to develop an organizational system to keep his room clean and keep track of his belongings.

Concluding Thoughts

Aaron is nearing the end of his sixth-grade year, and he is much happier at school. He has been turning in his assignments and he feels that he is learning much more in his classes. He told his learning support teacher and parents that he thinks that the help that he is getting is really making a difference both at school and at home. He is excited for the summer and is starting to get excited about seventh grade.

Questions:

1. What are the three types of ADHD?
2. What characteristics did Aaron demonstrate in elementary school that were indicative of ADHD?
3. Why do you think that Aaron was not diagnosed with ADHD until he was in middle school?
4. How does Aaron's ADHD impact him in school? In his personal life?
5. In addition to learning support services, several accommodations have helped Aaron. List the accommodations and discuss how they could be helpful for Aaron.

Challenge: Research common accommodations for students with ADHD. List five other accommodations that might be beneficial for Aaron at school, and explain why you think they will be helpful.

Challenge: Research typical behaviors associated with ADHD (both hyperactive/impulsive behaviors and inattentive behaviors). Make a list of the hyperactive/impulsive behaviors that Aaron displays. Make a second list of the inattentive behaviors that Aaron displays.

Reference

Centers for Disease Control and Prevention (CDC). (2024). *About Attention-Deficit / Hyperactivity Disorder (ADHD)*. https://www.cdc.gov/adhd/about/?CDC_AAref_Val=https://www.cdc.gov/ncbddd/adhd/facts.html

3

Autism Spectrum Disorder

Mary A. Houser, EdD

Autism spectrum disorder (ASD) is a complex neurodevelopmental condition involving persistent challenges with social communication, restricted interests, and repetitive behavior. Most children with ASD will show autistic symptoms early in life. These include, but are not restricted to, limited eye contact, not showing interest in others, and not responding to their names. Other behaviors such as hand flapping, rarely smiling, and overreacting to sounds might also be apparent (AutismSA, 2025, para. 5). Sometimes children with ASD will appear to develop typically until eighteen to twenty-four months of age, followed by a period of regression. Individuals who are mildly affected by their ASD might not be properly diagnosed until they are older.

While autism is considered a lifelong condition, the need for services and supports, because of these challenges, varies among individuals with autism (APA, 2025, para. 1). A spectrum disorder, such as ASD, ranges from mild to severe in its impact on an individual. Some students with ASD will require minimal support while in school, and others will require high amounts of support. Students with ASD may be placed in inclusive or self-contained classrooms in their neighborhood school. They may also be placed in separate schools or residential facilities, depending on the disorder's impact on them.

Autism Spectrum Disorder (ASD) #1

Table 3.1 Student Demographics

Student Name	Rahul Mookerjee
Gender	Male
Grade	11
Educational Placement	Autistic support (AS) classroom; part-time inclusive general education classroom
Geographic Location	Suburban
Parent/Siblings	**Parents:** Two parents (Jasmin and Summit Mookerjee)
	Siblings: Younger brother
School	Montgomery High School
LEA	Cranberry District
Academic Profile	**Reading:** Below grade level
	Writing: On grade level
	Mathematics: Above grade level

Who Is Rahul?

My name is Rahul. I am seventeen years old. I spend some of my time in school in a special education classroom with other kids like me at Montgomery High School. We live in a small town outside of a city in the Northeast. My parents are from New Delhi, India. They moved here together from India to go to college. My mom is a good cook. My dad works a lot. I don't have any brothers or sisters. I have a few cousins, and they sometimes visit us from India over the holidays.

When I was young, I was fascinated with dinosaurs. I loved everything about them. I read books on dinosaurs, looked at pictures of dinosaurs, and learned tons of facts about them. Still, to this day, they are the one thing I like to talk about the most. In my head, I will go through the list of the different types of dinosaurs over and over: Abelisaurous, Brontosaurous, Stegosaurous, Megalosaurous, Triceratops… ! There are so many different types of dinosaurs that most people have never heard of before. I sometimes close my eyes and see them running around and fighting each other. I like to talk about them, but people have told me this is a problem, and that I need to limit how much I talk about dinosaurs. I guess it gets on people's nerves. Strange.

I like my computer and most types of technology. Computers make sense to me. They don't change, and I find that comforting. I also like basketball statistics. Ask me anything about the NBA, and I can tell you. Shimmery things are also great. I have lights around my bedroom ceiling that shimmer. My dad helped me put them up. I like to squint my eyes when I look at them. It makes me happy. I also collect water bottles. Right now, I have twenty-seven of them in my room. I arrange them first by color, and then by size. I don't like it when people touch them.

I do some things that other kids my age don't do. I make random noises under my breath. Sometimes I do it loudly. I don't even think about it when I am doing it. When I am out in public, people look at me funny when it happens. I also like to clear my throat. Loud noises and bright lights bother me. I prefer to be in my room where it is calm and quiet. I also like to be alone. Most people think I am unhappy when I am alone, but that is not true. My mom always tells me I should make friends so I can be happy. I think it makes her sad when she sees me by myself. When I am with too many people, I get anxious, and I want to get away from them. I don't like making "small talk." I don't see the point in it. I have a dog. His name is Angus. He is my best friend.

School Life

I have been told by my IEP [individualized education program] team that my academic skill levels are all over the place. When I asked what that meant, I was told that I was pretty good in some things, but not so good in other things. I recently took an IQ test, and my parents told me my IQ was 110. I guess that is okay. I also took a pretty long test that was called the Woodcock-Johnson. Anyway, this test showed I was good at applied math problems (solving math problems) and math calculations. I was not so great at reading recall or editing sentences. Anything that deals with a lot of words, I am not very good at doing. So, it is safe to say if it involves math… good. If it involves reading and writing… not so good. For most of my life, I have struggled with both reading and writing. I can read the words, but I have problems understanding what the words mean. It takes me a long time to understand a story or a reading passage when we read it in class. Writing is hard for me because I am not great at holding a pen or pencil. I think my OT [occupational therapist] called that a "fine motor" problem. It physically hurts for me to write. In the past year or so, I have been allowed to use Microsoft Word on my laptop to do a lot of my assignments. That has been so helpful.

Most of the time, I stay in my classroom with the other students in my class. I go to geometry, specials, and lunch with everyone else. I wish I could go to more classes with them.

My parents and teacher told me I would stay in school until I am at least eighteen years old and maybe older. That is weird because my younger brother will finish high school before I do. They asked me if I want to go to a vocational program where I can learn more about computers when I finish high school. There is a program like this at a nearby community college.

I want to get a part-time job. I also want my own apartment someday.

Social Life

I have one friend. His name is Maximo. Maximo has ASD too and is in my class. We met back in elementary school and have been in the same class ever since. Max has a lot of baseball caps. When we are together, we like to play video games and hang out in my parents' basement. No one bothers us when we are down there. We don't talk a whole lot when we are together. Sometimes we will go out for pizza too. He's cool.

There is a girl in eleventh grade named Sadie whom I like. She sits in the back of the room in my music class. It is hard for me because I want to ask her out to a movie, but I have no idea how to even go up to start a conversation with her. I said "hi" to her the other day when I saw her in the hallway, but I don't think I said it loudly enough because she didn't look over at me. I had already passed her when I said it. My dad says to keep trying to get Sadie's attention. He wants me to practice talking to her with him. He said that it would make me feel more comfortable when I did it. I am not sure about that. I can talk without much of a problem, but I just don't know what to say to her. When I try to talk to her, I sometimes say stupid things.

A Personal Reflection

Sometimes people ask me what I want them to know about teenagers with ASD. These are the things I want them to know:

1. When I get mad, it is because I cannot always find the words to say what I want to say, and I get frustrated.
2. I get tired of people trying to fix me. I don't think there is anything wrong with me.
3. I like to have a daily routine, and I like it posted on the refrigerator where I can see it.
4. I do not like a lot of different foods. They sometimes smell weird and taste funny in my mouth. Do not make me eat it if I do not like it. It is painful.
5. Doing things over and over again helps me to relax. Let me do it.
6. Pillowcases never feel good on my face.

Questions:

1. Define autism spectrum disorder (ASD).
2. Describe Rahul as a person. What are his likes? Dislikes?
3. What autistic characteristics does Rahul display? Provide examples.
4. When Rahul describes himself, his thoughts seem to be "all over the place." Why might this be the case?
5. In your opinion, why did Rahul want us to know about what it is like to be a teenager with ASD?

Challenge: Write a one-page essay on the benefits and challenges of including students with ASD in an inclusive general education class.

Autism Spectrum Disorder (ASD) #2

Table 3.2 Student Demographics

Student Name	Trevor Riley
Gender	Male
Grade	3

Educational Placement	Full-time autistic support (AS) in special education classroom
Geographic Location	Rural
Parent/Siblings	**Parents:** Dad (David Riley)
	Siblings: None
School	Applecross Elementary School
LEA	Valley Views School District
Academic Profile	**Reading:** Well below grade level
	Writing: Well below grade level
	Mathematics: Well below grade level

Who Is Trevor?

Trevor is a nine-year-old Caucasian boy with an autism spectrum disorder (ASD) in the third grade. Trevor lives with his father in a rural farm community in the South. Trevor's dad works hard but he is not able to provide much more than food on the table and clothes for Trevor to wear. When Trevor was two years old, he began showing signs of regression, which meant he lost many of the communication, social, and motor skills he had developed up to this point. For example, Trevor had started talking and putting words together, but within a short period, he stopped talking altogether. When he was one year old, he would look at his father and smile when he saw him, but this stopped too by the time he was eighteen months old. He began toe-walking around the age of two, which continues to this day. By the time Trevor was three, he received the diagnosis of ASD, and was enrolled in an early intervention (EI) program, which he attended until he turned school age and began kindergarten.

At School

When Trevor began kindergarten, his expressive language skills were well behind his peers. By the age of five, neurotypical children are easily speaking in complete sentences and can express their thoughts and ideas. Although Trevor had good receptive language skills (i.e., understanding spoken language), he was only speaking in single words when school began. Trevor's cognitive abilities fell in the well-below-average range with a full-scale IQ of 75. He also displayed some of the more common characteristics of ASD, such as hand flapping, rocking, and spinning. Trevor did not play with his peers, but rather preferred to be alone. Most days during free play at school, he would sit in the corner of the classroom, throwing toys into the trash can. Loud noises bothered him, and he would often cover his ears, hum, and rock when he heard them. His gait was awkward, and he could often be found walking on his tiptoes as he moved about the classroom.

Perhaps one of Trevor's biggest challenges was how his lack of communication affected him from a behavioral perspective. Just like the other kids in class, Trevor had a lot to say, but he was not able to express himself like they did. His inability to effectively communicate caused him great frustration, which resulted in his being physically aggressive with other students in class. His teacher noticed him hitting, spitting at, and kicking other children. He would also screech when he became aggressive. Sometimes his screeching would startle the other children. It seemed every time he got upset, from not being able to communicate or from being overstimulated, he would lash out.

A New Communication Approach

Trevor's teacher gave a lot of thought to how he could help him. After careful consideration and conversations with Trevor's dad, his teacher decided to implement two specific interventions to help control his aggression. The first was the implementation of a new communication system for him: a communication app called Proloquo2Go. This communication app is a form of augmentative and alternative communication (AAC) that Trevor could download on his iPad, which would enable him to respond quickly to others. It had pictures, symbols, and a text-to-speech option, and all he had to do was select what he wanted to communicate by pressing buttons. Having this app on his iPad was also great because he could initiate conversations using it. This was a social skill goal that his teacher wanted to work on with him this year. His teacher thought that by having this system in place, it would allow Trevor to express himself and thereby lower his desire to be physically aggressive. Teaching Trevor how to use Proloquo2Go took some time, but Trevor liked his iPad, so it was a good fit for him. His teacher also liked the idea of putting a communication app on his iPad because it was less stigmatizing than some of the other AAC devices available. Carrying an iPad around was nothing out of the ordinary for a child his age to do.

Reinforcing Good Behavior

The second intervention was a new reinforcement system for Trevor. Reinforcement is used when the goal is to maintain or increase a behavior. His teacher wanted to positively reinforce him when he was acting appropriately, instead of punishing him every time he lashed out at others. He understood that it was more effective to focus on the positive behaviors Trevor was exhibiting and work to improve these. His teacher had learned that although he did receive some reinforcement when he behaved well during preschool, it was inconsistent. In other words, he only received a reward for some of his good behavior, but not for all of it. Also, the rewards he was receiving were always the same things, which led to him growing tired of them, and they lost their effectiveness. For example, Trevor's favorite toy was his Batman action figure. His preschool teachers gave it to him whenever he displayed appropriate behavior. After a while, Trevor was tired of his Batman doll and no longer wanted to earn it as a reward.

Trevor's teacher decided he would implement a token economy system for him. This would take the form of a token board. A token board is a visual tool that is used when an individual receives "tokens" for good behavior. When an individual earns a token, they place it on the token board. Once the token board is full of tokens, they may trade their tokens in for a prize. His teacher thought this would work well because it would allow Trevor to be rewarded consistently throughout the day. Also, Trevor would select his reward from his "choice board." A choice board is a board with icons or pictures of several different rewards from which to choose. On Trevor's board, he had pictures of several of his favorite activities, treats, and social reinforcement (e.g., high fives or fist bumps) to choose from. Each day, he would select a different reinforcement to work for and put a picture of its icon on his token board to remind him of what he could earn from displaying appropriate behavior. His board consisted of eight tokens. He had opportunities throughout the day (both scheduled and unscheduled) to earn tokens. At the end of the school day, if he earned all eight tokens, he could turn them in for one of his chosen rewards.

With these two new interventions in place, Trevor's teacher was hopeful he could improve his aggressive behavior. Trevor possessed many positive traits, and his teacher wanted to make sure that he was able to demonstrate these traits while minimizing or even eliminating the challenging behaviors he had been demonstrating.

Questions:

1. Describe Trevor's language skills. What effect did they have on his behavior?
2. Discuss some of Trevor's autistic traits other than his language challenges.
3. What is Proloquo2Go? How would using it help Trevor?
4. What is a token board? Why did the teacher decide to implement one with Trevor?
5. Do you think the interventions his teacher selected for him will help his behavior? Why or why not?

Challenge: Visit the PBIS.org website. Create an infographic that explains the three-tiered approach to positive behavior. Be prepared to share it with others in your class.

References

APA (2025). *What is autism spectrum disorder?* https://www.psychiatry.org/patients-families/autism/what-is-autism-spectrum-disorder

AutismSA (2025). *Autism first signs: A checklist for babies and toddlers.* https://autismsa.org.au/autism-diagnosis/autism-symptoms/signs-of-autism-in-babies/#

4

Culturally and Linguistically Diverse Exceptional Learners

Lesley N. Siegel, PhD

Our culturally and linguistically diverse exceptional (CLDE) learners represent a vast diversity of cultures, Native languages, and language learning needs, as well as disabilities spanning all Individuals with Disabilities Education Act (IDEA) categories. Students in U.S. schools are increasingly linguistically diverse. Approximately 10.6 percent of students in U.S. public schools are English learners (ELs), with Spanish being the most common Native language (76.4 percent), followed by Arabic, then Chinese (NCES, 2024). Data from the National Center on Educational Statistics (2024) reports that 15.8 percent of students who are English learners (ELs) are also students with disabilities. There is no such thing as a single profile of a CLDE learner.

Supporting our culturally and linguistically diverse learners with disabilities calls for additional knowledge and skills. In addition to a deep knowledge of disability, special educators must develop their understanding of language acquisition and the role of language within the context of the student's family and community (García and Ortiz, 2013; Hoover et al., 2008). Special educators must strive to embody culturally responsive practices, including validating and affirming students' cultural identity, drawing on students' Funds of Knowledge, and holding universal high expectations (Brown et al., 2019; Hoover et al., 2008).

Table 4.1 Student Demographics

Student Name	Mateo Montoya
Gender	Male
Grade	5
Educational Placement	Inclusive general education with learning support in a resource room
Geographic Location	Urban
Parent/Siblings	**Parents:** Two parents (Martha and Carlos) **Siblings:** Two older sisters
School	Hill View Elementary School
LEA	Los Lunas School District
Academic Profile	**Reading:** Below grade level **Writing:** Below grade level **Mathematics:** Above grade level

Who Is Mateo?

Mateo, "Matt," is an eleven-year-old fifth grader. He is a bilingual English and Spanish speaker, a second-generation New Mexican, and hopes to follow in his father's and oldest sister's footsteps to the University of New Mexico. Mateo's family is part of a close-knit community. Three generations have lived in Los Lunas since his grandparents settled there. Martha, Mateo's mom, is an accountant at a local firm, and his dad, Carlos, is an emergency room nurse. Mateo and his two older sisters are close to their abuelita, Rosa, who lives on an adjoining property. Mateo and his sisters cook dinner with their abuelita every Sunday for extended family and friends.

Mateo and his sisters were raised simultaneously bilingual in English and Spanish, and he is fluent in both languages. It was important to his parents that their children be able to communicate with their grandparents, extended relatives, and community members in Spanish, so Martha and Carlos spoke to their children both in English and Spanish from birth. Mateo is close to both his older sisters, and many weekends, Mateo's mom will take him and his middle sister to see his older sister, a freshman at the University of New Mexico, for Lady Lobo basketball games.

Mateo is a kind and outgoing child and makes friends wherever he goes. He has a group of close friends he grew up with, as well as friends from various clubs and activities. Mateo has an ever-growing interest in robotics. He's been building his robots since second grade and has attended robotics and computer summer programs for the past two years. Mateo and his best friend even started a YouTube channel dedicated to their love of robots. Mateo is part of an after-school robots and gamers club and hopes to take computer classes when he goes to middle school next year. In addition to his love of robots, Mateo is very creative and has developed an interest in photography. His older sister loves art and encourages Mateo; this spring, he is taking a photography class at the local community center. He also loves to ride his bike and skateboard around the neighborhood with his friends.

Mateo at School

Mateo is currently a fifth grader at High View Elementary, a K–5 school of roughly three hundred students. High View is a small school, and students from multiple cultural and ethnic backgrounds form strong bonds in the tight-knit school community where most of the students have been together since kindergarten. Approximately 68 percent of the students at High View are Hispanic, and almost all students speak or understand some Spanish. Both English and Spanish fill the hallways, lunchroom, and cafeteria, which contribute to the school being a culturally affirming space.

Mateo's fifth-grade teacher, Mr. Lopez, communicates with family members in both English and Spanish, and both languages are utilized to support students who are English learners in his classroom. At High View, over three-fourths of the teachers, administrators, and school staff are Hispanic and have some level of Spanish language proficiency.

Mateo loves school and overall performs well. He excels at math and all creative and social activities. His expressive and receptive language skills are strong in both English and Spanish. Reading has always been a bit of a challenge, but with additional support at home coupled with his love of school and very supportive teachers, Mateo was able to meet the standard in reading in first and second grade.

By the end of third grade, reading shifted more toward content instruction, and writing toward informational purposes, and Mateo's third-grade teacher observed him fall behind. The summer after third grade, Mateo's parents worked with him on reading and writing skills, but after the first few weeks of fourth grade, Mateo continued to demonstrate systematic struggles. Mateo started intensive interventions in reading and writing, but he was not making progress by the winter break. At this time, his fourth-grade teacher recommended an evaluation for special education services. Mateo's parents were hesitant about special education but agreed to have him evaluated.

A bilingual school psychologist assessed Mateo, and because Mateo is a fluent English speaker and has received all academic instruction in English, all assessments were administered in English. Assessment data was considered along with data from the twelve weeks of intensive intervention. Mateo qualified for special education services under the IDEA category of specific learning disability in the areas of reading and writing.

In March of his fourth-grade year, Mateo began receiving special education services in reading and writing. He spent forty-five minutes in a resource room setting three times a week, and his fourth-grade teacher provided additional accommodations. Mateo liked his special education teacher and the other kids in the resource room class, and he made steady progress. Mateo made strong gains in writing, and at his individualized education program (IEP) in the spring of fifth grade, the team discontinued special education services for writing. Mateo continues to receive special education services for reading.

As the end of fifth grade approaches, Mateo is scheduled to transition to Sunset Middle School, a grade 6–8 school of almost eight hundred students. Mateo is excited for the many clubs and activities at the middle school and all the elective classes. The middle school has a robotics club, a skateboarding club, and art electives. All of his fifth-grade friends will be going to the same middle school, as well as fifth graders from elementary schools across the district.

Mateo's parents have multiple worries about middle school. The collective and familial nature of High View Elementary helped Mateo thrive, especially as he navigated academic challenges and special education. His parents do not want him to be lost in the hustle of middle school, and they are apprehensive about the way special education services are provided at the middle school. At Sunset, students only receive special education as a class that meets for one period every day. This will be an increased level of services for Mateo and will also prevent him from taking an elective. Mateo's parents are very concerned that students who receive special education services have to give up electives, which are a large motivator for Mateo.

In addition to losing out on art, computers, and other electives, Mateo's parents are concerned that special education will isolate Mateo from the general education curriculum and his sixth-grade peers. However, they know that middle school's increased focus on academics, coupled with larger classes and the need for students to be academically independent, could jeopardize Mateo's progress without special education support.

Mateo's parents are committed to his being included in all classes at middle school. They do not want to remove Mateo from special education as he seems to be making steady progress and continues to benefit. Mateo and his parents do not want him to be denied the opportunity to take elective courses. Mateo's parents are fierce advocates for their son, but they are unsure of what they can expect in a large middle school and what choices they have to make to meet Mateo's needs.

Questions:

1. Define "CLDE" learners.
2. In what ways does Mateo's elementary school (High View) create a welcoming environment for all families?
3. Is English proficiency adding to Mateo's challenges in reading? How do you know?
4. What are the particular challenges for culturally and linguistically diverse students with learning disabilities?
5. In what ways does being in a learning environment with a similar cultural and linguistic profile shape a CLDE student's experiences?
6. Discuss how you will center Mateo's family's voice and their expertise as part of the IEP team. Give at least three specific examples.

Challenge: Research the linguistic diversity and special education profiles for a district you are familiar with. What questions does this raise? What do you need to know more about?

Overview of Los Lunas, New Mexico

Los Lunas is a city of 17,452 people located twenty-five miles south of Albuquerque, New Mexico. Demographic data from the U.S. Census 2022 ACS reports that 96.5 percent of Los Lunas residents are U.S. citizens. Ethnic and demographic data is as follows: 60.4 percent of the population is Hispanic; 30.4 percent is White (non-Hispanic); 3.09 percent is American Indian and Alaska (Non-Hispanic); 0.72 percent is Asian (Non-Hispanic); 1.32 percent is Black or African American (Non-Hispanic); and 3.53 percent is multiracial (Non-Hispanic) (Census Bureau, 2022).

References

Brown, M. R., Dennis, J. P., & Matute-Chavarria, M. (2019). Cultural relevance in special education: Current status and future directions. *Intervention in School and Clinic, 54*(5).

Garcia, S. B. & Ortiz, A. A. (2013). Transformative research in special education. *Multiple Voices for Ethnically Diverse Exceptional Learners, 13*(2), 32–47.

Hoover, J. J., Klinger, J. K., Baca, L. M. & Patton, J. M. (2008). *Methods for Teaching Culturally and Linguistically Diverse Exceptional Learners.* Pearson.

Los Lunas School District (n.d.). *About LLS.* Los Lunas Schools. https://www.llschools.net/about

National Center for Education Statistics (2024). English Learners in Public Schools. *The Condition of Education.* U.S. Department of Education, Institute of Education Sciences. https://nces.ed.gov/programs/coe/indicator/cgf/english-learners

U.S. Census Bureau (2022). *American community survey data.* https://www.census.gov/programs-surveys/acs/

5

Developmental Delay

Mary A. Houser, EdD

Developmental delay occurs "when a child's progression through predictable developmental phases slows, stops, or reverses" (Yale Medicine, 2025, para. 1). Simply put, this occurs when a child takes longer to meet their developmental milestones when compared to their peers. There are different types of developmental delays, such as delays in cognitive skills, social and emotional skills, speech and language skills, and fine and gross motor skills. In addition, there are global developmental delays, when there is a delay in development in two or three of these areas (Cleveland Clinic, 2025). Symptoms of a developmental delay depend on the delay the child is exhibiting. Examples of such delays include not rolling over, crawling, or walking when expected. Another example of a developmental delay is not starting to talk (e.g., first words) when anticipated or having challenges with fine motor or gross motor skills (e.g., trouble grasping objects or balance problems). There are different causes of developmental delays, such as premature birth, being exposed to toxins such as alcohol or drugs during pregnancy, low birth weight, poor nutrition, or insufficient oxygen during the birth process. Developmental screening is an important way to determine whether children are meeting their developmental milestones. Oftentimes, children are recommended for early intervention services when delayed development is determined. It is important to note that each state defines "developmental delay" differently (Young, 2023).

Table 5.1 Student Demographics

Student Name	Hao Wang
Gender	Male
Grade	Pre-kindergarten
Educational Placement	Special education early intervention (EI) preschool program
Geographic Location	Rural
Parent/Siblings	**Parents:** Two adoptive parents (Anna and Quon Wang) **Siblings:** None
School	Roseberry Elementary School (contains EI program)
LEA	Ramson Intermediate Unit
Academic Profile	Skill deficits in cognitive development, social-emotional development, communication development, and adaptive development

Who Is Hao?

Hao was born in San Francisco, California, to his twenty-year-old mother, Min. Min was a young, single mother who had substance abuse problems. She partook in recreational drugs such as cannabis and fentanyl during her pregnancy. Min led a reckless lifestyle, and after a series of romantic relationships, she became pregnant. As a result of her lifestyle, Hao was born several weeks prematurely. Min was unsure who fathered Hao due to having more than one partner at the time of conception. Unfortunately, Min did not have the financial means or parental prowess to care for Hao, and she decided after some convincing that it would be best if she put him up for adoption.

The Wangs

Mr. and Mrs. Wang tried to conceive a child for several years but were unsuccessful. They knew they wanted children and agreed that adoption would be a wonderful way to start a family of their own. When the adoption agency told them about Hao, they were certain they could provide him with a loving, stable home, and began the adoption process. With time and persistence, the Wangs eventually traveled to San Francisco to bring Hao back to his new home in rural North Carolina. Hao was two years old when the Wang family adopted him. When Hao arrived at his new home, his new bedroom was waiting for him. Adorned with stuffed animals, colorful decorations, and plenty of books and toys, Hao had everything he could ever want, including two parents who were overjoyed to have him. Fortunately, Mrs. Wang was able to take a few weeks off from work to adjust to having a new baby and get him settled into his new home. She spent her time taking him for walks through the neighborhood, reading to him, and playing with him and his new toys. She was so happy to have this time to spend alone with him, getting to know him.

Subtle Differences

Not long after his arrival, Mrs. Wang registered the two of them for a Mommy and Me (Kindermusik) music class at a nearby YMCA. She looked forward to showing off Hao to her friends who also had young children in this program. The Mommy and Me music class started the following week. When they arrived at class, all the moms and their young children were sitting around talking and laughing and enjoying their time together. The music leader began by introducing herself and explaining the class activities for the session. The intent of the first music class was to introduce the children to socializing with each other and to create a bonding opportunity with their mothers. Everyone in class was in a good mood and enjoyed their first music lesson together. The class leader gave the participants a series of simple instructions and played lively music as they progressed throughout the session.

The first exercise required the moms to get their child's attention. Mrs. Wang looked at Hao and gently called his name. She noticed that Hao did not look at her, which she thought was unusual. She tried again, but there was still no response. Hao seemed more interested in looking at the bright lights and his reflection in the large mirror in the front of the room. As Mrs. Wang looked around the classroom, she saw other children responding when their mothers said their names. Additionally, when the moms smiled at them, their children smiled back at them. This was something that Hao had never done. This was the first time Mrs. Wang noticed differences between Hao and other children his age. The music class ended, and it was time to go home. At dinner that evening, Mrs.

Wang told Mr. Wang about how Hao seemed different from the other toddlers in class that day. She told her husband that because she had not spent much time with young children herself, she did not notice there was anything unusual about Hao's behavior. Observations like this one would continue for both parents over the next few weeks.

Visiting a Friend

It was Saturday morning and one of Mr. Wang's friends, Paul, asked him if he wanted to bring Hao over to visit for a couple of hours because his wife had an appointment and could not bring their daughter, Emily, with her. Mr. Wang thought this would be a good idea because it would give Mrs. Wang some time alone to rest and to get a few things done around the house. When Mr. Wang arrived at his friend's house, Emily was in a playpen holding onto its sides and jumping up and down excitedly. She was so pleased to see her guests when they arrived! Emily was eleven months old but seemed quite advanced to Mr. Wang. Mr. Wang asked Paul when Emily started pulling herself up in the playpen, and Paul responded she had been pulling herself up for about two weeks and was also "furniture surfing" by moving around the furniture while holding on to it. Hao was a late walker and did not take his first steps until a few months ago close to his second birthday. This was considerably later than Emily's—by almost a year! Mr. Wang had heard that girls develop faster than boys when they are younger, so he did not give it much thought, but he did tell his wife about Emily when he got home that day.

Mrs. Wang was glad to see her husband and Hao when they returned home. Mr. Wang told his wife about how Emily was already showing signs of starting to walk and how advanced she seemed. The next day, it was time again for their Mommy and Me music class. Mrs. Wang was starting to be concerned about Hao's development. She made it a point during music class to take a closer look at the other children in class and the things they were doing. She knew that two of her friends had children very close in age to Hao, so she sat down next to them when the class started. Mrs. Wang then heard one of children say, "More, more!" when his mother showed him his tangerines for snack. Then he said, "No! No drink!" She was becoming concerned about Hao's development. He was still mostly babbling, and although he had a few words, he was certainly not putting words together like this young child. As she looked at the other children sitting nearby, they were also putting together words to communicate with their moms. She decided on the way home from music class to make an appointment with Hao's pediatrician, Dr. Miller, to discuss her and Mr. Wang's observations in recent weeks.

A New Pediatrician

Dr. Miller was the Wangs' new pediatrician. They had taken Hao to see another doctor, but he did not give them much time and attention at Hao's well-child check-ups. More importantly, he never mentioned that Hao was not meeting his developmental milestones on time. Dr. Miller was a patient and kind doctor. He listened carefully to Mrs. Wang as she told him about their concerns. The new pediatrician asked about Hao's birth mother and whether she had any information about her pregnancy and his early development. Dr. Miller discussed the concept of developmental milestones and how these are used as a tool to determine children's developmental progress. Together, they talked about the skills Hao has achieved over the past two years and what he still has to master. It appeared that Hao had delayed development in most areas. He recommended that Hao receive a developmental evaluation through the local school district's EI services. Dr. Miller assisted the Wangs in contacting the proper office and setting up an appointment.

The Diagnosis

After the evaluation was completed by the EI team, Hao was diagnosed with a global developmental delay. Having a global delay meant that he was significantly delayed in two or more areas of development. The team determined that Hao had delays in his cognitive development, social-emotional development, communication development, physical/motor development, and adaptive development. They had a meeting with the Wangs and discussed the importance of Hao being in an early intervention (EI) program to begin to catch him up on his skills. The early intervention team discussed the benefits of EI, such as preparing him for kindergarten, building greater independence, developing positive social-emotional skills, and improving his overall development. The Wangs agreed to this placement, and Hao began his new EI preschool the following week.

At first, Hao was scared when Mrs. Wang left him at the new preschool. He cried as she walked out the door for the first few days of preschool. Mrs. Wang's heart sank a little when this happened, but she knew that she and Mr. Wang were making the right decision to begin intervention with him. After a week or two in this new EI class, Hao began to thrive and loved going to school each day. He started showing interest in doing art projects, singing songs, and building with blocks. He also started to show interest in playing with another child who befriended him from the first day he attended. Over time, the Wangs began to see Hao developing new skills that he had not previously mastered. They realized then that they had made the right decision when they took him to Dr. Miller with their concerns.

Questions:

1. What is a developmental delay?
2. Explain Min's lifestyle and how it might have contributed to Hao's delayed development.
3. What did Mrs. Wang notice about Hao's development when comparing him to the other children at the Mommy and Me music class?
4. Mr. Wang noticed some differences between his friend Paul's daughter, Emily, and Hao, with respect to their rate of development. Discuss some of these differences.
5. Why did the Wangs decide to take Hao to the new pediatrician, Dr. Miller? What did Dr. Miller suggest they do to identify Hao's challenges?
6. Discuss the results of Hao's developmental evaluation performed by the EI team.
7. Do you think an EI preschool was a good choice for Hao? Why or why not?

Challenge: Research EI services in your local school district. Discuss family resources the district provides and how they might help parents of young children being identified with a disability.

References

Cleveland Clinic (2025). *Developmental delay in children.* https://my.clevelandclinic.org/health/diseases/14814-developmental-delay-in-children

Yale Medicine (2025). *Developmental delay.* https://www.yalemedicine.org/conditions/developmental-delay

Young, H. (2023). *Here are the 13 (or 14) official categories for receiving an IEP.* The IEP Attorney. https://iep-attorney.com/special-education-law-blog/here-are-the-13-or-14-official-disability-categories-for-receiving-an-iep/

6

Emotional Disturbance

Colleen E. Commisso, PhD and Alyssa Blasko, PhD, BCBA

Emotional disturbance (ED) is a disability category under the Individuals with Disabilities Education Act (IDEA). To be identified as a student with an emotional disturbance, a student demonstrates one or more of the characteristics below over a long period and to a marked degree. These characteristics include

a) an inability to learn that cannot be explained by intellectual, sensory, or health factors;
b) an inability to build or maintain satisfactory interpersonal relationships with peers and teachers;
c) inappropriate types of behavior or feelings under normal circumstances;
d) a general, pervasive mood of unhappiness or depression; [and]
e) a tendency to develop physical symptoms or fears associated with personal or school problems.

(IDEA, 20 U.S.C. § 1401 (2004), 20 C.F.R. § 300.8(c)(4)). Behaviors displayed by students with emotional disturbances can include internalizing behaviors (e.g., depression, fearfulness, loneliness, body complaints, anxiousness) and/or externalizing behaviors (e.g., physical aggression, verbal aggression, defiance, calling out, lying, substance abuse). Internalizing behaviors can be difficult to identify, given that they are often directed inward and may be difficult for a teacher to visually see. For example, a student might sit with a group but be too anxious to participate in the group.

Approximately 4 percent of students with disabilities are identified under the IDEA category of emotional disturbance (National Center for Education Statistics, 2024). Students with ED can be educated in a variety of educational placements based on the student's specific needs. This can include receiving education in the general education classroom, in separate classrooms, or in separate schools.

It is important to note that not all students who display behaviors are students who are diagnosed with emotional disturbance, and that not all students with mental health conditions are identified or should be identified with emotional disturbance.

Emotional Disturbance (ED) #1

Colleen E. Commisso, PhD and Alyssa Blasko, PhD, BCBA

Table 6.1 Student Demographics

Student Name	Matthew Stanton
Gender	Male
Grade	1
Educational Placement	Inclusive general education classroom
Geographic Location	Suburban
Parent/Siblings	**Parents:** Two parents (Mom and Dad)
	Siblings: Sister (age 8)
School	Silver Lake Elementary School
LEA	Red Oak School District
Academic Profile	**Reading:** Below grade level
	Writing: On grade level
	Mathematics: Below grade level

Who Is Matthew?

Hi! My name is Matthew, but I like to be called Matt. I am six years old, and I am in the first grade. I live in a town that is outside of a big city, and sometimes I get to go to the zoo where I can see rhinos and monkeys. I also get to go to the aquarium in the city. I like looking at turtles, jellyfish, and sharks. I have a mom, a dad, and a sister who is eight. I also have a dog, Max, who is fun to play with.

At Home

At home, I like to play with Legos, magnetic blocks, dinosaurs, and paint. I also like to play board games, play on my swing set, and play with Max, my dog. My favorite snacks are apple slices, fruit snacks, and Goldfish. I also like when I get to take swim lessons. My teacher always calls me a fish! There is also a playground close to my house that I walk to with my mom and dad. It has a wooden castle and two big red slides that come down from the top. The slides look scary, but I like going down them. They are super-fast! There is also a fun climbing wall that is tall, and I get mad when I cannot climb to the top of it. My mom always tells me that "it's okay" and "that was a great try," but I still get mad. At home, I often get in trouble when I am told to do something (homework, put my clothes away, get off my tablet, go to bed). When I do not want to do something, I will yell at my mom and dad or my sister, run away from them, throw things that are in the house, and try to hit them. When I do these things, my mom and dad will yell at me and put me in a timeout or put me in my room.

At School

At school, I have math, science, reading, writing, and social studies with Mr. Calderone, who is a general education teacher. I also have gym, music, art, and computers. My favorite subject is science because I like space and animals, but I hate math and reading. Gym is also fun, and I like to ride the scooters, do relay races, and play with the kickballs. I also like that our school has walking and jumping paths in our hallways. My favorite is the one that has the planets where you have to jump from one to the next. I have two friends in my class, Austin and Ryon, who are in my group and sit at my table.

At school, I get in trouble with Mr. Calderone because I like to talk to friends when he is teaching or when I am supposed to be getting work done. When I get math and reading work, I usually just put my head down or crumple up the work because I do not want to do it. I also sometimes yell, "No," or "I do not want to" when I have to read. When I do these things, Mr. Calderone sometimes sends me out of the classroom into the hallway for a timeout or down to Miss K, who is the emotional support teacher. I also sometimes hit or push other kids when they make me mad and do not do what I want. When this happens, I have to go to the office. Sometimes, Mr. Calderone will sit with me and help me do my work.

In the emotional support classroom, Miss K will help me do my work, and we will talk about better ways to tell Mr. Calderone that I need help or need a break. She gave me a card that says "break" on one side and "help" on the other side. Miss K has been talking to me about trying a new idea, she calls it Check-In, Check-Out (i.e., aka CICO, a Tier-2 intervention within a multi-tiered system of supports [MTSS] framework). Miss K will give me a point sheet during the morning homeroom time, and we will have a meeting every day during homeroom to "check in." Miss K will review the rules I am supposed to follow during the day and check in about my morning. I will carry this point sheet all day and receive points at the end of every class period to reflect my behavior. At the end of each day, I will "check out" with Miss K. In this meeting, Miss K will add all my points from the day, and I will get a prize (i.e., earn reinforcement for meeting my behavioral goals) if I meet my goal. I will get to pick a prize from the prize box or get five minutes doing something that I want to do (e.g., watch an animal video, do the paths in the hallway). Miss K will use all the point sheets to check how I am doing toward my annual individualized education program (IEP) goals. The point card I carry looks like this (see Table 6.2).

Questions:

1. What is an emotional disturbance (ED)?
2. Describe Matthew. What are his likes? Dislikes?
3. What characteristics of ED does Matthew display?
4. Why might Matthew be engaging in disruptive behaviors in math and reading class?
5. What are Matthew's strengths/interests? How could you use them to engage him in the classroom?

Challenge: The intervention that Matthew's teacher wants to use is called Check-In, Check-Out (CICO). Further research this behavioral strategy and describe its benefits. Are there any drawbacks? If so, please indicate them.

Table 6.2 Matt's Point Card

Matt's Point Card

Class	Behavior Goals			Points Earned	Point Criteria	Reinforcement
	Raise My Hand	Use My Break	Use My Help Card			
Homeroom					0 = I did not meet my behavior goal and needed more than 3 teacher prompts	If I earn 51 or more points, I get to:
Math						Pick a prize from the prize box
Science						Watch one animal video
Reading						Play with dinosaurs for five minutes
Writing					1 = I partially met my behavior goal and needed 2–3 teacher prompts	
Lunch						
Recess						
Social Studies					2 = I met my behavior goal with 1 or less teacher prompts.	
Specials						
Homeroom						
Total Points Earned						

Notes:

Challenge: Are Matthew's behaviors externalizing or internalizing behaviors? Explain.

Emotional Disturbance (ED) #2

Colleen E. Commisso, PhD

Table 6.3 Student Demographics

Student Name	Sarah Johnson
Gender	Female
Grade	8
Educational Placement	Full-time emotional support (ES) special education classroom
Geographic Location	Urban
Parent/Siblings	**Parents:** Single parent (Mom)
	Siblings: Two younger siblings
School	Roosevelt Middle School
LEA	Fairmont School District
Academic Profile	**Reading:** Above grade level
	Writing: Above grade level
	Mathematics: Above grade level

Who Is Sarah?

Sarah is a fourteen-year-old student in the eighth grade who lives in an urban area. She is the oldest of three children; her sister Macy is eight, and her brother Josh is six. Her mother, Debra, is a single mother who works two jobs. Each day, Debra makes sure her children have breakfast, are ready for school, and get on the bus. Then, Debra takes a forty-five-minute bus ride to work, works at a grocery store from 9 a.m. to 5 p.m., and takes the same bus ride home. After eating dinner with her family and making sure the children are in bed, Debra works online in the evening from 7:30 p.m. to 11 p.m. Given Debra's busy commute and work schedule, Sarah is responsible on most days for getting her siblings off the bus and providing them with a snack. She also helps them with homework and makes dinner for the family.

At School

In elementary school, Sarah was a quiet student who preferred to work alone rather than in groups and avoided talking to her classmates. She always seemed to want to do her best and would get frustrated if things were not done correctly or if she couldn't get something to be exactly how she wanted. On the playground, Sarah would sit alone or spend time swinging on the swings. Sarah earned good grades, enjoyed drawing, and rarely engaged in disruptive behaviors.

At the beginning of middle school, Sarah's teacher noticed that although Sarah got near-perfect grades, she never answered questions in class, always chose to work alone, and avoided talking to peers across settings (e.g., while working in group projects, sitting alone at lunch). She also noticed that in class, Sarah seemed to be "on edge." Sarah picked at her nails and seemed worried when entering class (e.g., looking around, hesitating to come in the door) and when sitting in class (e.g., scanning the room continuously). Sarah also started to get upset when she didn't earn as high grades as she wanted and often asked if she could redo work or do extra credit. Sarah started show up late for class and indicated that she was late because she didn't feel well and was in the bathroom or with the nurse.

Sarah's teacher went to the guidance counselor to discuss her concerns and contacted Sarah's other teachers to see if they were seeing similar behaviors. Several teachers reported that they were. Upon meeting with Sarah, the guidance counselor was also concerned about the anxious behaviors that Sarah was displaying. The school district decided to request permission to evaluate Sarah for an emotional disturbance and Debra gave written permission to evaluate. During the time that Sarah's evaluation was being completed, Sarah stopped showing up to all classes, except art. Debra was concerned about Sarah's grades and her progression toward graduation; she decided that she would allow her to enroll in the district's virtual school. After being identified with an ED, Sarah began attending the virtual school. She completed all of her virtual coursework in the emotional support online classroom; however, she attended her art class in an inclusive general education virtual classroom. Sarah is earning near-perfect grades, and her special education teacher discussed with the IEP team the possibility of her attending general education classes beyond art.

Questions:

1. What characteristics of ED does Sarah display?
2. Describe the collaborative efforts that were made in this scenario (among school personnel and with Debra). Do you think the collaboration was effective? Why or why not?
3. If you were a general education teacher and Sarah was going to be joining your classroom, what questions would you ask the emotional support teacher?

Challenge: If Sarah is joining the inclusive general education virtual classroom for instruction, what supports do you think she will need?

Challenge: Make a list of Sarah's challenging behaviors. Are these predominantly externalizing or internalizing behaviors? Explain.

Challenge: Is it more difficult for teachers to identify externalizing or internalizing behaviors? Explain why.

References

IDEA (Individuals with Disabilities Education Act). (2004). *Section 300.8*. https://sites.ed.gov/idea/regs/b/a/300.8/c

National Center for Education Statistics. (2024). *Students with disabilities*. U.S. Department of Education, Institute of Education Sciences. https://nces.ed.gov/programs/coe/indicator/cgg.

7

Gifted and Talented

Tara S. Guerriero, PhD

Students who are gifted and talented have the capacity to demonstrate high levels of performance in one or more of the following areas as compared to those of the same age, grade, and experience: intellectual ability, academic achievement (e.g., math, reading, writing), creative ability, leadership, visual and performing arts, and athletic capability (Gargiulo & Bouck, 2026; NAGC, 2025). Gifted and talented children often demonstrate these different capacities from a very young age (e.g., advanced early language skills or mathematical ability, advanced thinking or problem-solving skills, high levels of curiosity, early musical ability). Different districts and schools throughout the country have a variety of approaches to teaching and working with students who are gifted and talented (e.g., enrichment programs, accelerated programs, differentiated instruction). Gifted and talented students can show a wide variety of characteristics in a school setting; they may excel in school but may also get average grades or perform below their ability level.

Table 7.1 Student Demographics

Student Name	Gabriella Smith
Gender	Female
Grade	5
Educational Placement	Inclusive general education classroom; with gifted enrichment services in a gifted education classroom

Geographic Location	Suburban
Parent/Siblings	**Parents:** Two parents (Mom and Dad)
	Siblings: Older brother Carter (7th grade) and younger sister Katie (1st grade)
School	Lakeside Elementary School
LEA	Anderson School District
Academic Profile	**Reading:** Well-above grade level
	Writing: Well-above grade level
	Mathematics: Well-above grade level

Who Is Gabriella?

Gabriella is a ten-year old child who is in the fifth grade. She lives in a small suburban town with her dad, mom, older brother Carter (in seventh grade), and younger sister Katie (in first grade). Her parents are both professionals who have full-time jobs. Her mom works outside of the house three days a week and from home two days a week and her dad works fully from home. Gabriella is generally a happy child who loves being with her family, playing with her friends, playing on her travel soccer team (a team for which she tried out and made), practicing the piano and the glockenspiel (an instrument that is similar to a xylophone), and listening to music. Most people who know her would describe her as a "crafty" child, as she is always thinking of new things to make and design. She always says that she loves figuring out how things work and that she wants to be an inventor. She enjoys playing family games, putting together puzzles, and is an avid chess player.

At school, Gabriella spends most of the day in her regular fifth-grade classroom, with an hour of small group enrichment in the gifted classroom three days a week. Additionally, at the beginning of each day, she attends a sixth-grade accelerated math class at the middle school before being picked up by the school bus to go to her elementary school. Since the middle school has an earlier start time, she is still able to get to the elementary school before it starts. Gabriella has always been a "perfectionist;" she really wants to do everything perfectly and sometimes gets upset with herself if it isn't "right." For example, if she gets a problem wrong on her math test, she feels like she didn't do well at all. Or, in a soccer game, if she misses scoring a goal, she thinks that she didn't play well. This need for perfectionism can take a toll on her self-confidence from time to time, and her parents and teachers often remind her that she is doing a great job.

Gabriella also plays percussion in the school band. While she likes playing the drums, she really loves playing the glockenspiel. She has always loved music and was so excited to play in the school band. She has been playing the piano since she was little and her grandparents have a marimba that she has learned to play. When it came time for her to decide on an instrument for band, she wanted to choose something that was similar to the piano and the marimba; she decided to choose percussion so that she could play the glockenspiel. In addition to playing in her school's band, she auditioned for and made the fifth -and sixth-grade honors band.

The Early Years

As a young child, Gabriella had extremely advanced language skills; her vocabulary from a very young age seemed like that of a much older child. She put words together and said sentences well before what would be considered age appropriate. For example, when she was fifteen months old, when children are often saying single words or putting two words together, Gabriella often put together sentences such as "I get the emote (remote)." At two years, when children are typically putting together two to three words, Gabriella, said to her mom, "Please may I have my milk, please?" When her mom gave her the sippy cup, she went over to her brother and said, "My mommy gave me my milk."

Since her parents had flexible work schedules that included working from home, Gabriella did not go to daycare. Instead, when she was two, she went to nursery school in the morning for two days a week; she went three mornings a week when she was three; and she went to preschool for five mornings a week when she was four. She loved school, but when she was two and a half, she told her parents that she would try to talk to the other kids a lot but that they wouldn't say very much back to her. She asked if they didn't like her, but her parents explained that every child learns to talk at different times and that they may not be able to say as many things as she could. Around that same time, her teacher told her parents that one of the teacher's favorite parts of the day was when Gabriella would come over to her and tell her about her morning before school and things that she had done the night before. She said most of the kids in the class didn't have the type of language skills that Gabriella had.

This proficiency with language carried over to reading. Gabriella really took a liking to "reading" books when she was very little and she loved being read to. Upon seeing her interest in reading, her parents began teaching her to read when she was three. She was fully reading by the time that she was four. In preschool, Gabriella told her teacher that she could read and asked if she could read her a book; her preschool teacher didn't initially understand that she could actually "read" the book and was shocked when she started reading to her. Gabriella had a similar love for math and began counting and adding small groups together at a very young age. By the time she entered kindergarten, she was able to count to over two hundred and add and subtract small groups of objects.

Elementary School

Once she entered kindergarten and her teacher realized that she could read, her teacher would give her books to read instead of only listening to books, as many of the other children were doing. At one point, Gabriella came home and asked her parents why the reading center in her classroom was called the "reading center." She said that the kids were listening to books from their headphones and asked why it wasn't called the "listening center." Realizing that she needed more than what was being done in the classroom, her teacher had her meet in a small group with a math and reading specialist once a week to receive enrichment. Gabriella really liked being able to learn more difficult things.

As she moved into first grade, she would often come home from school and say that school was boring. She said that she didn't learn anything. Her parents would explain to her that she should find a way to make the activities at school more challenging for herself. Gabriella tried to do this, but sometimes the other kids sitting around her would ask why she was doing things differently from what the rest of the class was doing. She was having a hard time relating to the other kids in her class; they all seemed to be so happy about the work that the class was doing, but Gabriella didn't understand why. She was starting to get discouraged. She came home from school one day and said that her teacher told the class that children learn differently but that every child gets what they need. Gabriella asked her parents, "Why don't I get what I need?" Her parents relayed this conversation at the parent/teacher conference, and the teacher said that she would begin giving her more challenging activities from time to time. For much of her first-grade year, Gabriella didn't seem as excited about school as she had always been.

Identification and Eligibility for Gifted Services

When she was in second grade, her teacher realized how strong her academic skills were and recommended that she be screened for giftedness; upon examining the results, it was determined that she would have a full evaluation for giftedness. After her parents gave their permission to evaluate, Gabriella was given an evaluation and found to have very superior levels of performance both intellectually and academically (in the areas of reading, writing, and mathematics). She began receiving gifted services shortly thereafter that consisted of an hour, three days a week of small group enrichment in the gifted classroom. Her parents noticed a big change in her attitude toward school. She would come home much more excited and started to say how much she loved school.

Concluding Thoughts

While it took some time to get there, Gabriella has really started to thrive in school and has been able to feel as though she is learning and being challenged more frequently.

Questions:

1 List the possible areas that children who are gifted and talented might possess.
2 Describe Gabriella's strengths both academically and outside of school.
3 Why did you think that Gabriella's attitude toward school began to change in first grade?
4 Why could being a perfectionist lead to difficulties for a child?

5 When you were growing up, did you know anyone who was gifted, or who seemed to understand things more quickly than the other kids? What types of characteristics did they show?
6 Do you think that all kids who are gifted or talented love school and always get good grades? Why or why not?
7 Why did Gabriella ask if the other kids didn't like her when she was in nursery school? How do you think a teacher could help to make that situation better for a child like Gabriella?
8 Gabriella's parents were very involved in her schooling and advocated for her to the teachers. How might Gabriella's situation have differed if her parents weren't as involved? What can a teacher do to recognize giftedness in a child and help to provide enrichment?

Challenge: Research strategies for teaching gifted students (e.g., enrichment, acceleration). Choose three curricular areas (e.g., math, science, reading, English) and for each curricular area, describe a specific strategy that a teacher might use to help a child in the classroom who has skills beyond what is taught in the curriculum.

References

Gargiulo, R. & Bouck, E. (2026). *Special Education in Contemporary Society: An Introduction to Exceptionality.* (8th ed.). Sage Publications, Inc.

National Association for Gifted Children (NAGC) (2025). https://www.nagc.org/glossary-of-terms

8

Intellectual Disability

*Dawn R. Patterson, EdD and
Colleen E. Commisso, PhD*

Individuals with intellectual disabilities (ID) display needs in areas related to intelligence and adaptive behaviors (e.g., self-care skills, daily living skills, money management) with onset during the developmental period (birth to eighteen years). These needs present themselves in conceptual, social, and practical domains (Diagnostic and Statistical Manual of Mental Disorders-5th Edition [DSM-5], 2013).

Intellectual disabilities can have several different causal factors, including, but not limited to, genetics (e.g., Down syndrome), infections, environmental factors (e.g., toxins), substance use during pregnancy (e.g., alcohol, certain medications), trauma during birth (e.g., lack of oxygen), and injuries or accidents. The severity level of intellectual disability can range from mild (the most prevalent) to profound (the least prevalent) and is identified based on adaptive functioning due to the level of required support, rather than the intelligence quotient (IQ) (DSM-5, 2013).

Students with ID receive instruction within a range of educational placements from inclusive general education classrooms to self-contained classrooms in their schools. Some students with ID may also receive their education in a separate school. Instruction for students with ID is aimed at improving adaptive behaviors and can include academic skills, social skills, community-based instruction, and independent, functional living skills. Following their pre-K through 12 instruction, students with ID can often work in a variety of employment settings or attend college.

Table 8.1 Student Demographics

Student Name	Tyrese Moore
Gender	Male
Grade	Kindergarten
Educational Placement	Inclusive general education
Geographic Location	Urban
Parent/Siblings	**Parents:** Two parents (Mommy and Mum)
	Siblings: Older sister Nikki and younger sister Santangela
School	Thomas Jefferson Middle School
LEA	East City School District
Academic Profile	**Reading:** Below grade level
	Writing: Below grade level
	Mathematics: Below grade level

Who Is Tyrese?

My name is Tyrese, and I am the only boy in my house. My two sisters tell me that I am spoiled because of this, but I am also the middle child. My two moms tell me not to listen to my sisters, and that they are just jealous. My older sister Nikki goes to George Washington High School. I'm going there next year! My younger sister, Santangela, goes to William McKinley Elementary School, but next year she will be in my school, Thomas Jefferson Middle School. My mommy and mum met at the University of Toronto, Canada. They fell in love and got married before they moved to Chicago. All of us kids were born in the United States.

Medical Considerations

When I was two years old, I had a stroke. Due to the blocked artery to my brain, my brain did not get enough oxygen, and my brain cells started to die. I don't remember any of this, but that's what Mommy and Mum tell doctors. Thankfully, Mommy was home because I could have died. The dead brain cells caused me to have an intellectual disability. I don't notice my challenges; I'm just me. Sometimes, I get a little mad at myself because my thinking is a little slower than the other kids who are my same age. It takes me a little longer to learn, but I want to go to university just like Mum and Mommy.

At School

At school, I spend most of my time going to classes with the other eighth graders. My favorite class is science. I love when I get to work with different things, such as the microscopes, and do experiments. I liked social studies in seventh grade, but this year there is so much to know and memorize. I spend a lot of time at home with Nikki re-reading the chapters from the textbook. It's not homework, but Nikki doesn't mind helping me to re-read because she loved Ms. Lippanoga when she had her for social studies and Nikki wants to be a lawyer. At home, I can use the read-aloud feature on my digital textbook to answer the questions. I asked Ms. Lippanoga at the beginning of the school year if I could answer my questions from class at home and bring them back the next day for credit. Ms. Lippanoga said that would be ok. Nikki used to help me a lot with answering the questions, but now she mostly just sits with me in the room and helps me when I need it.

All my elective classes are so much FUN! I have theater arts right now, and last term, I took visual arts. In the elective classes, I feel smart because there is not a lot of textbook learning. It is much more relaxed, and I can talk and joke with my friends. I try to follow the rules, but sometimes I mess up, and my teacher will talk to me in private. My moms always find out and then one of them will talk to me, too.

I like math, putting numbers together to make bigger numbers, and combining money to make more money is even better, but I still don't always understand budgeting and not spending more money than what I have. Now, I mostly use a calculator for adding, subtracting, and multiplying. When I was younger, math was easier, but it is getting more difficult now. I spend half of the math block in the learning support special education classroom with some of the other kids from my math class. We all need the pace to go a little slower and the teacher to reteach some of the harder stuff, especially with some of the algebra. I can solve for x in a simple addition or multiplication problem, but when there is a number beside x and two different operations, like a plus and multiplication sign, it all starts to get a little confusing; Isiah and Robael agree with me. Mr.

Ramirez teaches the hard stuff in a way that makes sense to me, but it takes a couple of days, and I need it to be repeated over and over again. Math is getting harder and harder; I am having a hard time keeping up in math.

I am in Mrs. Habib's special education classroom for English language arts. Mrs. Habib spends a lot of time with me helping me with my reading comprehension. She says that if I want to go to college, I need to practice my reading more. I like graphic novels because the pictures are there, and there are fewer words on the page. *Super Pancake* is my favorite. The pictures make it easier to understand, not like my social studies textbook. There are nine other kids in Mrs. Habib's classroom. Some of them I see in some of my classes during the school day, and some of them I only see when I am in Mrs. Habib's class. I think that they are in her classroom all day.

Jonas and Gabriella are in my science class. This is fun because sometimes, when it is time for expressive writing, we are grouped to write about what we learned in science class.

After school, I have some chores at home, like emptying the dishwasher, vacuuming every Wednesday, and of course, cleaning my room. I'm pretty responsible with my chores, except maybe cleaning my room; no one ever looks under my bed.

My moms never let me be home alone. They are afraid that something is going to happen again. My other friends get to stay home alone, and they get to hang out after school. If I am playing video games in my room, I have to keep my door cracked. I am fifteen years old; I think that I am old enough to have some privacy and to hang out with my friends.

Next week, we are having a meeting at school about math. Mum is coming because Mommy will be out of town for work. I am worried about the meeting. Mum wants my math time to stay as it is, but I am having a hard time. I am going to the meeting. I want to hear what everyone has to say, and I want to make sure I can tell everyone how I am feeling.

Questions:

1. What are some of Tyrese's strengths and challenges in school?
2. How do the challenges align with his disability?
3. What strategies can be put in place to improve Tyrese's social life in school and at home?

Challenge: There may be a couple of different outcomes to the individualized education program (IEP) meeting focusing on math. One option is that the time in the special education learning support classroom could increase. Another option is that the current plan will remain the same. What are the benefits and challenges of both options? Explain them. Are there other options?

Challenge: Tyrese wants to go to college, but his reading comprehension and expressive writing skills are at the late third-grade level. He is also starting to have more difficulties with higher-level math concepts. In Tyrese's transition plan, college is listed as a goal. Do you think that college is a realistic expectation? Explain your rationale.

Reference

American Psychiatric Association. (2013). *Diagnostic and statistical manual of mental disorders* (5th ed.). American Psychiatric Association.

9

Learning Disability

Tara S. Guerriero, PhD

Students with learning disabilities (LD) have one or more deficit(s) in the way that they process information that comes in through their sensory system (i.e., hearing, vision, touch, taste, smell). The information comes in through their sensory system, but they have difficulties making sense of it. Processing deficits impact the way that they understand language and lead to difficulties in one or more areas of academic achievement including oral language, reading, written language, math, and nonverbal abilities. Students with LD traditionally have average or above levels of intelligence, suggesting that they have the cognitive ability to be able to learn; however, they have difficulties learning in one or more areas because of the way that their brain processes information. There are many areas of processing that could be impacted by a learning disability, including, but not limited to, visual processing or perception, auditory processing or perception, haptic processing (processing of information related to touch and movement), and the integration of information between the different modalities (e.g., visual/auditory integration).

Each student with a learning disability may have a different learning profile based on their areas of strength and need. For example, there can be three different students, all of whom have a learning disability in the area of reading, but for very different reasons. One student may have a visual processing deficit that makes it difficult to visually discriminate between different letters in the alphabet, while another student with auditory processing deficits may have difficulties with phonological processing and perceiving the sounds that the letters make. A third student may have difficulties when they have to integrate auditory information and visual information, thus making it difficult to connect the visual letter to the sound that it makes (process required for phonics). In order to truly understand the strengths and needs of a student with LD, it is important to get a clear picture of the processing strengths and needs that are contributing to their academic performance.

Table 9.1 Student Demographics

Student Name	Anna Jones
Gender	Female
Grade	7
Educational Placement	Inclusive general education classroom; with learning support services in the learning support classroom
Geographic Location	Rural
Parent/Siblings	**Parents:** Two parents (Mr. and Mrs. Jones) **Siblings:** Younger brother James (5th grade)
School	Ridge Middle School
LEA	Fairley School District
Academic Profile	**Reading:** Below grade level **Writing:** Below grade level **Mathematics:** On grade level

Who Is Anna?

Anna is a twelve-year old child who is in the seventh grade. She lives in a rural town with her mom, dad, and younger brother James (in fifth grade). Mr. and Mrs. Jones work in and help to run the family diner in town that is owned by Anna's grandparents. Since it is one of the busiest restaurants in town, the whole family spends much of their time helping out at the diner. Her family would describe Anna as a joyful and loving child. She loves being around people and greeting everyone who comes into the diner. Living in such a rural area, she knows almost everyone that comes in. When she isn't at the diner, she enjoys playing the clarinet, singing in the chorus and her church choir, spending time with her friends, and running. She is planning to be on the cross-country team in high school.

Anna has a lot of friends and is generally a really positive person, but sometimes she gets discouraged when she can't read or write in the same way as her friends. For example, all of her friends got matching diaries that they decorated, and they write in them every day. Anna doesn't like writing in her diary; she would rather just say her thoughts out loud and record them on her phone so that she can listen to them and remember them. Sometimes, this makes her feel different from her friends. Her friends don't seem to care, but it still bothers her.

At school, Anna is a good student who strives to do her best; she says that her favorite subjects are math and science and that her least favorite subject is English. She loves social studies too but has a hard time keeping up with all of the reading that is required. She is in all grade-level classes with the exception of English, where she has considerable difficulties and is in a lower-level class that focuses on basic reading and writing skills. She receives learning support services in the areas of reading and written language in a learning support classroom for one period a day. Anna has a lot of friends at school, and sometimes it bothers her that she has to go to the learning support classroom instead of taking a language like most of her friends. She also loves playing in the seventh- and eighth-grade band at school. She started learning to play the clarinet when she was in fourth grade and continues to love it. She has a hard time reading the music, but she can hear the notes so well that she has learned to play by sound.

The Early Years

As a baby and young toddler, Anna met all of the typical developmental milestones in the areas of social/emotional development, cognitive development, motor/physical development, and language/communication development. She was always such a happy child who loved being with people. She also loved listening to music and singing. There was rarely a time when she didn't have music playing in her room. When Anna was three, she started attending preschool two mornings a week. She loved learning and all the games that they played. She particularly liked the morning meeting when they sang the good morning song and talked about what they did the night before.

She also liked the crafts that they did, but sometimes she had a hard time understanding how to make the crafts. For example, she was supposed to draw a picture of a house, but she had a hard time fitting in the windows and doors. She didn't quite understand the size of them. They did a lot of floor puzzles in school, and she understood the picture of what the puzzle was, but she couldn't tell the differences in the shapes; it was hard for her to see how the pieces fit together. She learned the ABC song really quickly, but when they started working on their letters, she had a hard time learning them. The teacher would show them different letters, and they were supposed to say the name. Some of the letters looked so much alike that she couldn't tell the difference between them. For example, she couldn't tell the difference between a **W** and an **M** and a little **d**, **p**, and **b** all looked the same to her. She didn't understand how all of the other kids were able to tell them apart.

These difficulties continued into pre-kindergarten (pre-K) and kindergarten. When they worked on learning the sounds of the letters and connecting them to the written letter, she knew the sounds that the letters made, but she couldn't connect them to the written letter. For example, she knew the sound that a "b" made, but she couldn't tell if it was supposed to look like **b**, **p**, or **d**. They all seemed the same; they had a line and a circle. The teachers said to look to see if the circle was at the top of the line or the bottom and whether it was to the right or to the left of the line. This was so hard for her because she didn't know which was the right and which was the left and she had a hard time seeing if it was at the top or bottom of the line. Her teacher told her that she could remember her right from her left by looking at her hands and seeing which one made an **L** when she held out her thumb and pointer finger. It didn't matter which hand she used; they both looked like an **L** to Anna, so it didn't help her very much.

In first and second grade, she had more and more trouble with letters and had a really hard time learning to read. Writing was also difficult for her. She couldn't figure out the direction in which the letters should go. She was able to trace letters with her finger or a pencil, but she couldn't make a lot of them on her own.

Diagnosing, Eligibility, and Support

In the middle of second grade, the school recommended that they conduct a comprehensive evaluation to see if she had a learning disability. Her parents agreed and gave their written consent for the evaluation. It was determined that she had a learning disability in the areas of reading and written language with a deficit in visual perception. She had strong auditory and haptic perception as well as strong memory skills, but her visual processing made reading and writing difficult for her. She began receiving learning support services in the areas of reading and written language for thirty minutes, three days a week. She worked on learning left/right orientation and letter identification. There were a number of strategies that she tried including "drawing" the letters in shaving cream or in the air so that she could feel the difference between them. She also started wearing a watch on her left arm which helped her to tell the difference between her right and her left. As she learned left/right orientation, she began saying (or singing) the orientation of the letter as she drew them in the air or in shaving cream. For example, for the small letter **p**, she would say (or sing) "straight line from the top to the bottom, circle at the top right." Since she had such good memory skills, she began to learn the letters much better with a combination of drawing and saying or singing them. This helped with her reading and her writing.

Making Considerable Progress

As she has gotten older, she has noticed that reading has become easier, but it takes her a long time to read because she can't automatically see the letters without really thinking about them. Over the years, she has focused on learning orthographic patterns (e.g., *-tion*, *-ing*, *-dis*, *-ight*), which helped her to focus on the whole word rather than all of the individual letters. This method of learning orthographic patterns in combination with her strong visual and auditory memory skills has really helped her to recognize words more quickly and easily. Another strategy that she uses to "get her ideas out" when writing is to say everything that she wants to write using the talk-to-text function on her computer. She then listens to it back and writes it as she hears it. She is able to stop and start the recording as much as needed. She also listens to audiobooks to help her to learn information more quickly. She currently receives learning support services for forty-five minutes per day in a learning support classroom as well as accommodations in each of her classes. Her support services focus on a combination of teaching strategies to help her to improve her reading and writing as well as accommodations (e.g., talk-to-text and audiobooks) to make sure that she is learning the content. Although she continues to need learning support in reading and writing, she has made considerable improvement and she says that she now feels like "a reader."

Questions:

1. What is a processing deficit as it is related to learning disabilities?
2. Describe Anna's processing strengths and needs.
3. Why did you think that tracing letters in shaving cream was a beneficial strategy for Anna?
4. Why is it important to understand the student's learning profile and strengths and needs before determining the best strategies to use?
5. Why would puzzles be difficult for a child like Anna?

Challenge: What are some other strategies that could be beneficial for improving Anna's reading and written language? How could her love of music be incorporated into her learning?

10

Multiple Disabilities

*Dawn R. Patterson, EdD and
Colleen E. Commisso, PhD*

There is no single medical diagnosis for multiple disabilities (MD). It is a category of eligibility for a student to receive special education services. According to the Individuals with Disabilities Education Act (2004), there are fourteen different eligibility categories for children and young adults with disabilities to receive special education services. Multiple disabilities is one of those categories.

> Section 300.8 (c) (7) defines this eligibility category as "concomitant impairments (such as intellectual disability-blindness or intellectual disability-orthopaedic impairment), the combination of which causes such severe educational needs that they cannot be accommodated in special education programs solely for one of the impairments. Multiple disabilities do not include the combination of deaf blindness," this is a separate eligibility category.
> (IDEA, 20 U.S.C. § 1401 (2004), 20 C.F.R. § 300.8(c)(7))

Each state interprets this disability category using various specifications. For example, some states may consider a student with a combination of autism, intellectual disability, speech-language disorder, and/or attention deficit hyperactivity disorder eligible for special education services under the category of multiple disabilities. Other states use different criteria, requiring more intensive specialized support, such as a combination of intellectual disability, orthopedic impairment, students with special healthcare needs, speech-language impairment, deaf, blind, and/or other disorders and/or syndromes. The Multiple Disabilities #1 case study focuses on the former, while the Multiple Disabilities #2 case study focuses on the latter.

Multiple Disabilities (MD) #1

Table 10.1 Student Demographics

Student Name	Markeith Buchanan
Gender	Male
Grade	Kindergarten
Educational Placement	Full-time multiple disabilities support (MDS) in separate school
Geographic Location	Suburban
Parent/Siblings	**Parents:** One adoptive parent (Mother) **Siblings:** Two older brothers
School	Tyson Developmental School
LEA	Williamston School District
Academic Profile	**Reading:** Well-below grade level **Writing:** Well-below grade level **Mathematics:** Well-below grade level

Who Is Markeith?

Hello, everyone. My name is Markeith, and I am six years old. When I was born, I was diagnosed with fetal alcohol syndrome. The doctors could see this by my facial structure, which included short palpebral fissures (the distance between upper and lower eyelids is shorter than normal), flat upper lip, smooth philtrum (groove in the upper lip that runs from the top of the lip to the nose), and flat nasal bridge. Also, my biological mother was an alcoholic, and she binge drank every weekend, all weekend. When I was about fifteen months old, my foster mother realized that I was not meeting my developmental milestones. Some of these concerns included the limited sounds that I was making to communicate, using crawling as my primary method to move around, reaching for items with a full palmar grasp, being fed with a bottle, and crying when people left the room. I also had a lot of energy; I liked to move and had a very difficult time paying attention to anything. Finally, I don't like light touches; this makes me cry because it feels like pins and needles. The doctor told my foster mother that I have an intellectual disability. When I was two years old, I was adopted by my foster family. I have two older brothers; both are also adopted and have disabilities.

I go to a school that only has kids like me. I am in kindergarten, but there are friends in my class who are in first or second grade. Each day when I go to school, I do the same activities in the same order. I like this because I am learning to do these activities on my own and learn new skills. I love attention, I love people, and I am always happy. My mama says that I am a bundle of joy, but my brothers find me annoying because I am always in their toys. Eventually, I learned how to talk, but my sentences are about three to four words in length and are based on my routine. For example, most of the time I can say what I want or need, like when I want something to eat. Sometimes, I have a lot to say, but some of my words come out jumbled together, and people do not understand me. I think that is because I am trying to get all my words out, but my brain is trying to make all the words. When this happens, I grab what I want. I heard Mama say that I have a speech and language impairment.

At School

At my school, there are only kids with disabilities; they are all my friends. I am learning how to write my name, rote count to ten, say the alphabet, identify shapes and colors, answer questions, use words to express myself, and sit for five minutes during different activities like circle time, coloring, and arts activities. Right now, I can count up to four. I know the letters M-A-K-T-I-H, and I know *circle* and *yellow*. I have my desk with all my learning materials like my pencil, crayons, and eraser that looks like a monkey. I spend most of my day there, unless we are having group activity time. At school, there is a pretend area. I like to play with the baby dolls by pretending to feed them with a bottle, hold them, and walk around the classroom with the baby under my arm.

I meet with someone two times a week who helps me learn how to say my words. I also meet with someone who helps me work on moving my fingers and holding things in my hands, like my pencil. I also like going with Miss April because we work together, so I can stand on one foot and jump, and it is lots of fun. I wear blue pull-ups because I don't always know when I have to go to the bathroom. I have a tube (gastrointestinal, G-tube) to make sure that I get proper nutrition, but I can eat with my mouth too. Sometimes I have a hard time swallowing, and I can be a picky eater. Sometimes, I will pull my G-tube out when no one is looking. I get a lot of attention when this happens. My mama has me wearing a onesie so that I cannot get to my G-tube, and someone watches me all the time.

At school, there are four other kids in my class; three of them cannot walk around like I can, and they sit in special chairs with wheels, and one walks around like me. Sometimes we play together. I have music and art in my classroom, but I go to PE in the gym. Ms. Pam is always with me. She is the teaching assistant. She knows me and I trust her; she helps me learn, but she is not the teacher in the classroom. Ms. Pam treats me like her son. When she is absent from work, there is a substitute, and I feel confused and anxious.

I like school because I have so many friends. I don't have friends at home, just my two brothers. I play in the backyard at home sometimes because Mama is always very busy. When school is over, I go to an after-school program with many of the other kids from my school. When I am there, I talk to a lot of the adults and other kids, make puzzles, complete shape sorters, and do other activities where I am putting items into a container. Sometimes I count when I do this and sometimes I just talk and laugh. If I pull my G-tube out at my after-school program, they have to call my mama. Sometimes she will take me home, and other times, she will put it back in and then go back to work; she's a nurse. I love school and my after-school program. Learning is fun, but recess and running are especially fun. I think everyone is my friend and I like interacting with them, but I don't know how to play very well with other kids.

Questions:

1 Identify and describe each of Markeith's disabilities.
2 If someone asked you, "Tell me about Markeith," how would you describe him?
3 When thinking about his kindergarten-second-grade classroom, what activities would you plan for him?

4 How can you improve Markeith's communication skills?
5 What does Markeith mean when he states that he thinks everyone is his friend and that he likes interacting with them, but doesn't know how to play very well with other kids? What can you do to help with this interest?

Challenge: Please respond to the following:

- What educational professionals work with Markeith as a member of his team?
- Describe each person's role and why it is important to collaborate.
- How will this collaborative work benefit Markeith?
- Identify three general goals that can be implemented by different team members.

Multiple Disabilities (MD) #2

Table 10.2 Student Demographics

Student Name	Mahsumah Basu
Gender	Female
Grade	11
Educational Placement	Full-time multiple disabilities support (MDS) in separate school
Geographic Location	Rural
Parent/Siblings	**Parents:** Two parents (Mr. and Mrs. Basu)
	Siblings: Fraternal twin sister, Jiya
School	Indian Flatlands Separate School
LEA	Country Wide School District
Academic Profile	**Reading:** Well-below grade level
	Writing: Well-below grade level
	Mathematics: Well-below grade level

Who Is Mahsumah?

I am Mahsumah and I am determined. People call me Sumah, and my fraternal twin sister is Jiya. When I was born, I wasn't supposed to live.

We were born 147 minutes apart; some things did not go the right way during my delivery. Umm (Mama) has told us that Jiya came right away; she was easy, but I was stuck in the birth canal. I was not in the right position, and the doctor had to try to turn me in Umm's belly. Once I was lying the right way, I started to go out, then my shoulders got stuck inside my mother. The long delivery resulted in me not getting enough oxygen, causing my profound intellectual disability and blindness. Umm knew immediately that my name would be Mahsumah, which means "determined." When I was three days old, I fought an infection for two weeks, which led to my quadriplegia. I am determined, and that has been evident throughout my life.

Umm told us stories about how we played together as infants. Umm would hold each of us in an arm; Jiya would intentionally reach my foot to give me a nudge, and I would gurgle in response. As we got older, Jiya would crawl toward me to physically interact with me, and I would make different sounds. Jiya, Umm, and Baba (dad) learned what each of my different sounds meant. This is the same today; I never learned how to talk. I have many thoughts, but because of my physical limitations, which affect my mouth, tongue, and respiratory abilities, I cannot talk.

I am in eleventh grade, in Mrs. Smith's high school multiple disabilities classroom at Indian Flatlands Separate School. I have attended the same school since I was three years old. Due to my many different needs, there is only one school in this rural area that has the level of support that I need for my learning and health. Shortly after returning home from the hospital at three weeks old, I began receiving many different services. First, there was nursing care, then physical therapy, then occupational therapy and speech-language therapy; I had all of my therapies at our home.

Now that I am in high school, I am still receiving all of the same services in school. During the school day, I have to change positions frequently, but because I cannot move my own body, the teachers, teaching assistants, and physical therapist move me out of my wheelchair, to a standing position, to a side-lying position, and into the walker. I must get out of my wheelchair and into these different positions so that my muscles stay strong and do not contract, to keep my bones strong, and to decrease any chances of skin breakdown. After my therapy, all of the adults give me a choice of which position I want to be in based on which feels the best to me.

I am able to stretch out my right arm. I have learned that if someone asks me a yes or no question, I can stretch out my right arm to answer "yes." I started doing this after second grade, when the speech and language and physical therapists collaborated to teach me an authentic response mode. I was extremely happy about this because, before this, I only did what everyone said to do. If I do not respond to a question that is asked, people know that the answer is no. When I am given a choice between two items, and if my answer is no to both of them, then I am asked again in about fifteen minutes. If my answers are still no, then the person asking will decide for me. When I was younger, this happened all the time; now, I simply decide for myself, because I do not like being told what to do.

I enjoy getting in the walker, especially at school, because I can walk up and down the hallway and see what is happening in all the other classrooms. The side sleeper feels good because I can stretch out on my right side or left side, and it alternates every time I am in this position. The stander makes me feel strong and tall, even though I am only 4 feet 11 inches. Jiya is only 5 feet 2 inches, so I don't mind. In each of these positions, I am secured with various straps because I cannot control my own body except for my right arm and my head. I also wear ankle foot orthotics because it is important that my feet are in the correct position, and that my heel is down in the back of my orthopedic shoes, especially when I am walking or in the stander.

When I am in my stander, I have literacy time with two other students. During the story time, there are specific objects related to key points in the story to help me understand new vocabulary words. Reading comprehension time is one of my favorites because I like to hear the stories and think about the characters. I think that the other two students have pictures to see also, but they both have very good vision, unlike me. Learning about the story while I am standing distracts me from the amount of time that I have been standing. In my class, we also learn math, science, and social studies. Mrs. Smith has been a wonderful teacher for the past two years. She knows that I want to learn, and she treats me with respect. She uses objects in every lesson to make sure that I am learning as much as possible. We have so much specialized equipment in the school because all of us must receive a meaningful education. We don't all learn the same.

When I was younger, I used to wear a pull-up, but I realized in second grade that I could feel the urge to go to the bathroom, and that when I ate at regular times, I typically needed to go every two hours. Again,

I could be me, and the speech-language therapist and occupational therapist were able to attach a single message switch to the right side of my wheelchair, coming from my headrest, with a single message, "I have to go to the bathroom, please." The switch is close to my head, so that I can tilt my head to the right to let people know, especially if the people around me have lost track of time. I am determined because with a single person's assist, I can push myself up when my footrests are removed from my wheelchair and my feet are placed on the platform. My arms are placed around the helping person's neck. While I am in a standing position, pitched forward, the person helping will get my pants down and lower me to the toilet seat. I love this because Jiya goes to the bathroom independently. I have other opportunities to communicate using different augmentative and alternative communication aids, but they must always be paired with an object. I want to know what I am saying before I communicate.

Jiya is planning to go to college after she graduates from twelfth grade. She wants to be a pediatrician and she has been applying to colleges that are two to four hours away. I am happy for her, but I am also starting to feel sad. We are so close, and I have learned so much from her. She has always told me everything and helped me understand her world. We have always gone to different schools, but we have been together most of the time. I have gone to her soccer games, and we have gone to the movies together. We lie in bed together, and she tells me stories. She even told me about her first boyfriend. She has told me that she is sad to go away to school and leave me behind. I will be in school until my twenty-second birthday. I am happy about that because I like school. Umm has reassured both of us by saying that we can go visit Jiya any time we want. I don't know what I will do after I finish school.

Questions:

1. Identify and describe Mahsumah's disabilities.
2. Describe Mahsumah's personality and provide evidence.
3. Mahsumah requires many different pieces of equipment for her to stay healthy, communicate, and learn. Identify each of these in a list, select two, and describe them, including their importance.
4. Describe the relationship between Mahsumah and Jiya.

5 Mahsumah lives in a rural area. Do you think that if she lived in a different geographic location (e.g., suburban or urban) that she would have different opportunities? Explain.

Challenge: Please respond to the following:

- Mahsumah is very aware of her sister's transition to college. What can Mahsumah's Umm, Baba, sister, and teacher do to prepare Mahsumah for this?
- How can they prepare for Mahsumah's post-secondary transition? Conduct research to identify options for Mahsumah's post-secondary life and develop a plan to inform her about the information learned.
- If you were Mahsumah's teacher and you were teaching a lesson about the life cycle of a plant, list some of the materials that you would use. Explain why.

References

Individuals with Disabilities Education Act, 20 U.S.C. § 1400 (2004)
IDEA (Individuals with Disabilities Education Act). (2004). *Section 300.8.* https://sites.ed.gov/idea/regs/b/a/300.8/c

11

Other Health Impairment: Epilepsy

Colleen E. Commisso, PhD

Other health impairment (OHI) is a disability category under the Individuals with Disabilities Education Act (IDEA, 2004). This definition includes the following:

> having limited strength, vitality, or alertness, including a heightened alertness to environmental stimuli, that results in limited alertness with respect to the educational environment, that—
>
> a) Is due to chronic or acute health problems such as asthma, attention deficit disorder or attention deficit hyperactivity disorder, diabetes, epilepsy, a heart condition, hemophilia, lead poisoning, leukemia, nephritis, rheumatic fever, sickle cell anemia, and Tourette syndrome; and
> b) Adversely affects a child's educational performance.
>
> IDEA, 20 U.S.C. § 1401 (2004), 20 C.F.R. § 300.8(c)(9)

Table 11.1 Student Demographics

Student Name	Alexandra (Alex) Peters
Gender	Female
Grade	11
Educational Placement	Inclusive general education classroom

Geographic Location	Urban
Parent/Siblings	**Parents:** Two parents (Mom and Dad)
	Siblings: Two brothers (ages 14 and 19)
School	Pine Crest High School
LEA	Pine Crest School District
Academic Profile	**Reading:** On grade level
	Writing: On grade level
	Mathematics: On grade level

Who Is Alex?

Alex is a sixteen-year-old girl who attends her local high school in a large metropolitan city. The first five years of Alex's life were very typical. She was born on her due date and met all her developmental milestones as a baby, toddler, and young child. Her parents described her as a happy child who enjoyed playing with age-appropriate toys and being outside. She and her family enjoyed going to local parks and activities within the city, such as visiting the aquarium and zoo. Before going to kindergarten, Alex attended a local pre-K program and knew her letters, numbers, shapes, and how to count to ten.

When Alex was five, she started attending her local elementary school. At her first parent-teacher conference, the teachers indicated that Alex was friendly, got along with her classmates, and had a few close friends that she played with during recess and free time within the classroom. They also said that she worked hard and wanted to do her best on academic tasks. Alex's parents indicated that she often had play dates with friends from school, got along with her siblings, and was helpful at home. At home, Alex enjoyed baking with her mom, doing puzzles, and playing outside.

Medical Considerations

A few months following the parent-teacher conference, Alex's parents noticed that there were sporadic moments that were concerning but difficult to identify. Alex would suddenly lose awareness of her surroundings, displaying unusual behavior such as staring blankly for short periods, but Alex's parents thought that she was daydreaming or being absent-minded.

Concerned, Alex's mom reached out to her classroom teacher and asked if they were seeing anything similar. Alex's teacher responded, indicating that they didn't notice anything, but that they would keep an eye out. A few weeks later, Alex's teacher emailed Alex's mom that she noticed that Alex seemed to be staring into space and was unresponsive when prompted for a few seconds. Over the next three weeks, these episodes became more frequent at home and school. Her parents became increasingly worried, and they sought medical advice. They scheduled an appointment with Alex's pediatrician, who, after seeing Alex, referred her to a neurologist for additional testing.

The Diagnosis

After a series of tests, including an EEG (electroencephalogram), the diagnosis was confirmed: she had epilepsy, a neurological disorder characterized by recurrent, unprovoked seizures. The diagnosis was a difficult moment for Alex's parents, who were faced with the uncertainty of how this condition would affect her long-term health and development. The seizures were identified as focal seizures, which involve one part of the brain and can present as a sudden loss of awareness or jerking movements, among other symptoms.

Treatment and Supports

Following the diagnosis, Alex began an individualized treatment plan. Initially, her doctors prescribed medications to control the seizures, which were designed to regulate the electrical activity in her brain that caused the seizures. This process to find the right medication included many obstacles. Alex experienced multiple side effects from several different drugs, including fatigue, weight gain, and difficulty concentrating.

While the medications helped reduce the frequency of her seizures, they did not eliminate them. Over time, her doctors and parents worked together to adjust the treatment plan. She also underwent several rounds of lifestyle modifications, including sleep regulation, reducing stress, and minimizing any potential triggers for seizures, such as flashing lights or prolonged screen time. These early years were marked by constant medical appointments and testing as her care team sought the optimal balance of medication and lifestyle adjustments. As she continued kindergarten and into first grade, Alex missed almost 20 percent of school days due to appointments or side effects; however, Alex's parents and teachers were proactive in ensuring as much as possible that her seizure disorder did not interfere with her educational development. Over time, however, it became clear that the condition posed challenges. Episodes of focal seizures often occurred in the classroom, leading to concerns from both Alex and her peers. On several occasions, she would suddenly zone out during lessons, which led to questions and, at times, misunderstandings from classmates and teachers. Alex would also miss instruction/directions during these episodes, and sometimes, following episodes, she would need to take breaks in the nurse's office, causing additional missed instructional time. Given the impact on her education, Alex was evaluated and classified with "Other Health Impairment" during first grade, making her eligible for special education services under IDEA.

To support Alex, the following adaptations were included within her individualized education program (IEP):

- Alex sat near the front of the classroom so that teachers could easily monitor her and provide help if a seizure occurred.
- Alex was allowed to have access to the nurse after a seizure if she needed to rest.
- If Alex missed class time, her teachers also gathered any materials (e.g., notes, assignments, activities, etc.) to be sent home.
- When the class was using their iPads for learning, Alex was given the option to use physical materials (e.g., handouts, manipulatives) to mitigate the impact of the bright lights of the iPad.
- Alex received learning support to assist her in developing memory strategies and learning how to refocus when she lost concentration because she faced difficulties with memory and concentration during flare-ups, which were common side effects of both her medication and the seizures themselves.
- A flexible assessment policy was implemented, allowing her to take exams in a quiet environment and offering extended time for assignments.

During middle school, Alex became increasingly self-conscious of her condition, often having feelings of isolation, especially since her classmates noticed her seizures and began to question her frequent absences. In response, Alex developed a sense of resilience and learned to explain her condition in simple terms, which helped to reduce misunderstandings and foster a supportive environment among her peers.

Upon entering high school, Alex had become quite familiar with her condition. Seizures remained a part of her life, but she had learned to manage them with the help of her medical team and the support of her family and school. Although the frequency of seizures had decreased with the right combination of medications, they still occurred from time to time, often triggered by stress or changes in routine. Alex continued to receive adaptations to navigate the ups and downs of living with epilepsy. During high school, Alex continued to engage with a tight-knit circle of friends who were understanding of her condition and helped her feel less isolated. However, some challenges persisted in group settings, such as school dances, sports, or overnight field trips. Alex was sometimes hesitant to participate in activities where she felt her condition might interfere. However, with her parents' encouragement and a strong support network at school, she gradually became more involved in extracurricular activities, including the yearbook and the school newspaper. These activities gave her a chance to showcase her strengths and form meaningful relationships, helping her to feel more like a typical teenager, rather than just a person with epilepsy.

Questions:

1. What initial characteristics did Alex display that concerned Alex's parents and then her teachers?
2. What are important factors for teachers to consider about students who take medications, or when students are trying to figure out which medications work best for them?
3. What adaptations did Alex receive? What other adaptations do you feel could support Alex?
4. How did her epilepsy impact Alex's social relationships?

Challenge: While this didn't necessarily happen with Alex's peers, what types of reactions might peers have to a child with medical conditions like epilepsy? What could a teacher do to help children better understand the impacts (e.g., medical, social, behavioral, academic) of such conditions?

Challenge: Research the steps that should be taken to properly respond when someone is experiencing a seizure. Make a list describing these steps.

References

Individuals with Disabilities Education Act, 20 U.S.C. § 1400 (2004)
IDEA (Individuals with Disabilities Education Act). (2004). *Section 300.8.* https://sites.ed.gov/idea/regs/b/a/300.8/c

12

Orthopedic Impairment: Cerebral Palsy

Mary A. Houser, EdD

According to the Individuals with Disabilities Education Act (IDEA), Orthopedic impairment (OI) means "a severe orthopedic impairment that adversely affects a child's educational performance. The term includes impairments caused by congenital anomaly (e.g., clubfoot, absence of some member, etc.), and impairments from other causes (e.g., cerebral palsy, amputations, and fractures or bones that cause contractures)."

IDEA, 20 U.S.C. § 1401 (2004), 20 C.F.R. § 300.8(c)(8)

The largest category of orthopedic impairment is cerebral palsy. Cerebral palsy (CP) is a group of neurological disorders that become present in infancy or early childhood that affect body movement and muscle coordination. "Cerebral" refers to the brain, and "palsy" refers to problems related to motor function. CP causes issues related to the developing brain and interrupts the brain's capacity to maintain posture and balance and control movement. CP can range from mild to severe (National Institute of Neurological Disorders and Stroke, 2025). Students with orthopedic impairments may or may not require special education services.

Problems with movement and posture are common to all individuals with CP. Some examples of symptoms include ataxia (i.e., a neurological disorder characterized by the loss of coordination and control of voluntary muscle movements), spasticity (i.e., a neurological condition characterized by stiff or rigid muscles and exaggerated reflexes), weakness in arms or legs, and differences in muscle tone. Related conditions to CP include intellectual disability, seizure disorder, and delayed growth and development, to name a few. Most individuals with CP are born with it; however, it is possible to acquire CP after birth due to brain infections, brain damage early in life, and head injury (National Institute of Neurological Disorders and Stroke, 2025).

Table 12.1 Student Demographics

Student Name	Michael Montgomery
Gender	Male
Grade	Pre-kindergarten
Educational Placement	Special education early intervention (EI) preschool program
Geographic Location	Suburban
Parent/Siblings	**Parents:** Two parents (Mary Auer and John Montgomery) **Siblings:** None
School	Sangry Lane Learning Center
LEA	North Hills Central School District
Academic Profile	Skill deficits in physical development, cognitive development, communication development, social-emotional development, and adaptive skills

Who Is Michael?

The Pregnancy

Mary and her boyfriend, John, were excited about the upcoming birth of their baby. They had been trying to get pregnant for over a year, and their dreams finally came true late one September when Mary took a pregnancy test, and the result came back positive. It seemed like they had waited a lifetime to receive this good news. Mary's pregnancy was mostly uneventful, and she made sure to take good care of herself and attend her regular pregnancy check-ups with her obstetrician, Dr. Sallis.

A Premature Birth

One evening, about seven weeks before their baby was due, Mary began experiencing back pain, cramping, and bleeding. This felt unusual to her as she had not experienced anything like it before. She called her doctor, Dr. Sallis, who told her to come to the hospital so he could examine her. He performed a full physical examination and conducted several tests. When he was done, Dr. Sallis had a concerned look on his face. He told Mary and John that Mary's placenta had separated from her uterus (i.e., placental abruption) and that an emergency C-section was necessary. Mary was immediately taken back for surgery, and their son, Michael, was born a short time later. Although Dr. Sallis worked as quickly as he could to deliver Michael, some oxygen deprivation had already occurred during the birth process.

Over the next two years, Mary and John noticed that Michael was developing differently from other infants and toddlers his age. He had floppy muscle tone (hypotonia) in his arms and legs. This meant that Michael's arms and legs had a "rag doll" appearance. His limbs were limp and lacked tension. He rolled over and crawled later than expected. He did not lift his head when he should have, and he had stiff joints and problems swallowing his baby formula when fed. As a toddler, he continued to have swallowing problems. He was not walking by the age of eighteen months. Michael was also demonstrating some signs of a mild intellectual disability, such as a lack of curiosity. He was not naturally inquisitive about seeing new things or going to new places with his parents. He also exhibited coping problems. For example, if he did not want to go to the grocery store with his mother, he would break down and have a tantrum while at the store until Mary was forced to leave in order to stop his crying. Michael was also not talking like other toddlers his age. He would say a few words here and there, but he was not spontaneously putting words together. Around the age of two, Michael's pediatrician diagnosed him with cerebral palsy (CP), an orthopedic impairment.

The Diagnosis

The diagnosis of CP was a shock to Michael's parents. Because Mary and John did not know anyone with CP, there was so much for them to learn about it. It seemed overwhelming at times. Dr. Sallis spoke to them about the different types of CP (spastic, dyskinetic, and mixed). He also explained the different subtypes of CP and how they are based on the part of the body that is primarily affected (e.g., diplegic, hemiplegic, quadriplegic, monoplegic, and paraplegic). He talked about the fact that Michael might benefit from certain medications, occupational and physical therapy, and speech therapy. Dr. Sallis mentioned the benefits of assistive technology that might also help Michael in school. Lastly, he spent quite a bit of time discussing the possible need for a walker and how this would help Michael's ambulation. He stressed the fact that Michael was young and that early intervention would be critical to his progress.

Mary and John were stressed and anxious after they received Michael's diagnosis. They worried about finding an appropriate school program for Michael and the financial burden that might result from having a child with a disability. In addition, they could not help but think about what the future might hold for him. Would he ever live on his own? Hold a job? Have a family?

Early Intervention Services

Michael is now three years old and receives early intervention services in a self-contained special education preschool in his local suburban school district. There are six other preschoolers with varying disabilities in his class. His parents are relieved that they live in a school district that provides high-quality early intervention programs at no additional cost to them. When Michael turned three, an individualized education program (IEP) was developed for him. This program included goals for his motor skills, communication, and social-emotional skills. Michael's goals would be regularly assessed and adjusted to ensure his progress throughout the year. Both of Michael's parents were actively involved in the planning of his IEP and considered valued members of his IEP team. An important aspect of Michael's early intervention program is the related services he receives that specifically address his CP. Michael receives occupational therapy (OT) a few times per week. Areas he is currently addressing include the following:

- **Fine motor control:** for example, painting, sorting objects, and coloring
- **Crossing the midline:** for example, throwing and kicking a ball, playing Simon Says, and making windmills
- **Self-care skills:** for example, washing his face with a washcloth and getting dressed

Michael also receives physical therapy (PT) a few times a week. The following are some areas he is working on and the activities he performs:

- **Stretching:** for example, hamstring stretch and quadricep stretch
- **Range of motion:** for example, shoulder flexion
- **Strengthening:** for example, resistance training
- **Gait training:** for example, parallel bars, and bodyweight supporting treadmills

Concluding Thoughts

Michael is showing improvement and will continue to receive preschool special education services until he transitions to kindergarten at the age of five. In the next year or so, his IEP team will begin discussing transition planning to prepare him for kindergarten. At this time, his IEP team will meet to discuss his preschool progress and the different types of educational placements that will be considered for elementary school.

Questions:

1. What is cerebral palsy?
2. What caused Michael's cerebral palsy?
3. Describe the cerebral palsy characteristics Michael displayed as an infant and as a toddler.
4. Provide examples of the various activities Michael engages in during his occupational therapy sessions and his physical therapy sessions.

Challenge: Interview an occupational therapist or a physical therapist. Ask them to elaborate on their experiences working with individuals with cerebral palsy.

References

IDEA (Individuals with Disabilities Education Act). (2004). *Section 300.8.* https://sites.ed.gov/idea/regs/b/a/300.8/c

National Institute of Neurological Disorders and Stroke (2025). *Cerebral palsy.* https://www.ninds.nih.gov/health-information/disorders/cerebral-palsy

13

Sensory Impairments

Tara S. Guerriero, PhD and Mary A. Houser, EdD

In this chapter, auditory and visual impairments are grouped together as sensory impairments. Case studies depicting individuals with deafness, deaf-blindness, hearing impairment, and visual impairment are included. The following is the Individuals with Disabilities Education Act (IDEA) definition of each of these impairments:

1. **Deafness** is "a hearing impairment so severe that it impairs a child's ability to process linguistic information through hearing, even with amplification, and this adversely affects their educational performance" (IDEA, 20 U.S.C § 1401 (2004), 20 C.F.R. § 300.8(c)(3)).
2. **Deaf-blindness** "means concomitant hearing and visual impairments, the combination of which causes such severe communication and other developmental and educational needs that they cannot be accommodated in special education programs solely for children with deafness or children with blindness" (34 CFR 300.8(c)(2)).
3. **Hearing impairment** is "an impairment in hearing, whether permanent or fluctuating, that adversely affects a child's education performance but that is not included under the definition of deafness in this section" (IDEA, 20 U.S.C. § 1401 (2004), 20 C.F.R. § 300.8(c)(5)).
4. **Visual Impairment including blindness** "is impairment in vision that, even with correction, adversely affects a child's educational performance. The term includes both partial sight and blindness" (IDEA, 20 U.S.C. § 1401 (2004), 20 C.F. R. § 300.8(c)(13)).

Sensory Impairments: Deafness

Mary A. Houser, EdD and Tara S. Guerriero, PhD

Deafness is considered a complete loss of hearing. It might be caused by genetics, complications during pregnancy (e.g., infections), certain medications used during pregnancy, and accidents or illnesses. Deafness might also be caused by the underdevelopment of the outer ear (microtia) or the absence of the ear canal (atresia). There are four types of deafness: sensorineural, conductive, mixed (sensorineural and conductive), and auditory neuropathy spectrum disorder (ANSD).

Characteristics of deafness include challenges in understanding speech, delayed language development, reliance on visual communication, social isolation, and the need for individualized education. Students who are deaf typically have individualized education programs (IEPs) and can be educated in a variety of educational placements. Most deaf students attend their neighborhood public schools. Some other educational placement types, such as residential schools, charter schools, and day schools, cater to students with profound hearing loss.

Table 13.1 Student Demographics

Student Name	Jackson Brown, III
Gender	Male
Grade	6
Educational Placement	Inclusive general education
Geographic Location	Urban
Parent/Siblings	**Parents:** Mom (Janet Brown)
	Siblings: Younger sister Lily (age 8)
School	Liberty Middle School
LEA	Ft. Honor School District
Academic Profile	**Reading:** Below grade level
	Writing: Below grade level
	Mathematics: On grade level

Who Is Jackson?

Jackson is an eleven-year-old, sixth-grade middle-school student who attends Liberty Middle School in the Bronx, New York. He lives with his mother, Janet, and his younger sister, Lily. Jackson was born with permanent deafness. His hearing loss was due to the pregnancy complications Janet experienced. She contracted cytomegalovirus (CMV), an infection from a herpes virus, in her early pregnancy, which is a known cause of sensorineural deafness (affects the inner ear).

Jackson started demonstrating signs of deafness in both ears from birth. He lacked a startle reflex, which is a natural reaction to a loud sound. Jackson did not turn his head in the direction of the sound either. He failed his newborn hearing screening before he and Janet were discharged from the hospital. A follow-up test was done (e.g., auditory brainstem response) to confirm his deafness diagnosis. This diagnosis came both as a relief and also created a sense of fear for Janet. She was relieved because she finally got an answer to why Jackson was not responding to his name when she said it and lacked a startle response at the sound of loud noises. She was fearful, however, of what his future would hold as a person with a profound hearing loss. Janet also experienced guilt when the doctor told her it was likely due to her contracting CMV.

Early Years

As a very young child (nine months old), Jackson began receiving early intervention (EI) services. These services included speech-language therapy and an educational program for young children who were deaf. His mother and sister were also given family resources and support. Receiving help was important because his family members had no knowledge of deafness or how to best interact with Jackson, a child who could not hear. When Jackson turned one, he received cochlear implants in both ears. Cochlear implants are commonly used for children with a profound hearing loss. These devices bypass the damaged ear and directly stimulate the hearing (i.e., auditory) nerve, which in turn, sends an electronic signal to the brain, which then interprets the signal. Jackson also began to learn American Sign Language (ASL) during this time. This would become his primary language.

When Jackson turned three, he attended a specialized preschool for students who are deaf and remained there until he started kindergarten. Once Jackson started kindergarten, he attended his neighborhood elementary school. His IEP team determined that a self-contained classroom setting would be his least restrictive environment. He was also included in all specials (e.g., art, music, PE). During his elementary years, Jackson worked hard to be successful. During that time, he made significant progress both academically and socially. His reading comprehension, although still delayed, improved. His vocabulary usage and ability to express himself got better. Jackson also began making friends with other students in class. This was not previously possible.

Middle School

Now that Jackson is entering middle school, his IEP team has decided they want him to be placed in an inclusive general education setting with his hearing peers. Janet, in particular, wants Jackson to be educated with other typically developing children. Being placed in an inclusive general education classroom in middle school was an exciting new step for Jackson, but it would come with a lot of changes. The school would be larger than his elementary school. He would have multiple teachers. Jackson would be introduced to a whole new group of students in an inclusive general education class. The expectations for independence would also be higher.

For Jackson to be successful in his inclusive general education middle school placement, several adaptations will be needed. These will assist in providing equal access to instruction and assessment. Because of his deafness, Jackson will benefit from adaptations in the general education setting from both an academic and social perspective. Here are some of the changes that will take place:

- **The Teachers' Roles:** Jackson's teachers need to implement several accommodations for him. Jackson should be seated in the front row of the class, so he is closest to his teachers and away from the possible distractions caused by the rest of the class. They should always get his attention before speaking. Jackson's teachers must avoid turning their backs on him during instruction. They will also need to repeat comments or questions, as needed. They will need

to use visual aids, in addition to oral instruction, to support his learning. They will also need to collaborate with his sign language interpreter, as needed.
- **Sign Language Interpreter:** Jackson will be provided with a sign language interpreter in his class. This person helps to translate the instruction given by the teacher into Jackson's primary language: ASL. He also helps to facilitate meaningful interactions between Jackson and his peers as he bridges the gaps between spoken and signed communication. He will work closely with Jackson's teachers to ensure he is relaying all important instructions.
- **Speech-to-Text:** Speech-to-text allows Jackson to talk, and his words get automatically translated into text on his laptop. This will help Jackson speak and get his thoughts down quickly. It provides him with greater independence in his writing assignments. He uses Dragon NaturallySpeaking. He downloaded the software on his laptop, and it was ready to use.
- **Captioned Media:** Captions allow students with hearing challenges equal access to video content by providing text so that they can better understand the audio content of the media they are viewing. All of Jackson's media-related assignments and assessments will have captioned media.
- **Testing Accommodations:** Jackson will not be required to complete any type of oral assessments. He will be provided with extended time on tests. He will be allowed to take breaks as necessary. He will be allowed to use his assistive listening device (ALD) and captioned media, as needed. He will also be permitted to take tests in a separate environment, which will help to minimize distractions.

Concluding Thoughts

A lot of things changed for Jackson from the time he was diagnosed with deafness until the start of middle school in his new inclusive general education classroom. He had received quality education, good medical care, and benefited greatly from family support, which significantly aided in the gains he has made since being a young child. If he continues to progress as he has up to this point, the sky is the limit for him.

Questions:

1. Define deafness.
2. What signs of deafness were apparent at Jackson's birth?
3. Discuss how Janet felt about receiving Jackson's diagnosis.
4. Identify the different educational placements Jackson was in, beginning at nine months old up to middle school.
5. Discuss the adaptations Jackson will receive in his inclusive general education middle-school placement.

Challenge: If you were a special education teacher in an inclusive general education classroom, how else could you create a more inclusive classroom for your deaf students?

Challenge: Research three evidence-based practices (EBPs) for teaching students with deafness. Create an instructional video of you presenting these EBPs.

Sensory Impairments: Deaf-Blindness

Mary A. Houser, EdD and Tara S. Guerriero, PhD

Deaf-blindness is a rare condition that occurs when an individual has combined hearing and vision loss, thus limiting access to both auditory and visual information (National Center on Deafblindness, 2025, para. 1). It is one of the disability categories recognized under IDEA. Deaf-blindness is most commonly caused by prematurity complications and hereditary disorders and syndromes. Examples of such causes include Down syndrome, trisomy 13, Usher's syndrome, toxoplasmosis, AIDS, herpes, syphilis, and fetal alcohol syndrome. Congenital anomalies such as hydrocephaly and microcephaly (i.e., neurological impairments affecting brain development and head size) might also be the cause of this disorder. There is a significant range in one's ability to both hear and see with this disorder. Some children with deaf-blindness have sufficient vision, in their environments, to recognize familiar faces and read large print. Others might be affected more profoundly, resulting in lack of vision or ability to hear. Similarly, individuals with deaf-blindness might be able to adequately hear familiar sounds, understand speech, and even develop some speech themselves. Others with deaf-blindness might not develop these abilities (Miles, 2008). Like other children with disabilities served under IDEA, children with deaf-blindness must be educated in their least restrictive environment. For some students with deaf-blindness, this will be an inclusive general education classroom or a self-contained classroom in a neighborhood school; others will attend separate schools for the deaf and blind, and some will attend residential facilities to best serve their needs.

Table 13.2 Student Demographics

Student Name	Allie O'Brien
Gender	Female
Grade	Kindergarten
Educational Placement	Special education early intervention (EI) preschool program
Geographic Location	Rural
Parent/Siblings	**Parents:** Three parents: Tom O'Brien and Brian Callahan (adopted dads) and Kelly Simmons (birth mother)
	Siblings: None
School	Moynihan School for the Deaf and Blind
LEA	Mountain Bridges School District
Academic Profile	Skill deficits in physical development, cognitive development, communication development, social-emotional development, and adaptive skills

Who Is Allie?

Allie is a three-year-old girl with deaf-blindness who lives in rural Oklahoma. She was born two months prematurely. Shortly after birth, Allie presented with some significant challenges that would affect her development. During the birth process, Allie did not receive enough oxygen, resulting in hypoxia (which can lead to various health concerns). Additionally, Allie was diagnosed with hydrocephaly, which occurs when there is a buildup of cerebrospinal fluid in the brain's ventricles. Allie was also diagnosed with Usher's syndrome (impacts vision and hearing) later in her first year, which was determined through genetic testing. Due to her prematurity and health problems, Allie needed to spend several weeks in the neonatal intensive care unit (NICU) until she was stable enough and ready to come home.

The Adoption

One evening, shortly after Allie's birth, Allie's mother, Kelly, was having dinner with her friends Tom and Brian. The dinner conversation centered around Kelly's concerns about raising Allie. Kelly was distraught. She said that she was afraid of raising a newborn with a severe disability, and she was not sure how she could financially support Allie because she had just gone through a divorce. Kelly shared that she was hardly able to support herself, let alone a child with a disability. She discussed her limited options with Tom and Brian, which included the possibility of putting Allie up for adoption. Tom and Brian listened compassionately to their friend, and after they went home that evening, they had a long talk about how they could help Kelly. Their discussion revolved around the idea of them adopting Allie. Tom and Brian had been wanting to adopt a child for a long time, but the circumstances had never been right. They knew that it would be very difficult for Kelly to give Allie up for adoption to a perfect stranger, but maybe she would feel differently if it were them who were caring for Allie. Tom and Brian thought that by adopting Allie, this would allow Kelly to be part of her life as she grew up. When Tom and Brian approached Kelly about adopting Allie, she was initially shocked by their offer but soon realized this might be an ideal situation. Before Allie came home from the hospital, they began the adoption process, and as luck would have it, the adoption was completed over the next few months.

Allie's Deaf-Blind Characteristics

When Allie came home from the hospital, she was small and underweight. Tom and Brian commented on how little she looked in her car seat as they placed her in it to ride home. Before they left the hospital, Tom and Brian were given lots of paperwork from the discharge nurse. This included contact information for some of the new specialists Allie would need appointments with, in addition to scheduling follow-up appointments. Tom and Brian also received literature on how to interact with an infant with deaf-blindness. This was something neither of them had ever considered when thinking about parenting a child. Both Tom and Brian knew extra care would be necessary to provide Allie with everything she needed to thrive, but they were ready for the challenge.

Once they got her home, Tom and Brian began to notice some of Allie's unique characteristics. Allie exhibited several classic symptoms of an infant with deaf-blindness. These characteristics included the following:

- Not turning her head toward the sound
- Failure to make eye contact
- Failure to reach out toward people or objects
- Dislike of certain textures
- Not wanting to be touched by parents or others
- Banging her head on her crib
- Minimal crying

Tom and Brian recognized that many of these characteristics were not typical for infants because both of them came from large families, had younger siblings, and remembered what they were like as babies. They commented to each other about the distinct differences between Allie and other members of their families as very young children.

Early Intervention and School Life

Allie began receiving EI during her first year of life. Tom, Brian, and Kelly were instrumental in the development of her individualized family service plan (IFSP). An IFSP is a legal document that outlines how to promote Allie's growth as a young child, assist her family in supporting her, and outline her special education and related services. Allie's EI services consisted of physical therapy, speech therapy, occupational therapy, and instruction from an early intervention special education teacher and a deaf-blind specialist. Allie's EI services occurred at the family's home, which is often the ideal location for very young children with disabilities to receive early intervention. Several days during the week, one of the education professionals would come into their home and work with Allie. This model worked well because very young children tend to make good progress in their natural environments (e.g., home).

Tom and Brian also received support from their school district, which helped them parent a young child with deaf-blindness. Perhaps the best resource they received led them to join a parent support group for children with deaf-blindness. This allowed Tom and Brian to share their concerns and victories when raising Allie with other parents raising children with complex support needs.

When Allie turned three, it was time for her to go to an early intervention preschool program at school. This was a big deal not only for Allie but also for her parents. Although Tom and Brian were excited for Allie to be part of a class at school, they worried about her because she had never been anywhere without one of them before. What would being away from home be like for Allie? Would she be scared? Would she be safe? Would everyone treat her with as much love and care as they did?

Because she was now three years old, Allie would transition to an IEP (from an IFSP), which would be developed by her new IEP team. Together, they developed goals for Allie to achieve over the next year. After her IEP team met with the members of her IFSP team and consulted with Allie's parents, it was determined that a separate preschool specializing in deaf-blindness would be the most appropriate educational placement for Allie. Her IEP team also discussed their desire to eventually have Allie attend a neighborhood school and be included with her typical peers for at least part of the school day.

Here are some examples of the skills that Allie worked on at her EI preschool:

1 Allie will visually attend to a single photograph of her favorite object for at least five seconds to indicate she wants that object.
2 Allie will use her pincer grip to obtain small objects.
3 Allie will explore solid embossed objects on a page with her hands.

Shortly after her third birthday, Allie began attending the Moynihan School for the Deaf and Blind. This separate school served children three to twenty-one years of age who received the diagnoses of blindness, deafness, or deaf-blindness. Allie's preschool teacher specialized in early intervention and teaching students with deaf-blindness. Allie would be taught a life skills curriculum that included instruction in adaptive skills such as communication skills, basic reading and writing, hygiene, and social skills. The Moynihan School for the Deaf and Blind also offered many excellent support services that would help Allie acquire important life skills. These support services included assistive technology specialists, braille specialists, adaptive physical education specialists, orientation and mobility specialists, and ASL specialists. Moynihan School for the Deaf and Blind also provided vision specialists, audiologists, physical therapists, occupational therapists, and speech and language therapists. More than anything, the education professionals who worked at the Moynihan School used instructional strategies that were specific to children with deaf-blindness. Tactile learning strategies became a primary way of instructing Allie. These learning strategies employ a hands-on approach where Allie used real, everyday objects to learn concepts by exploring using her sense of touch. Tactile tracing was another common instructional strategy used where Allie would trace letters, numbers, and objects with her fingers in various materials such as sand and textured papers. They also worked on orientation and mobility skills that taught Allie how to safely and independently move about the classroom (e.g., learning spatial concepts). Neither Tom nor Brian had ever seen a school that offered so much help to their students. After visiting the school and seeing how much help Allie would receive there as a student, they were excited for her to get started. That evening, they phoned Kelly and shared the good news.

A few weeks after Allie began school, Tom, Brian, and Allie invited Kelly to go for a walk at a local park with them. As they strolled around the paved path, they reminisced about how much had taken place since Allie's birth and how much they had accomplished as a team. They spoke of the mutual love they had for Allie and shared their dreams for her future.

Questions:

1 What is deaf-blindness? What might have contributed to Allie's deaf-blindness?
2 State four examples of deaf-blindness characteristics that Allie exhibited as an infant.
3 Allie received an IEP when she turned three years old. List two new skills listed in her IEP that she would be working on that school year.
4 Allie's transition to an early intervention preschool was a big change for the family. What concerns did Tom and Brian have about her attending school?

5 Describe the Moynihan School for the Deaf and Blind. Why would this be a good choice for Allie?
6 What type of curriculum would Allie be learning at the Moynihan School for the Deaf and Blind? Why might this be appropriate for a child with deaf-blindness?

Challenge: Research support groups for deaf-blindness at the local and state levels in your state. In a format of your choosing (e.g., PowerPoint, Prezi, Google slides) report back on your findings.

Sensory Impairments: Hearing Impairment

Tara S. Guerriero, PhD and Mary A. Houser, EdD

Those with hearing impairments who have functional hearing that allow them to be able to hear and understand speech may be described as hard of hearing (Gargiulo, 2026). There are many factors that can cause hearing loss (e.g., maternal infections before birth; complications after birth; differences in the formation of the heart, face, or ears; an accident or head injury) (Centers for Disease Control and Prevention, 2024). The severity of hearing loss can vary substantially between individuals from mild to profound, with the hearing loss for those considered to have a hearing impairment being milder.

Table 13.3 Student Demographics

Student Name	Gia Bailor
Gender	Female
Grade	8
Educational Placement	Inclusive general education; with accommodations provided for hearing impairment
Geographic Location	Suburban
Parent/Siblings	**Parents:** Two parents (Mr. and Mrs. Bailor) **Siblings:** Two younger sisters and three older brothers

School	Greenwood Middle School
LEA	Ashton School District
Academic Profile	**Reading:** On grade level **Writing:** On grade level **Mathematics:** Above grade level (honors class)

Who Is Gia?

Gia is an eighth grader at Greenwood Middle School and she lives with her dad, mom, two younger sisters, and three older brothers in a small suburban town in the Midwest region of the United States. Gia is an energetic and outgoing child who loves participating in as many extracurricular activities as she can (e.g., soccer, tennis, basketball, playing the violin in the school orchestra, being in the school chorus, Girl Scouts). Academically, Gia is a conscientious student who always tries to do her best; she is on grade level in all of her classes with the exception of math, her favorite subject, in which she is in an honors level class.

The Accident

During the summer before eighth grade, Gia and her parents were on their way back from the grocery store when their car was hit by another car whose driver had gone through a red light. The Bailors were hit toward the back of the driver's side of the car, where Gia was sitting in the back seat. The accident resulted in bruising on the left side of her face, a minor concussion, and a mild hearing loss on her left side. As her bruises and head healed, she continued to have difficulties clearly hearing sounds that were coming from her left side. She described the sound coming in through her left ear as muffled, like it would sound if she were covering her ear with her hand.

Persistent Difficulties with Hearing

For the most part, Gia's hearing loss changed very little in her life; she is still able to participate in school and all of her extracurricular activities as she always has because she can hear everything clearly from her right ear. However, there were a couple of situations in which her hearing loss impacted her. She noticed that she had difficulties hearing when people talked to her from her left side. If they didn't talk loudly enough, she wouldn't be able to hear what they were saying. Sometimes, other kids would get mad at her saying that she was ignoring them when she didn't even know that they were talking to her. She also had difficulties in class depending on where her desk was placed. If she was sitting all the way to the right side of the classroom (when facing the front of the classroom), she often had difficulties hearing the teacher and others in the class.

Another way that her hearing loss impacted her was when she was using her laptop in school. Each student had a laptop, and they often needed to use it during their classes. When they needed to listen to something with sound on their laptop, they used their headphones; Gia had a lot of difficulties with headphones because many of the sounds cut out. Sometimes sounds would only go to the right or left ear through the headphones. She felt like she was missing a lot of what was said.

Accommodations

Even though her difficulties were relatively minor, the Bailors decided to set up a meeting with the school to talk with them about what Gia was experiencing. Her teachers hadn't realized that she was having these difficulties with her hearing. The school and her parents decided that she didn't need to have a comprehensive evaluation to determine whether she was eligible for special education services for a hearing impairment under IDEA because Gia didn't need specially designed instruction to succeed in school. They did, however, determine that she was eligible to receive accommodations through a Section 504 service agreement under Section 504 of the Rehabilitation Act of 1973 (often referred to as Section 504).

According to the U.S. Department of Education OCO (2025), the goal of Section 504 is to prevent discrimination to individuals with impairments in programs or activities that receive federal financial assistance. Individuals who have "physical or mental impairment that substantially limit one or more major life activity" (U.S. Department of Education OCO, 2025, para. 5) are eligible for accommodations under Section 504. Examples of major life activities are "walking, seeing, hearing, speaking, breathing, learning, and working" (U.S. Department of Education OCO, 2025, para. 5, number 11, para. 2). For Gia, hearing loss would be considered a physical impairment, and a major life activity would be considered hearing.

A Section 504 service agreement was developed for Gia that indicated that she would be given the opportunity to choose where she would sit in each class to maximize her hearing in the classroom. Additionally, whenever she was required to listen to something on her laptop, she was able to listen to it directly from the laptop (without using headphones) either in a corner of the room or in a different location in the building. These accommodations have proven to be very successful in minimizing the impacts of her hearing loss. Gia was also told that if she noticed any other situations that were impacting her at school, she could talk with her teachers, and the school would update her Section 504 service agreement, accordingly.

Questions:

1 What was the causal factor of Gia's hearing impairment?
2 Why did the school and the Bailors decide not to pursue an evaluation for special education services for a hearing impairment under IDEA?
3 How did Gia's hearing loss impact her academically? Socially?
4 Are there any difficulties that you think Gia could have with the extracurricular activities (e.g., soccer, tennis, basketball, playing the violin in the school orchestra, being in the school chorus, Girl Scouts) as a result of her left-sided hearing loss?
5 Describe the difference between a hearing impairment and deafness.

Challenge: Research the following levels of hearing loss: mild, moderate, severe, and profound. For each level, describe the characteristics and how each may impact students educationally.

Sensory Impairments: Visual Impairment

Tara S. Guerriero, PhD

There are many types of visual conditions that may result in a wide range of severity levels of vision loss. One condition that young children may develop is amblyopia. According to the National Eye Institute of the NIH

(U.S. Department of Health and Human Services, 2024), amblyopia is a type of vision that occurs when there is a breakdown in the connection between one eye (sometimes both eyes) and the brain. The brain has difficulties recognizing sight from the affected eye and begins to rely on information from the stronger eye. Vision in the affected eye can become severely weakened if steps are not taken to correct it. The cause of amblyopia can differ from person to person. According to Johns Hopkins Medicine (2025), one possible cause of amblyopia is a strabismus, which is a misalignment of the eyes that causes one eye to drift inward or outward. While this may occur in very young infants when they are tired, if it persists and is not treated, the brain may begin to ignore information coming from the misaligned eye resulting in amblyopia. One major impact that reduced vision in one eye can have is the reduction of depth perception and 3-D vision, as it is the combination of vision from both eyes that allows for individuals to see depth.

Table 13.4 Student Demographics

Student Name	Max Perkins
Gender	Male
Grade	9
Educational Placement	Inclusive general education classroom with accommodations provided for visual impairment
Geographic Location	Urban
Parent/Siblings	**Parents:** Two parents (Josh and Melanie Perkins) **Siblings:** Older brother Nathan (eleventh grade)
School	Manor Area High School
LEA	Oakley School District
Academic Profile	Honors level courses across all subjects

Max's Early Years

Max is fifteen years old and in the ninth grade; he lives with his dad, Josh, his mom, Melanie, and his older brother, Nathan. Josh and Melanie met in college where they were both student athletes; Josh played baseball while Melanie played soccer. After college, they both moved back to their hometowns; after two years of being in a long-distance relationship, they got married and moved back to the city that their college was in to pursue their careers in finance. They soon decided to start a family and had Nathan. When Nathan was about two, with hopes of expanding their family, they moved to a larger apartment. When Max was born, Nathan was so excited to have a little brother. Max was an advanced child, meeting many of his developmental milestones earlier than what is considered typical; for example, he began walking when he was just under nine months old. His parents assumed that he was a cautious child because he always preferred to hold onto something when he was walking or running. For example, he loved to run around the coffee table while holding on. When he was about fourteen months old, they began to notice that his right eye would cross inward when he was really tired; as the month went on, his eye was crossing more and more at other times of the day. They talked to the doctor at Max's fifteen-month well-child visit, and the doctor referred them to a pediatric ophthalmologist to evaluate his eyes. It was determined that Max had a strabismus, or a misalignment of the eyes that caused his eye to cross inward. The doctor was able to test Max's vision and determined that he needed glasses. The glasses prescription was going to help straighten his right eye and help with his vision. The first day that Max had his glasses was one of the hardest days of Josh and Melanie's parenting life; every time they put his glasses on him, he took them off. After a whole day of this, they were afraid that he would never keep his glasses on. The next day, he kept his glasses on and didn't try to take them off; his glasses became part of him from then on.

At his follow-up appointment with his ophthalmologist, the doctor was concerned that he would develop amblyopia (i.e., breakdown in the connection between the eye[s] and the brain), as the vision in his right eye was weak, even with his corrective lenses. In addition to benefits that the glasses were providing, he was also going to start wearing a patch over his left eye (his stronger eye) for four hours per day to force the brain to recognize vision from his right eye. The patches were one-time use patches that looked like large bandages with fun designs; the Perkins called them his special stickers. When he was very young, he saw his ophthalmologist every six to twelve weeks to check his progress; he was slowly making progress and typically got a new glasses prescription each year. When he was five, he had surgery to tighten the muscles in his right eye and help with alignment. As he got older, it became harder and harder to find four hours a day when Max was home to wear his patch, and he really disliked the way that it made him feel. When he wore his patch, he felt disoriented, and it was hard for him to do things that required detailed vision like reading. However, the Perkins insisted that he wear it every day; they told him that a few years of not liking a patch would lead to a lifetime of being able to see better. Max had a second surgery when he was nine and continued to wear a patch until he was almost eleven years old, at which time it was determined that it wouldn't continue to help his vision. While the vision in his right eye had improved considerably, he still had better vision in the left eye. This caused some difficulties with his depth perception and his understanding of three-dimensions. Max's vision impacted him the most in three areas of his life: in school, in sports, and in the city in which he lives.

School Life

Max has always loved school and learning; when he was in kindergarten, he was excited every morning to go to school. He had already learned how to read, so school didn't seem as hard for him as it did for the other kids who hadn't yet learned to read. He continued to excel in first and second grade, but he noticed that as the print got smaller, he had a much harder time seeing it. He also noticed that it was hard for him to see things in fine detail, which made activities like writing and completing small puzzles more difficult for him. His teacher and parents agreed that he should be referred for a comprehensive evaluation to see if he needed special education services for his visual impairment.

While he did have a visual condition, the evaluation showed that he was not eligible for special education services under IDEA because he didn't demonstrate a need for modifications or specially designed instruction. It was determined that he would, however, benefit from accommodations that were provided under Section 504 of the Rehabilitation Act of 1973. The team (that included his parents) developed a Section 504 service agreement that allowed for him to use a computer with a magnifier that would help with his visual difficulties. Any physical work (e.g., worksheets, books) that was too small for him to see would be provided to him electronically. If there was something that was not able to be provided in an electronic form, he was given a large format version of it or he was able to use a magnifier that was backlit. Additionally, an accommodation was put into place that allowed for his desk to be close to the front of the room so that he could see the board.

As he got older, his accommodations continued to help him. His difficulties with three-dimensional vision sometimes hindered his ability in his art class and in his math class when he needed to understand 3-D forms on paper. However, his accommodations provided for programs on the computer which would show the 3-D figures with more depth and color contrast, thus allowing him to better "see" the dimensions. He is currently in ninth grade, and he continues to have accommodations for his vision, but they have allowed him to continue exceling in school, without being hindered by his vision.

Athletics

Mr. and Mrs. Perkins, Nathan, and Max have always been big sports fans; they have season tickets for their college basketball and football teams, and they spend much of their family time at the park playing different sports. When Max was three, he wanted to start playing soccer like his brother Nathan and his mom. He loved it, and played every week at the community park. At that age, they mostly played fun games and tried to dribble the ball.

He continued playing soccer and when he was four, he was so excited to start playing T-ball. He was going to play baseball just like his dad. His excitement for baseball soon started to wane because he said that he couldn't see the ball when he was in the field, and when he was hitting, he couldn't see the bases. He also said that he was frightened when someone would throw the ball toward him. He played for the whole session (ten weeks), but he really didn't like it and said that he didn't want to play anymore.

He continued to play soccer, and when he was in kindergarten, he was able to play on a team. He did great in practice, but the Perkinses noticed that he would just stand in the middle of the field during games. He seemed to be really confused and disoriented during the games. As he got older, he realized that he was getting confused during the games because he couldn't tell when the ball was coming close to him, and he couldn't adjust his eyes to all of the movement on the field. As his eyes improved, he found it much easier and when he was about ten, he really started to make gains as a soccer player because his vision had improved to the point that it didn't affect him very much on the field.

He continued to play in middle school and made the junior varsity (JV) team during his first year of high school. This is quite an accomplishment because his school is large and there are only three teams, a first-year team, a JV team, and a varsity team. Many of the first-year students who tried out weren't able to make one of the teams. His coach says that he is playing so well that he has a good chance of making the varsity team in tenth grade. He has come so far from a young child who was confused on the field to one of the better players in the school.

Navigating the City Life

The third area in which his visual condition has had great impacts lies in his ability to navigate the city in which he lives. He lives in a heavily populated city and his family walks or takes public transportation, taxis, or rideshares nearly all of the time. Similarly to his early experience with T-ball and soccer, when he was young, he had considerable difficulties with his vision and depth perception in the city. When he was walking in crowds of people, he would become disoriented and confused by all of the movement, and he found it really hard to visually track what was going on around him, especially if people were moving quickly.

When he was using public transportation, he often couldn't keep track of where he was and what stops were coming up. At night, the contrast between the lighting and the darkness made it very difficult for him to see what was going on. Similarly to his experience with school and sports, as his vision improved, his difficulties with his environment started to improve, as well. Now, he is able to navigate his city without difficulty both because his eyes have improved so substantially, and because he has had so much experience navigating his city that he has really learned to compensate for any residual vision difficulties.

Concluding Thoughts

It has taken Max a long time to get to where he is with his vision and he has had to work really hard to overcome his difficulties (e.g., wearing a patch for over nine years, enduring surgeries, wearing glasses, using different types of accommodations at school), but he is exceling in nearly every aspect of his life much due to the early care that he received as soon as his visual condition presented itself.

Questions:

1. What is a strabismus? Amblyopia?
2. When Max was really young, why do you think that Max preferred to hold on to something when he was walking or running?
3. Max really took to his glasses early on, even though he was very young. Why do you think he didn't get upset about wearing them?
4. Compare and contrast Max's vision when he was young to when he was older. What contributed to the improvements in his vision?
5. Why would Max's vision difficulties have made him feel disoriented or confused in crowded spaces or on the soccer field?

Challenge: Research the requirements for special education services under IDEA and accommodations under Section 504 of the Rehabilitation Act of 1973. Why wasn't Max eligible for special education services under IDEA? Why was he eligible for accommodations through a Section 504 service agreement?

Challenge: Depending on the level of severity of a visual impairment, students may need to be educated in different environments or educational placements to meet their needs. Research possible types of educational placements for students with visual impairments and compare and contrast how different educational placements might meet the needs of different students.

References

Centers for Disease Control and Prevention. (2024, May). *About hearing loss in children.* https://www.cdc.gov/hearing-loss-children/about/index.html

Gargiulo, R. & Bouck, E. (2026). *Special education in contemporary society: An introduction to exceptionality.* (8th ed.). Sage Publications, Inc.

IDEA (Individuals with Disabilities Education Act). (2004). *Section 300.8.* https://sites.ed.gov/idea/regs/b/a/300.8/c

Johns Hopkins Medicine. (2025). *Strabismus*. https://www.hopkinsmedicine.org/health/conditions-and-diseases/strabismus#:~:text=Strabismus%20

Miles, B. (2008). *Overview of deaf-blindness*. DB Link. https://www.nationaldb.org/media/doc/Overview-Deaf-Blindness_a.pdf

National Center on Deafblindness (2025). *Deafblindness overview*. https://www.nationaldb.org/info-center/deaf-blindness-overview/

U.S. Department of Education – Office of Communications and Outreach (OCO). (2025, January 13). *Frequently asked questions: Section 504 free appropriate public education (FAPE)*. https://www.ed.gov/laws-and-policy/civil-rights-laws/disability-discrimination/frequently-asked-questions-section-504-free-appropriate-public-education-fape

U.S. Department of Health and Human Services. (2024). *Amblyopia (lazy eye)*. National Eye Institute. https://www.nei.nih.gov/learn-about-eye-health/eye-conditions-and-diseases/amblyopia-lazy-eye

14

Speech or Language Impairment

Tara S. Guerriero, PhD

Speech or language impairments (SLI) includes types of communication disorders that impact an individual's ability to produce and/or understand language. A **speech disorder** is an impairment that includes articulation disorders (i.e., the ability to articulate speech sounds), fluency disorders, and/or voice disorders. A **language disorder** is an impairment that impacts the ability to use or understand language (e.g., spoken, written, signed). Language disorders may impact the form (phonology, morphology, syntax), content (semantics), and/or function/usage (pragmatics) associated with language (ASHA, 1993).

Table 14.1 Student Demographics

Student Name	Sara Reader
Gender	Female
Grade	5
Educational Placement	Inclusive general education classroom with speech and language support outside of the general education classroom
Geographic Location	Suburban
Parent/Siblings	**Parents:** Two parents (Mom and Dad) **Siblings:** Younger sister Reagan

School	Wheaton Elementary School
LEA	Millbrook School District
Academic Profile	**Reading:** Above grade level
	Writing: Above grade level (written expression content and ideas); Grade level (spelling)
	Mathematics: Above grade level

Who Is Sara?

Sara Reader is a fifth grader who has been diagnosed with an articulation disorder, which is a type of speech disorder. Sara lives with her dad, mom, and younger sister, Reagan, in a single-family home in a small suburban town. Her dad is a consultant for nonprofit organizations, and her mom is a certified public accountant. Sara has always been a very talkative and outgoing child who loves to be with people. She loves playing soccer, basketball, and tennis. She has also been taking piano lessons for the last three years. The family spends a lot of time together (e.g., playing board games, watching movies, and playing in the yard) and getting together with other families in the neighborhood.

The Early Years

When Sara was first learning to talk, she developed language really quickly. Both her receptive (listening) and expressive (speaking) language skills were much stronger than most kids her age. Her vocabulary was strong and she was very good at finding the words that she wanted to say and expressing her thoughts. As she got older, her parents noticed that she was having difficulties pronouncing multisyllabic words (e.g., elementary, basketball, family). She would omit sounds or syllables in the words (e.g., "emantwy" instead of elementary, "basetball" instead of basketball) and/or put the syllables in the wrong order (e.g., "falimy" instead of family, "ephelant" instead of elephant, "sgabetti" instead of spaghetti).

In addition to difficulties with multisyllabic words, she wasn't able to say her "Rs," instead pronouncing the "R" sound as a "W" sound. For example, she pronounced her name as "Sawa Weadew" and she called her sister "Weagan." When Sara was little, everyone thought that her speech was really cute, but as she got older, it became clear to her parents and teachers that her speech difficulties were extending well beyond what would be considered typical for her age. Her parents and teacher also noticed that she was starting to shy away from social situations (e.g., talking to other kids at recess, during lunch, and on the bus; playing with friends outside of school), saying that she was embarrassed by the way that she talked. She asked her parents if they could start driving her to school because the older kids on the bus called her "a baby" because of the way that she talked and they sometimes even imitated and made fun of her speech.

Evaluation, Eligibility, and Support Services

When she was in third grade, the decision was made by her parents and the school that she be evaluated by a speech and language pathologist and school psychologist to determine whether she had a speech and language impairment. The evaluation indicated that she had an articulation disorder, or deficits in the ability to articulate speech sounds. Her articulation disorder impacted both her speech production and her written language in the area of spelling (she relied heavily on sounding out the words, incorporating the mispronunciations into her spelling). Since the evaluation resulted in evidence of an articulation disorder and evidence of need for specially designed instruction, she became eligible for special education services under the Individuals with Disabilities Education Act (IDEA) in the category of "Speech and Language Impairment."

Following the comprehensive evaluation, toward the end of third grade, the individualized education program (IEP) team that included her parents, her teacher, a special education teacher, the speech and language pathologist, the school psychologist, and the principal convened to develop her IEP. Sara started receiving speech and language support three times a week for twenty minutes outside of her general education classroom because it was determined that that would be her least restrictive environment (LRE). One reason why receiving services outside of the general education classroom was determined to be her LRE was because it would allow her to receive services without bringing further attention to herself and her speech difficulties. She had small group instruction two days per week and individual instruction one day per week. Over the past two years, she has tried many different strategies to improve her articulation. The following are just some of the beneficial strategies that she has engaged in during her support sessions:

- She listens to recordings of her speech and notes any articulation errors that she has made in multisyllabic word production. For each misarticulated multisyllabic word, she completes the following:
  - She listens to a correct model of the word, while also reading the word.
  - She then says each syllable of the word slowly in isolation, focusing on the motor planning and movement that is needed to articulate the different sounds.
  - Then, she puts the syllables together as a whole word and repeats the word several times.
  - Lastly, she says it in the context of a sentence.

The combination of listening to a model and reading the word really helps her to be able to sequence all of the sounds and say the word in context.

- Using a similar technique that was described above, she works on articulating sets of words (e.g., connec*tion*, adap*tation*, rela*tion*, comput*ation*) with the same morphological endings (e.g., *tion*, *sion*, *ness*). This helps her to sequence multiple multisyllabic words that follow a pattern.
- When working on the letter "R" she focuses on the motor movement, tongue, and lip placement. She also uses a mirror to watch her movement when saying the sound.
- She uses her strong reading skills and visual memory to help with her spelling skills instead of relying on sounding out the words. This has really helped with accuracy in spelling.

Concluding Thoughts

Sara has made so much progress over the last two years. She has greatly improved her ability to make the "R" sound. When she is talking very quickly or is tired, she will often mispronounce the "R" sound, but for the most part, she is able to produce it in her everyday speech. Her ability to articulate multisyllabic words has improved, as well. If she slows down her speech, she can generally pronounce most multisyllabic words. Similarly to the "R" sound, she continues to demonstrate errors when she is talking quickly or when she is tired. She feels much more confident in her speech and feels better about social situations. She will continue to receive services into sixth grade to help with any residual difficulties that she has, but it is likely that she will be able to discontinue her speech and language services during her sixth grade year.

Questions:

1. Define a speech disorder and identify the three different types.
2. Define a language disorder.
3. What is the difference between a speech disorder and a language disorder?
4. Why do you think Sara started to have difficulties in social situations? Why might Sara's speech difficulties have been more pronounced in a social situation as compared to a reading or social studies class?
5. Why do you think that Sara's speech disorder impacts her spelling skills but not her reading skills?

Challenge: Define the following: articulation disorder, fluency disorder, and voice disorder.

Challenge: Research strategies for improving articulation disorders. Identify and describe three strategies that you think could benefit Sara and provide a rationale for why they would be beneficial.

Reference

American Speech-Language-Hearing Association (ASHA) (1993). *Definitions of communication disorders and variations.* https://www.asha.org/policy/rp1993-00208/?srsltid=AfmBOophywQ65FQ9qtPamKpgkgNVYkNGTZXmYJZtkWjKfBxr7B1zi4lx

15

Trauma-Informed Practice

Colleen E. Commisso, PhD

---

*DISCLAIMER: This section includes case studies that discuss children who have experienced traumatic events. Reading and discussing information on traumatic events can cause individuals to have strong emotional responses.

Adverse childhood experiences (ACEs) are traumatic events experienced in childhood. It is important to note that various groups (e.g., CDC, The National Child Traumatic Stress Network [NCTSN]) include different examples of ACEs and that one list is not necessarily inclusive of all ACEs a child could experience. Examples of ACEs can include, but are not limited to the following:

- Abuse: physical, emotional, or sexual
- Neglect: physical or emotional
- Exposure to domestic violence
- Loss of a parent from death, abandonment, divorce, incarceration, or military service
- Witnessing violence in the home or community
- Living with someone who has a mental health need
- Experiencing a natural disaster
- Societal variables such as lack of access to healthcare, financial difficulties, being unhoused or moving frequently, and discrimination.

Approximately 64 percent of adults have indicated that they have experienced at least one type of ACE before the age of eighteen (Cleveland Clinic, 2023).

ACEs can have many lasting impacts on a child's brain and health, including mental health concerns or chronic health conditions, as well as the failure to meet developmental milestones (Cleveland Clinic, 2023). It is important to understand that the impact of ACEs on an individual can vary depending on the severity, frequency, and duration of the event(s) as well as protective factors (e.g., coping skills and resilience). It is also important to know that individuals who have experienced ACEs can respond differently and exhibit different signs of trauma.

The Cleveland Clinic (2023) describes signs of ACEs, including but not limited to fear, mood changes, difficulty showing affection, difficulty learning, anxiety, depression, post-traumatic stress disorder (PTSD), phobias, insomnia, and engaging in high-risk behaviors (e.g., substance use, sexual behaviors).

Trauma-Informed Practice #1

Table 15.1 Student Demographics

Student Name	Jonathan Hess
Gender	Male
Grade	Kindergarten
Educational Placement	Inclusive general education classroom
Geographic Location	Suburban
Parent/Siblings	**Parents:** Lives in two separate households: Household #1: Dad; Household #2: Mom and Mom's boyfriend
	Siblings: Younger brother (age 3)
School	Elmwood Elementary School
LEA	Stone Bridge School District
Academic Profile	**Reading:** Below grade level
	Writing: Below grade level
	Mathematics: Below grade level

Who Is Jonathan?

Jonathan is a five-year-old kindergarten student who recently started his first year in his local elementary school. Jonathan is energetic and loves playing outdoors, whether it's running, climbing, or riding his bike. His interests also include building blocks or LEGO, drawing simple pictures, and playing with action figures or toy cars. He also likes to watch cartoons or shows about animals. Jonathan displays some interest in academic skills related to learning letters and numbers. He displays independence skills that are similar to peers of the same age. For example, he can get dressed independently, brush his teeth independently, and follow multistep directions.

The Family Dynamics and Schedule

Before the start of school, Jonathan's father found out that his mother had cheated on him. They are currently separated and in the process of getting a divorce. Additionally, Jonathan's parents' work schedule is often challenging for the family. His father works eight-hour swing shifts that rotate every three weeks. Currently, his father's shift begins at 5 a.m. His mother is a hairstylist and works inconsistent hours. Jonathan and his three-year-old brother rotate back and forth between parents, currently spending every other week and weekend with each parent.

Jonathan gets on the bus each day from his mother's house regardless of which parent he is currently with. With his father's current work schedule, Jonathan's morning schedule when he is with his father is as follows:

- At 4 a.m., a paternal family member (typically an aunt) comes to his home before his dad leaves for work.
- At 6 a.m., the family member wakes up both children, gets them ready for school, feeds them breakfast, and packs their lunches.
- At 6:45 a.m., the family member drives both children to their mother's and her boyfriend's house. Sometimes their mother does not answer the door initially, and the family member with Jonathan and his brother has to call their mom on the phone to get her to answer the door.

- From 6:45 a.m. to approximately 7:45 a.m., Jonathan and his brother are often left alone to play or watch TV while his mother goes back to bed until she wakes to take Jonathan to get on his bus to go to school. When this happens, Jonathan feels sad because he wants to spend time with his mom. He does not get to see her very often, and when he does, he feels like she does not want to spend time with him.

After school, the expectations and schedule can vary greatly depending on which house Jonathan is at.

- *At his dad's house*, Jonathan and his brother have a snack and play games or watch TV with their dad until dinner. They have dinner together at the table and talk about their day; then, Jonathan and his dad work on his reading and homework. If there is time, they may watch more TV. Then, they complete their nighttime routine, which includes bathing, brushing their teeth, and getting to bed at a regular time.
- *If his dad is working after school during a week that they are at his house*, Jonathan and his brother go to their paternal grandparents' house. There, Jonathan typically has a snack after getting there, and then while Jonathan's grandmother makes dinner, she tries to help Jonathan get any worksheets completed while he sits at the kitchen table. Usually, she has Jonathan do a few items on the worksheet and then take a short break. During the break, Jonathan is allowed to play in the living room with his brother, and there is a timer that is set for five minutes. After the timer goes off, his grandmother prompts him to come back and work on the next few items on the worksheet. On some nights, one of Jonathan's aunts, who is a new teacher, comes over and helps Jonathan complete his work. If Jonathan is staying the night at this house, Jonathan and his brother will read with his grandmother or aunt before going to bed. Depending on his dad's work schedule, Jonathan and his brother will go back to his dad's house and complete their nightly routine.
- *At his mom's house*, Jonathan and his brother often have a snack and then watch TV until dinner. If Jonathan has homework (as discussed in following description), it often does not get completed. For example, Jonathan's paternal grandmother saw that on the nights Jonathan was with his mom, his reading log was not signed.

- *If his mom is working after school during a week that they are at her house,* Jonathan and his brother go to his maternal grandmother's house. There, Jonathan and his brother typically have a snack and watch TV until dinner. After dinner, Jonathan's grandmother usually tries to have Jonathan complete one of his worksheets, and then they usually read before going to bed. If Jonathan's mom picks him and his brother up before bed, reading together typically does not occur.

At School

At school, Jonathan's teachers have noticed that from the moment he walks into the classroom, Jonathan is moving. His backpack bounces against his back as he hurries to his seat. He often wiggles in his chair, tapping his feet on the floor, his hands unable to stay still as he fidgets with his pencil. Jonathan sometimes also calls out answers to questions, even when other peers have their hands raised; he also sometimes makes off-topic comments during class. Jonathan's teachers have been providing him with verbal reminders of expected behaviors, such as "Remember we want a quiet raised hand." During recess, Jonathan's favorite time of school, he often plays tag with his peers, swings on the monkey bars, and enjoys climbing on the playset.

Academically, Jonathan has displayed difficulties across subjects and has been recommended for Title I Reading supports. For these supports, Jonathan meets with the reading specialist and a few other students, one time per week for forty minutes, where they review letter sounds. When it is time to complete independent work, Jonathan often says that he doesn't know what to do and that the work is too hard. Jonathan's teachers often spend time supporting Jonathan to complete the work. For homework, students are asked to read with a parent for at least fifteen minutes and ask that a parent sign the student's reading log. Additionally, the students typically have one or two other activities for math or writing that usually total approximately twenty minutes.

Jonathan's teacher also indicated that sometimes Jonathan appears to be thinking about other things and acts "jumpy" when there are raised voices. They also said that Jonathan doesn't appear to make connections with them, even though they try to talk about his interests, and he does not seem to want affection in the form of hugs or high-fives. One day in class, when doing an activity about family, the students had to draw their house. Jonathan expressed to his teacher that he didn't know which house to draw because he had so many. After talking to Jonathan, the teacher realized the complexity of Jonathan's home situation. He asked the guidance counselor to meet with Jonathan.

When meeting with the guidance counselor, Jonathan expressed that he does not understand why he must go to different houses and that his mom often says mean things about his dad. He also told the guidance counselor that he is worried about what he is doing after school because he does not know which house he is going to, and that he often switches between houses or goes to one house after school and then sleeps somewhere else.

The guidance counselor contacted both of Jonathan's parents to ask if it was all right for him to check-in with Jonathan a couple of times per week; Jonathan's parents both agreed that this would be helpful for Jonathan. They agreed that they would all meet together with Jonathan's teacher and guidance counselor after a couple of weeks. After meeting with the guidance counselor a few times, Jonathan told him that the night before his first day of kindergarten, his mom was at his dad's house, throwing clothes and toys out onto the front yard. He indicated that his dad and mom often argue when they pick him and his brother up, and that he gets worried about what is going to happen. The guidance counselor started to consider the possible reasons for the difficulties that Jonathan was having in school and discussed what he had observed with Jonathan's parents and teacher in the follow-up meeting.

Questions:

1. What are Jonathan's interests?
2. What age-appropriate independent skills does he currently demonstrate?
3. Describe what traumatic events Jonathan has experienced.
4. Discuss Jonathan's current living situation. How might it impact him in school?
5. Beyond his living situation outside of the school, what concerns do you have about Jonathan's school life?
6. Based on the concerns that you identified in #5, what would you do to support Jonathan within your classroom? What strategies would you try?

Challenge: Create a short audio recording explaining to Jonathan's parents the concerns that you have seen in the classroom and what strategies you are going to try.

Challenge: Research the Neurosequential Model of Education's (NME) six Rs and describe what you could do to support Jonathan in alignment with these categories.

Trauma-Informed Practice #2

Table 15.2 Student Demographics

Student Name	Eva Jones
Gender	Female
Grade	10
Educational Placement	Inclusive general education
Geographic Location	Urban
Parent/Siblings	**Parents:** Three parents; lives with dad and stepmom; visits mom regularly
	Siblings: Older brother and two stepsiblings
School	Central City High School
LEA	Brighton United School District
Academic Profile	**Reading:** Below grade level
	Writing: Below grade level
	Mathematics: Below grade level

Who Is Eva?

Eva is a sixteen-year-old student who attends a separate school that provides academic instruction and intensive therapeutic support, including group and individual therapy. Eva and her team are currently discussing her return to her local urban public school.

As an infant, Eva was often left unattended for hours at a time while her brother was at school. Her biological mother had depression and was using alcohol and taking prescription pills. When Eva was left alone, her mother was frequently with friends who also drank alcohol and took prescription pills. Eva's mother was sometimes with these friends at another friend's house or the bar. It is unclear how often this occurred or for what lengths of time. Eva's mom does not have recollections of these times in detail.

When Eva was approximately eight months old, her dad came home early from work to find her alone, crying in her highchair. Although there were snacks within reach, it was clear that Eva had been there for hours. She had a soiled diaper that was full, and she had extreme diaper rash from sitting in feces throughout the day. Eva's mother came home later, and when Eva's father asked where she had been, she replied, "I had some errands to run, it wasn't long." Eva's father utilized sick leave and personal days to move his children out of the home and into his parents' house until he could find a home for their family. Eva's dad and mom separated after this event (they were not married). Initially, Eva's mother was angry regarding the removal of the children from the home and often tried to come to visit the children at their new home. This resulted in a court order barring Eva's mother from having contact with the children for six months. To regain visitation, Eva's mother had to demonstrate attendance at parenting classes and treatment for her depression and substance abuse.

Eva and her older brother had little to no contact with their biological mother until Eva was about two years old. Initially, these visits were supervised and only occurred for two hours at a time at a local playground or at Eva's mother's house. Eva's mother was granted these visitations because she demonstrated consistency in taking a parenting class and seeking help for her substance use and depression. When Eva was four, her father started dating a woman who would eventually become her stepmother. She had two children from a previous relationship.

At School

When Eva entered elementary school, she engaged in hyperactive behaviors. She was unable to sit for longer than a few minutes and often became disengaged from instruction/activities, and would almost seem like she was in another world. She would not respond to the teacher's directions, and when a teacher approached her or put a hand on her shoulder, Eva would jump away as if it were painful. Eva was also not completing schoolwork, often saying that it was boring. At home, her stepmom noticed that Eva had difficulties transitioning from one thing to another (e.g., going up and getting ready for bed) and she also had difficulties with displays of affection (e.g., hugs, snuggles, etc.).

In third grade, Eva was evaluated for a suspected emotional disturbance based on the behaviors that she was demonstrating. She was found to be eligible for and began receiving special education services. She met with an emotional support teacher two times per week, with the school social worker once per week, and was able to miss class and spend additional time in the emotional support classroom as needed. Eva worked with the emotional support teacher on skills related to her behaviors, such as asking for a break when needed and self-monitoring her behavior to see if she was engaging in instruction. When with the social worker, Eva spent time discussing her childhood and trauma that she experienced, and its current impact on her.

During elementary school, Eva also began displaying academic skills above her typical peers as well as an intense interest and excitement for learning. She also strived to be perfect on all her coursework and would often become frustrated if she lost any points on a test or assignment. Eva's teachers discussed the possibility that Eva might be gifted like her dad and stepmom. Through the gifted testing, Eva's IQ was found to be 138. As a result of her high IQ and strong academic skills, Eva began receiving gifted services, which included small group meetings with other students receiving gifted services. She also worked with the gifted teacher for extension activities in various topics. Additionally, Eva was provided enrichment activities in class to replace the core curriculum when she had already demonstrated mastery of the skill(s) being taught.

In middle school, not much changed regarding Eva's support or teacher feedback on what they observed. Eva did begin displaying a particular interest in science, math, and English. She enjoyed reading, writing, and investigating math and science concepts such as geometry and genetics.

From the time Eva was five years old, she has lived with her dad, stepmom, biological brother, and stepsiblings. She has visited her mom every other weekend, and time has been shared on holidays or other special events. Her biological parents, although divorced, have been civil to one another and have worked with each other so Eva and her brother could be with either family for vacations and other special events (e.g., birthdays). Eva's biological mother and stepmother have been welcoming to one another, and both believe that each of them serve an important role in the children's lives.

Before entering high school, Eva's father and stepmom became very concerned because Eva was starting to engage in self-injurious behavior and was isolating herself. She would spend days in her room, only coming out to get food and then going back into her room. Eva recognized that she did not like feeling this way and wanted to feel better, and she agreed to start going to therapy two times per week. Eva and her parents met with the school district, and everyone agreed that for her ninth-grade year, Eva's educational placement would be in a separate school. At the separate school, Eva was able to participate in a combination of both face-to-face instruction (elective classes and social studies) and online instruction (advanced English, advanced science, and advanced math). Typically, students at this therapeutic school do not take online courses; however, given Eva's academic levels and her desire to engage in academic instruction, this option was provided.

Questions:

1. Discuss Eva's social, emotional, and academic characteristics throughout her life up until this point.
2. Describe what traumatic events Eva has experienced in her life. How did her family play a role in those experiences?
3. What behaviors/characteristics did Eva display in school and at home that indicate that she was having difficulties related to the trauma that she experienced?

Challenge: Research trauma-informed supports. Make a list and describe three types of supports that could be beneficial in helping Eva to be successful in returning to the local public high school considering her traumatic experiences.

Challenge: Research the Neurosequential Model of Education (NME) and describe how the impact of trauma on the brain relates to Eva's situation.

Reference

Cleveland Clinic. (2023, February 7). *Adverse childhood experiences (ACEs) and childhood trauma.* https://my.clevelandclinic.org/health/symptoms/24875-adverse-childhood-experiences-ace

16

Traumatic Brain Injury

Mary A. Houser, EdD

Traumatic brain injury (TBI) is a disability category under the Individuals with Disabilities Education Act (IDEA). TBIs result in a significant injury when an individual experiences a blow to the head, and this affects how the brain works. In some cases, a TBI can result in death. Recent studies indicate that upward of 475,000 children aged between zero to fourteen will experience a TBI each year. TBI has been referred to as the leading cause of childhood death and disability (Araki, Yokoto and Morita, 2017). TBIs are considered "penetrating" (open-head) or "non-penetrating" (closed-head) and categorized as mild, moderate, or severe.

The effects that a TBI can have on a student will vary depending on its severity and the area of the brain that has been affected. Some common problems associated with TBIs are difficulties with executive function (e.g., attention, self-regulation, goal setting, and social problems) and organization problems (e.g., planning, prioritizing, and analyzing). Students might also experience cognitive problems such as memory problems, information processing, and language challenges. Students may also fluctuate in their educational performance demonstrating highs and lows. Finally, students might also experience memory issues such as recalling and/or retaining information (Bowen, 2018). Educators must consider several things once a student has experienced a TBI. Examples include the school reintegration process (i.e., the student returning to school after the accident), a possible change in classroom setting, a possible comprehensive evaluation for special education services, new instructional methods, and managing the effects TBI has on the student's social skills.

Table 16.1 Student Demographics

Student Name	Lauren Hillam
Gender	Female
Grade	4
Educational Placement	Inclusive general education classroom
Geographic Location	Rural
Parent/Siblings	**Parents:** Two parents (Marcia and Martin Hillam)
	Siblings: None
School	Brandywine Elementary School
LEA	Parksberry School District
Academic Profile (Pre-accident)	**Reading:** On grade level
	Writing: On grade level
	Mathematics: Above grade level
Academic Profile (Post-accident)	**Reading:** Well below grade level
	Writing: Well below grade level
	Mathematics: Well below grade level

Who Is Lauren?

Lauren is a nine-year-old girl in the fourth grade who lives in a rural town in the country. She fell in love with horses when she was a young child. From the moment she saw them at a local horse stable, she became infatuated with them. Lauren collected picture books about horses, watched horse videos, and spent her free time drawing pictures of herself riding different horses. She begged her parents to take horseback riding lessons. At the age of six, Lauren began taking lessons at a local horse farm. She also volunteered to help feed the horses just so that she could spend time at "the barn." When she turned eight years old, her parents purchased a horse for her. Lauren was ecstatic! Her horse was an off-the-track thoroughbred named Cinnamon. Having her horse meant that Lauren could go horseback riding whenever she wanted to and spend more time with her horse. They soon became best friends.

Over the next year or so, Lauren's riding skills flourished. She continued taking riding lessons and was riding almost every day. She loved the sport so much that she began contemplating becoming a large animal veterinarian when she grew up. All day at school, she eagerly waited for the bell to ring so she could go see her horse. Riding her horse was one of the most important things in her life. Lauren learned how to jump Cinnamon over fences and soon became what is known in the equestrian world as a "jumper." Simply put, this meant Lauren spent her time learning how to jump Cinnamon over fences in a quick and deliberate sequence. The faster and more accurate she could become at completing jump courses, the stronger a rider she would become. It was not long before Lauren began entering local horse shows where she and Cinnamon competed.

Competing in horse shows took practice, and a lot of it. Since she was young, Lauren's mother, Mrs. Hillam, would take her to ride her horse. Unless Lauren was taking a lesson, it was often just Lauren in the ring, riding alone. Typically, it was a joy to be out at the horse farm where she rode. It was always quiet and peaceful there. The soft sound of the horse's hooves hitting the dirt echoed through the ring, and Lauren always looked so happy. That was until one day, when Lauren experienced a very challenging event.

The Accident

It was a Friday. Like always, Lauren's mother took her to ride her horse, and Lauren happily gathered Cinnamon from the pasture and tacked her up. The two of them headed into the ring and began their normal warm-ups. First walking, then trotting, and then cantering. It seemed like just another day. Lauren then began her jumping sequences. There were five to six jumps to complete in each course that day. Lauren decided she would ride this one specific course that she would likely perform at an upcoming competition. The first run went smoothly, and she cleared all the jumps, but she knew she needed to pick up the pace to be competitive at her upcoming horse show.

After a short break, Lauren and Cinnamon began the same course again. They carefully maneuvered around the first and second jumps. They approached the third jump faster than they had the last time, but as they moved over the jump, Lauren felt very unsure of her bearings, lost her balance, and catapulted off the horse, landing headfirst into an adjacent fence. Her helmet hit the fence with enormous force, and Lauren landed on the ground. She couldn't move, and everything around her went black. Mrs. Hillam ran over to her, yelling her name, but Lauren did not respond. She had been knocked unconscious, and although she was beginning to regain consciousness by the time her mother got to her, she was very disoriented.

Her mother dialed 911, and an ambulance arrived in a matter of minutes. Fortunately, there was a hospital only a few miles away. The paramedics arrived and carefully lifted her into the ambulance. Soon, they arrived at the emergency department. Lauren was immediately taken and examined by an emergency room physician. The doctor conducted different tests to determine the extent of her injuries. These tests included the Glasgow Coma Scale (which examines the severity of a brain injury by assessing a person's ability to follow directions and move their eyes and limbs) and a CT scan of her brain.

After all her tests were completed and evaluated, Lauren was diagnosed with a brain injury. More specifically, she had what is referred to as a closed-head brain injury. She was admitted to the intensive care unit, where she spent the next week being treated. As the days progressed with proper treatment, Lauren gained strength, and doctors were finally able to send her home to recover. She rested at home for the next several weeks and went to her doctor check-ups and underwent additional tests. Finally, it was time to think about returning to school.

Returning to School

Life was different for Lauren when she returned to school. Everything seemed changed from before the accident, and she began experiencing new symptoms as a result. The following are some of the changes that were noted:

1. **Information processing**: difficulty processing multistep directions and problems learning new concepts; difficulties processing information auditorily
2. **Difficulty concentrating**: inability to attend for long periods, even to things that were of particular interest to her; problems attending to the teacher's instructions for long periods of time
3. **Impulsivity**: making decisions quickly without considering consequences and "thinking through" her actions
4. **Irritability**: becoming easily frustrated when she did not understand something; becoming impatient and lashing out at both her teachers and her peers

5 **Sensitivity to light:** needing sunglasses consistently when outside
6 **Anxiety:** "on edge" about her everyday activities, such as going to school
7 **Awareness:** failure to correctly interpret nonverbal cues; missing subtle social cues from her teacher to pay attention or get started on her classwork

Lauren's school reintegration took significant planning on behalf of the school and her parents. Lauren temporarily went back to her regular education classroom while a pre-referral team, comprised of her general education teachers, parents, school psychologist, and special education teacher, met to determine the next steps for her education. A comprehensive evaluation including assessments particularly designed to be used with students who have been diagnosed with a brain injury was conducted. In addition to cognitive testing, assessments about motor function, communication, and psychosocial behavior were also administered. The team compared these test results to her pre-injury performance. The team found her eligible for special education services under the category of "Traumatic Brain Injury" (TBI) as a result of both her brain injury and the need for changes to her educational programming.

The team determined that Lauren should receive special education services for English language arts (ELA), math, and social skills instruction. Based on the comprehensive evaluation results, Lauren's achievement in ELA and math had been impacted by her accident. Before her accident, Lauren was on grade level for reading and writing and above grade level in math. Now, due to the blow to her head, she was demonstrating achievement two to three years below grade level in these subjects. Her injury was also making it difficult to effectively manage her emotions. This was something she had not previously experienced. The team also discussed the benefits of Lauren seeing a psychologist outside of school to address her problems with anxiety. Lauren would need to work hard to regain her losses, and the individualized education program (IEP) team would need to strategically plan her comeback.

Mr. and Mrs. Hillam wanted Lauren to be placed in a general education classroom. They wanted things to be as close as possible to the way they were before her injury. The team agreed this placement would be a good place to start. For her to be successful, there were several accommodations Lauren would now receive. Lauren would sit at the front of the class to avoid being distracted by her classmates. To help her process information more effectively, she would receive guided notes from her teachers for all new content. Lauren was also permitted extended time on assignments and tests because it now took her longer to complete academic tasks. She also would receive a daily checklist from each of her teachers to keep track of what was due. Lauren would take scheduled breaks during class time to help prevent her feeling anxious, overwhelmed, and fatigued. Because doctors indicated that her abilities from her brain injury should improve over time, frequent progress monitoring will be important moving forward to gauge her improvement.

A Change in Social Life

Lauren's social life also changed since her accident. Her friends that she once was close to seemed to taper off. They were not as interested in spending time with her as they had been before the accident. Perhaps it was her new impulsivity and irritability that her friends didn't like. Or maybe it was her new challenges in social situations that caused them to stay away. Whatever the case, the social consequences of her TBI were one of the hardest things for Lauren to adjust to. Lauren understood there was a difference in her social life pre- and post- accident. She spent significant time with a therapist making sense of the changes she was experiencing and learning how to navigate relationships in light of the new challenges resulting from her accident.

Questions:

1. What is traumatic brain injury (TBI)?
2. Discuss Lauren's experience in the emergency department. List one of the tests that was performed in the emergency department on Lauren and what it assessed.
3. What characteristics of traumatic brain injury (TBI) did Lauren demonstrate?
4. How did Lauren's academic abilities and social skills differ from pre-accident to post-accident? How were her social skills impacted by the injury?

5 What type of educational placement did Lauren move to post-injury?
6 List some accommodations Lauren receives in her new classes.

Challenge: Research TBI and compose a list of instructional approaches that have proven effective for individuals with this disability.

References

Araki, T., Yokoto, H. & Morita, A. (2017). *Pediatric traumatic brain injury: Characteristic features, diagnosis, and management.* NIH. https://pubmed.ncbi.nlm.nih.gov/28111406/

Bowen, J. (2018). *Classroom interventions for students with traumatic brain injuries.* Brainline. https://www.brainline.org/article/classroom-interventions-students-traumatic-brain-injuries

Part II

Case Studies by Special Education Topic

Introduction to Part II

Would you like to learn about how disabilities and other learning needs factor into processes and procedures related to core special education topics? Current and future special education and general education teachers must have a firm grasp on processes and procedures related to foundational/introductory knowledge in special education. Part II allows the reader to understand these topics in the context of real-life situations as they are an integral part of being a well-informed and effective educator.

Each specific topic included in part II will have a brief introduction to the topic, which highlights some important features of that topic to refresh the reader's understanding of the concepts. As mentioned in the preface, some of the part II case studies refer to students who were introduced in part I of this book. They appear as either the subject of the case studies themselves or as reference points in the comprehension questions associated with the case studies.

Please refer to the "Crosswalk Table" (located at the beginning of the book) for information about which students from part I will be included in part II.

Specific topics covered in part II of this book include the following:

Table Part II.1 Chapter 17 Case Study Topics

Chapter 17: Laws
- Every Child Succeeds Act (ESSA) and State Testing Requirements
- Family Educational Privacy Rights and Education Act (FERPA)
- Individuals with Disabilities Education Act (IDEA): Addressing Procedural Safeguards and Manifestation Determination
- Individuals with Disabilities Education Act (IDEA): Dispute Resolution: Mediation and Due Process
- Individuals with Disabilities Education Act (IDEA): Least Restrictive Environment and Team Decision Making
- Section 504 of the Vocational Rehabilitation Act of 1973

Table Part II.2 Chapter 18 Case Study Topics

Chapter 18: Individualized Education Programs (IEPs)
- Annual Goals, Present Levels, and Progress Monitoring
- Case Management
- IEP Meetings (2)
- Specially Designed Instruction (SDI) (2)
- Transition (Secondary)

Table Part II.3 Chapter 19 Case Study Topics

Chapter 19: Early Intervention (EI) and Individualized Family Service Plans (IFSPs)
- Diagnostic Processes
- Early Childhood Special Education Service Delivery
- Family Response to Disability Diagnosis

Table Part II.4 Chapter 20 Case Study Topics

Chapter 20: Collaboration and Inclusive Practices
- Co-Teaching and Consultation
- Home-School Collaboration
- Paraprofessionals
- Teaching Across Student Populations

17

Laws

This chapter includes several case studies related to the topic of laws, which includes the following:

- Every Child Succeeds Act (ESSA) and State Testing Requirements
- Family Educational Privacy Rights and Education Act (FERPA)
- Individuals with Disabilities Education Act (IDEA):
  - Addressing Procedural Safeguards and Manifestation Determination
  - Dispute Resolution: Mediation and Due Process
  - Least Restrictive Environment and Team Decision Making
- Section 504 of the Vocational Rehabilitation Act of 1973

Introduction to Laws Related to Disability and Additional Learning Needs

Special education law and laws affecting individuals with disabilities are central to the processes and procedures of special education in today's schools. This chapter focuses on some of the most important laws for students with disabilities. The laws portrayed in this chapter have resulted in pivotal outcomes regarding how individuals with disabilities are treated and receive their public schooling.

This chapter examines the following laws:

1 **Every Student Succeeds Act (ESSA)** (2015): a federal law that replaced the No Child Left Behind Act. Although it is not a special education law, ESSA has a direct effect on students with disabilities.

ESSA ensures students with disabilities have access to the general education curriculum and are held to high standards through testing. In this case study, the reader will examine the guidelines for providing accommodations for state testing as well as alternatives to the regular state testing for students with disabilities as prescribed in ESSA.

2 **Family Educational Privacy Rights and Education Act (FERPA)** (1974): a federal law that specifically protects the confidentiality of students, including students with disabilities. FERPA ensures that students' records and all identifiable information about the student remain privileged. This case study explores the process of navigating FERPA regulations when responding to family inquiries (not from the parent/guardian) about a student's educational records.

3 **Individuals with Disabilities Education Act (IDEA)** (2004): a federal law that is considered the backbone of special education. It consists of several core concepts of special education, such as the least restrictive environment, free appropriate public education, nondiscriminatory evaluations, zero reject and child find, procedural safeguards, and parental rights. It also provides for mediation and due process for conflict resolutions between a family and the school system. In this chapter, four case studies address different aspects of IDEA including dispute resolution (mediation and due process), least restrictive environment, and procedural safeguards (manifestation determination).

4 **Section 504 of the Rehabilitation Act of 1973:** a federal civil rights law to protect individuals with disabilities by providing for accommodations. The primary premise of this law is that any agency receiving federal funding may not discriminate against individuals with disabilities. In this case study, 504 plans/service agreements are examined as they apply to students in the public-school setting.

Every Student Succeeds Act (ESSA) and State Testing Requirements

Tara S. Guerriero, PhD

Bobby was one month away from graduating from college with a degree in special education and he was really looking forward to starting his career as a special education teacher. He was in his student teaching placement working with his mentor teacher on the draft of an individualized education program (IEP) for Kerry, a seventh grader with a learning disability in the area of math, that would be shared with the IEP team. They were currently working on the section that focused on state testing. This is a section of the IEP that indicates whether the pre-K through grade 12 student will (a) take the regular state assessment *with* or *without* accommodations, (b) participate in an alternative assessment, or (c) not take the state assessment due to grade-level.

ESSA State Testing Requirements

In his program, Bobby had learned that the state testing requirements were regulated by the Every Student Succeeds Act (ESSA), which is a law that requires students in grades 3–8 and one time in high school to be evaluated in the areas of reading/language arts and math. Additionally, it requires students to be evaluated in the area of science one time during each of the grade bands (e.g., elementary school, middle school, high school). Each state develops learning standards, and the goal of the state assessment is to evaluate student proficiency according to those standards. The ESSA does allow for 1 percent of the students with the most significant cognitive disabilities to be evaluated using an alternative assessment that measures a different set of criteria (or standards) (Every Student Succeeds Act, n.d.).

Determining State Testing Needs for Kerry

Bobby knew that Kerry would not be taking the alternative assessment because her intelligence (IQ) was in the above-average range, which meant that she was not a student with a significant cognitive disability. In Bobby's state, seventh graders take the state test in the areas of reading/language arts and math. Bobby was to determine whether Kerry needed accommodations to be able to access the test in the same way she would if she did not have a learning disability. Accommodations don't change the expectations or information that is measured on the regular state test, but they do help the student to be able to access the test in a way that they might if they didn't have a disability.

Bobby spent some time reading through the accommodations matrix and accommodation guidelines provided by the state (PDE, 2025).

The regular test with accommodations allowed for several different types of accommodations including (a) presentation accommodations (e.g., braille, enlarged text, audio, directions read aloud); (b) response accommodations (e.g., responding in the test booklet, having a scribe record the answers, typing responses, voice-to-text, use of a calculator); (c) timing accommodations (e.g., extended time, frequent breaks); and (d) setting accommodations (e.g., noise-canceling headphones, a small group setting, a setting outside of the regular classroom).

In thinking about the types of accommodations that Kerry would need, Bobby considered her math difficulties. As a result of her learning disability, Kerry had difficulties with both math computation (computation associated with addition, subtraction, multiplication, and division) and math fluency (accuracy and speed). Additionally, Kerry sometimes felt overwhelmed when completing math problems and needed to take breaks while working on math. She also had considerable difficulties in the area of math when there was a lot of noise around her.

Bobby determined that Kerry's learning disability wouldn't impact her ability to take the reading/language arts assessment in the same way she would if she did not have a disability; therefore, she did not require any accommodations for that assessment. On her IEP, it was indicated that she would take the reading/language arts assessment without accommodations. Alternatively, her disability would impact her ability to take the math assessment, so her IEP indicated that she would take the math assessment with accommodations. After looking at all of the allowable accommodations, Kerry was provided the following:

- **Response Accommodation:** the use of a calculator on sections that allow a calculator
- **Setting Accommodation:** testing in a separate setting outside of the regular classroom
- **Timing Accommodations:** extended time (to accommodate her difficulties with math fluency) and frequent breaks

As Bobby spent time looking at the allowable accommodations, he realized how important it is to really take the time to decide which accommodations would best fit students according to their strengths and needs. This would allow them to be able to take the test in a way that was as close as possible to the way in which a student without a disability would take the test. He also thought that sometimes it's difficult to read about the education laws and really understand them and their importance; however, the outcomes of the laws really do make a difference and are there to support students. With respect to ESSA, it allows students with special needs to not only demonstrate progress but gives them the opportunity to show it in a way that is in alignment with their abilities.

Questions:

1. How does ESSA provide for students with disabilities in regard to state testing requirements?
2. Describe the grade requirements for state testing according to ESSA.
3. Explain why Kerry is not eligible for an alternative assessment.
4. Why is Kerry eligible for accommodations in math but not in reading/language arts?
5. Make a list of the accommodations that Kerry will receive for math.
6. Discuss your thoughts on why Bobby made the choice to have Kerry take the math portion of the state assessment in a separate environment.
7. Why isn't Kerry taking the science assessment?
8. Consider Sara (speech and language impairment case study, chapter 14, p. 115), Aaron (OHI: attention deficit hyperactivity disorder case study, chapter 2, p. 15), and Mahsumah (multiple disabilities #2 case study, chapter 10, p. 75). Who do you think would be the most likely to take an alternative assessment? Explain why.

Challenge: Research the allowable accommodations that are available for the state test in your state and list eight allowable accommodations and how they might benefit students.

Family Educational Rights and Privacy Act (FERPA)

Tara S. Guerriero, PhD

Melissa is in the fourth year of her career as a special educator at Hallow Elementary School, where she teaches in a learning support classroom. She was recently presented with a situation that she hadn't encountered before, and while it felt really uncomfortable, she thought that she had handled it correctly. Callie Hill is a ten-year-old student on Melissa's caseload who lives with her dad, mom, and older sister. Melissa has been working with Callie for two years and has a good relationship with Callie's parents.

The Dilemma

Melissa recently got a call from Callie's grandmother, Betty, requesting a copy of Callie's most recent IEP as well as information about her grades. Betty said that she was really interested in helping Callie with her homework and would genuinely benefit from having more of her educational information.

Melissa was initially caught off guard by the request, but she quickly thought about the rules of sharing information according to the Family Educational Rights and Privacy Act. FERPA is a law that is intended to protect the privacy of a student's educational records. Sharing educational records with anyone other than the student or the student's parent(s)/legal guardian(s) (if the student is a minor or dependent) is a violation of the student's rights under FERPA. She is allowed to share general policies and information (e.g., what an IEP is, general information about how grades are calculated), but she can't share any specific educational information with anyone without written permission from the parent(s) or legal guardian(s), or the student (if the student is eighteen years of age or older).

Melissa explained to Betty that she wasn't able to share Callie's educational records with her because it would violate the FERPA regulations. She further explained that other options that Betty could consider would be to (1) talk to Callie's parents and ask for the information directly or (2) ask Callie's parents to give the school written permission to allow the school to discuss Callie's educational records with her. Betty became upset and said that she just wanted to help her granddaughter. She said that she was only thinking of Callie's best interests. Betty said a quick goodbye and immediately got off the phone.

Talking with Callie's Parents

After speaking with Betty, Melissa thought that it would be a good idea to call Mr. and Mrs. Hill to share what had happened. She explained the

FERPA regulations and apologized that Betty had become upset. The Hills were unaware that Betty had called and thanked Melissa for letting them know. They apologized that Betty had put Melissa in that situation and said that Betty should have never called her. They further told Melissa that they were so thankful that she didn't give Betty any information and that they wouldn't be giving permission to the school to speak with Betty about any of Callie's school records.

Although the Hills had no obligation to share their private family information with Melissa, they wanted to explain to Melissa the difficult situation that they were facing with Betty. They shared the following with Melissa:

> Betty had asked the Hills for a copy of Callie's IEP because she wanted to include it in an application for the school that she wanted Callie to attend. The Hills said that they wouldn't give her access to the IEP and that they didn't want her to complete an application for the private school. Betty had been concerned that Callie wasn't getting the support that she needed and wanted to pay to send Callie to a private school that was near Betty's house. To further complicate the situation, the school that Betty wanted Callie to attend was forty-five minutes from the Hills's house. It would be extremely difficult for the Hills to get her to school every day.
>
> The Hills explained to Betty that while they were grateful that she would so generously pay for a new school, they disagreed with her opinions about Callie's education and support. They further shared that they were happy with Callie's school, teachers, and support services; they felt that Callie had been making great progress in school. They told Betty that they wanted Callie to stay at her current school and that Callie really liked her school and didn't want to switch schools, either.

A Resolution Between the Hills and Betty

Following their conversation with Melissa, the Hills called Betty and told her that Melissa had let them know about her phone call. They explained that although Betty has always been a big part of both their and Callie's life, Betty couldn't make educational decisions for Callie. They reiterated again that they were so thankful that Betty had taken such an interest in Callie's education but that they had to think of what they thought would be best for both Callie and their family. Betty was hurt and said that she only cared about Callie's well-being; she wanted to help in any way that she could, but she understood that it was ultimately their and Callie's decision to make. Although she was apprehensive about the Hills' decision and completely disagreed with them, Betty agreed to stop pushing the idea of a new school in an effort to maintain a good relationship with Callie.

Concluding Thoughts

In the end, Melissa reflected on the whole experience. She was so happy that she knew the FERPA regulations and that she had reacted the way that she did. If she had let her feelings of sympathy take over and agreed to Betty's request, she would have not only violated the law but also made the situation more difficult for Callie and her family. This was the first time that she had been tested in this way and she hoped that she wouldn't be presented with this type of situation again in the future.

Questions:

1. What is the purpose of FERPA?
2. Explain why Melissa wasn't able to provide Betty with information about Callie's education?
3. Describe how you would feel as a teacher if you were to get a call like the one that Melissa got from Betty. How do you think that you might react?
4. Why is it important to get *written consent* rather than *verbal consent* from the parent(s)/guardian(s)/student to share educational information?
5. Why do you think the Hills said that they wouldn't provide the school with written approval to share Callie's information with Betty?

Challenge: Consider Jonathan (trauma informed #1 case study, chapter 15, p. 122) and his family structure. Both his mom and dad are his biological parents. Should they both have FERPA rights?

Challenge: Research the Family Rights and Privacy Act (FERPA) and create a pamphlet for teachers with important facts about FERPA that all teachers should know.

Individuals with Disabilities Education Act (IDEA)

The following case studies are included within this section:

- Addressing Procedural Safeguards and Manifestation Determination
- Dispute Resolution: Mediation and Due Process
- Least Restrictive Environment and Team Decision Making

Addressing Procedural Safeguards and Manifestation Determination

Mary A. Houser, EdD

Dr. McDoughal's Foundations of Special Education Class

"Today we will be discussing a pivotal law in the field of special education: the Individuals with Disabilities Education Act of 1990 (IDEA)," announced Dr. McDoughal. "There are several core components of this law, and you will be responsible for learning these." The pre-service teachers in his foundations of special education course looked around at each other, feeling a little intimidated, but at the same time excited to learn about how this law changed the lives of school-age children with disabilities.

Dr. McDoughal began his lecture. He started with the history of special education and the lack of adequate and appropriate education that individuals with disabilities had received in the past. He introduced P.L. 94-142 (Education for All Handicapped Act) and professed that this law was the beginning of a better educational system for them. "One of the most important things for you to understand is that before 1975 and the enactment of P.L. 94-142, children with disabilities had no specific rights when it came to receiving a public education that addressed their disabilities. Many of these children lived in institutions under horrible conditions. Such institutions claimed to provide 'training' to them, but in reality, they did not. It was by no means an education equivalent to what their neurotypical peers were receiving back then."

The Individuals with Disabilities Education Act (IDEA)

Dr. McDoughal continued and stated that IDEA was an amended version of P.L. 94-142. He explained the amendments of IDEA and spoke about its core components: the concept of a free and appropriate public education (FAPE), the least restrictive environment (LRE), nondiscriminatory evaluation, zero reject, procedural safeguards, and parental rights and participation. Dr. McDoughal spent ample time defining each of these concepts while making references to Supreme Court cases that led to these decisions. He went on to discuss the impact IDEA had on the processes and procedures of special education. He wanted his students to understand the importance and impact of this law. This was something he was passionate about.

Procedural Safeguards

Monica, a first-year special education preservice teacher in his class, listened carefully as Dr. McDoughal spoke about IDEA, but one of IDEA's core concepts intrigued her more than the others. It was the core concept of procedural safeguards.

"Dr. McDoughal, can you tell us a little more about procedural safeguards?"

"Certainly, Monica. Is there something you want to know about them?"

"Well, actually, there is. The other day, I was at a coffee shop, and I overheard some mothers talking about something called a 'manifestation determination' hearing. They said a child with an emotional disturbance had recently been suspended from school for starting a fire in the school's bathroom. Is a manifestation determination a procedural safeguard?"

Dr. McDoughal smiled. He was pleased Monica made the connection that manifestation determination is a procedural safeguard in Pennsylvania, where their university was located.

Dr. McDoughal explained that procedural safeguards are given to the parents of children with disabilities and offer a full explanation of all the rights available to parents of a child with a disability (ages three to twenty-one) when their child has been referred for or is receiving special education services. He added, "Manifestation determination is a parental right. It is a procedural safeguard that is used to determine whether the child with a disability's inappropriate behavior is a result of his disability."

Monica was not sure she understood exactly what Dr. McDoughal was saying, but she continued to listen.

"You see, class," Dr. McDoughal continued, "this is something that must be determined before a child with a disability can be excluded from school. It would not be right, for example, to suspend a child with a disability from school if it was the disability that was causing his poor behavior in the first place. Let me give you an example. At an elementary school where I was a third-grade special education teacher in a self-contained classroom several years back, there was a boy named Trevor. (Note: Trevor was introduced in the ASD #2 case study in chapter 3, p. 25)

"Trevor had an autism spectrum disorder (ASD) and was a great kid but had several challenging behaviors. He would do things like pull his classmates' hair, scream if he did not get his way, bite others, and engage in some other aggressive behaviors if he was feeling under duress. We all worked hard with Trevor because we wanted him to be successful at school, and we also had to look out for other students' safety in class. As time went on, Trevor's challenging behavior did improve slightly.

"After we got back from our holiday break one January, his IEP team decided they were going to have Trevor try an inclusive general education classroom for mathematics. Mathematics was an area in which Trevor excelled, and with the support of a paraprofessional, the team felt he might be successful there. The IEP team followed the IDEA core concept of LRE that I spoke about earlier by placing him in a less restrictive placement for math. Although the IEP team was eager to have him with his typical peers, they were also cautious. Some situations tested Trevor's ability to maintain self-control.

"The first two weeks in his new math class went well for Trevor. However, it took a decent amount of effort for him to adjust to a classroom with a lot more students in it, and now there were two teachers in the classroom, which was something he had not experienced before. At times, the class was overstimulating for him, but he had a good paraprofessional who could tell when he started to experience sensory issues and needed a break.

"Trevor's problems began around the third week in his new math placement. It was a Thursday. Trevor had not slept well the night before, and he came into school that day feeling a little groggy. He was in my classroom for first and second periods and did okay completing his assignments. Then, it was time for him to go to math. We waited for his regular paraprofessional to come and get him to take him to math, but she did not show up. She was absent that day, and a substitute paraprofessional stopped by to get him. This change in his routine seemed to upset Trevor. Neither of them had ever met or even seen each other before. Nonetheless, off they went to math class.

"Trevor entered the room and went to his seat, as he usually did. The substitute paraprofessional followed behind him. The class started with a review of the preceding day's lesson: adding double-digit fractions. Trevor tried to relax and concentrate on the math instruction but found it difficult to do. The students in class were louder than usual that day, and the hum of fluorescent lights vibrated in his ears as he sat there. He made noises under his breath to try and drown out the humming noise. Then, suddenly, a fire drill alarm shrilled, sending Trevor into a panic. He immediately jumped up, shoved his desk with all his might, ramming into two of his female classmates, and then turned and punched the boy sitting next to him, causing a bloody nose. The substitute paraprofessional did not know what to do. She had never seen a child respond this way before to what seemed to be just a regular day at school."

The students in Dr. McDoughal's class were wide-eyed and eager to hear what happened next. *Did Trevor get suspended? Was he allowed to remain in his new inclusive math placement? How will the school react to a student with ASD acting aggressively to the point of harming another student in class?* They pondered question after question.

Manifestation Determination

Dr. McDoughal continued. "Trevor was immediately removed from the classroom and taken to the principal's office to calm down. He sat in the principal's office for quite some time. His mother came to school, and they talked with the principal about what had happened. The next day, Trevor returned to school. His IEP team was notified about the incident, and a manifestation determination hearing was scheduled. This hearing had to be scheduled within ten school days of the incident that occurred in math class.

"In the meantime, Trevor was not removed from school due to his aggressive behavior. He was placed in an interim alternative educational setting until the hearing occurred. This happened to be back in my classroom."

"A hearing?" exclaimed Monica. "What happens at a hearing? Who attends?"

Dr. McDoughal explained that the hearing would be conducted at the school. A representative from the local education agency (LEA), members of the IEP team, and Trevor's parents were all in attendance. Dr. McDoughal revealed, "These hearings typically occur when suspension and expulsion are considered as the disciplinary action. Since Trevor injured one of the girls when he shoved his desk and gave the boy a bloody nose, an option for the school was to consider suspending Trevor.

"There are several steps in the manifestation determination hearing process. They begin by discussing the sequence of events that led up to his physical aggression that day and the event itself. They reviewed Trevor's past disciplinary actions. They examined his IEP and his positive behavior support plan (PBSP) to determine whether he was receiving the behavioral support he needed. They also discussed whether he had been displaying aggressive behavior recently.

"I was able to relay that there was a substitute paraprofessional that day, and there was also a fire drill that could have triggered some of his inappropriate behavior. I also told them he came into school very tired that day. His parents talked about how it is more difficult for him to maintain self-control if he is tired and overstimulated."

"Well, what happened?" Monica questioned.

"Well, after a thorough investigation of the incident, the team determined that Trevor's behavior that day *was* a manifestation of his disability. In other words, there were characteristics of his ASD that contributed to him acting aggressively toward his classmates as a result of being overstimulated and overwhelmed in that classroom," Dr. McDoughal explained.

"Does that mean he did not get suspended from school?" another student asked.

Dr. McDoughal responded, "Trevor did not get suspended from school due to his behavior. Instead, a subsequent IEP meeting occurred, and the IEP team decided to add some additional accommodations to his PBSP while he was in his inclusive general education math class to help reduce some of his stress. These included having Trevor use noise-canceling headphones, taking sensory breaks, and having a quiet area in the classroom where he could go to if he was feeling overwhelmed. His parents also added they would try to see that he got enough sleep at night so he would be his best at school."

"There is a lot to know about IDEA," Monica commented. "Manifestation determination is only one of the procedural safeguards to know about, and there are all those other core components of the law, too."

"Yes, indeed," furthered Dr. McDoughal. "It is a complex law, but a very necessary one. It has changed the lives of students with disabilities in profound ways. It has guaranteed them they will receive the type of education that best meets their individual needs."

Questions:

1. List the core components of the Individuals with Disabilities Education Act (IDEA) of 1990.
2. What is a manifestation determination? How did Dr. McDoughal teach his preservice students about this concept?
3. Explain the event(s) that led to Trevor's manifestation determination hearing. Identify all factors that could have contributed to his physical aggression that day.
4. What topics were discussed in Trevor's manifestation determination hearing? Who attended this meeting?
5. What was the outcome of Trevor's manifestation determination? Was he suspended from school?
6. The IEP team met again after the hearing to discuss ways to improve Trevor's experience in his inclusive math class. What accommodations were added to his positive behavior support plan?

Challenge: With a partner, select one of the core components of IDEA (e.g., LRE, FAPE, nondiscriminatory evaluation, etc.) and create a twenty-minute mini-lesson to share with your classmates. Be sure to include an explanation of the component, a brief history of how it came to be, and examples of how it is implemented in public schools in the United States.

Dispute Resolution: Mediation and Due Process

Colleen E. Commisso, PhD

Determining the specially designed instruction (SDI), including accommodations, modifications, and related services for a student with a disability, is a collaborative team process. As a collaborative team process, the student (as appropriate and/or required by law), the student's parent(s)/guardian(s), and the school district work together to develop the student's IEP. As part of this process, disagreements about the student's program can occur. To support families and school district's conflict resolution, they can agree to mediation. Alternatively, if they do not agree to mediation or if mediation does not lead to a successful outcome, either the parent(s)/guardian(s) or the school district can seek due process.

Mediation

Mediation is a process that utilizes a neutral third party (i.e., a mediator) to support families and school districts in resolving disputes about a child's education plan. Mediation is provided free of charge (to both parties) through state resources, and these meetings typically last between three to five hours (Office for Dispute Resolution, 2021). Mediation is sometimes a step that is utilized before due process or in an attempt to avoid due process. Before a mediation meeting, parents and school personnel should keep their schedule clear for the entire day, arrange logistics so individuals can attend (e.g., child care, substitute teachers), bring any documents, organize the information, consider potential options, and try to have a positive attitude. During the mediation meeting, the mediator helps facilitate the discussion, meets with all parties together, meets with both parties privately, finds areas of agreement, and writes down the agreements in a legally binding document (Office for Dispute Resolution, 2021).

Due Process

Due process is a formal, legal process within special education that is utilized to resolve disputes between school districts and parents regarding a child's special education services under the Individuals with Disabilities Education Act (IDEA). This process could be utilized by parents or school districts regarding the identification, evaluation, educational placement, or provision of a free and appropriate public education (FAPE).

A due process hearing is similar to a trial in which a hearing officer acts as a judge. During the hearing, both sides (typically represented by an attorney) provide evidence and testimony for the record to state their case (e.g., provide an overview of the issue, key findings within the evidence). After all testimony is given, a hearing officer has until the predetermined decision due date to render a legally binding decision. Either party (i.e., the family or school district) can appeal the hearing officer's decision.

It is important to note that due process should be the last resort for families or school districts. All other options (e.g., state complaints, IEP facilitation, mediation) should be considered and possibly explored before due process. Furthermore, it is important to remember that even if the parent(s)/guardian(s) and school district enter into due process, in many cases, even after a hearing officer's decision has been provided, the school district and family will still need to work closely together. Continued collaboration is necessary and critical for a student's progress.

General Information

The following provides an overview of the participants involved in the scenario and the details of the initial situation and ensuing conflict:

Participants

- Jalen: nine-year-old student with ASD
- Dana and Marcus Greene: Jalen's parents
- Brenda Toller: School district's special education director
- Alicia Lopez: School psychologist
- Crystal Johnson: Special education teacher
- Matt Garcia: General education teacher
- Julia Sanchez: Occupational therapist for the district
- Ken Ramirez: Mediator
- Rachel Gross: Parent's attorney during due process scenario
- Leah Nwosu: Private occupational therapist brought by the parents

Initial Situation and Conflict

When Dana and Marcus Greene received their son Jalen's IEP home with him in his backpack, they both felt a familiar tightness in their chests. Jalen, a bright nine-year-old with ASD, had always struggled with sensory processing and communication (both receptive and expressive communication). While he did well in some subjects, he needed significant support during transitions and group activities. The Greenes believed he needed a one-on-one aide, additional accommodations and modifications, as well as more occupational therapy time to meet his goals.

However, the IEP didn't reflect that. They were frustrated to see some of the provisions that were incorporated into the IEP, including (1) a reduction of his occupational therapy time (from two 30-minute sessions per week to just one per week); (2) a denial of the request for a dedicated one-on-one aide (suggesting that classroom staff could support him collectively); and (3) the lack of inclusion of the accommodations and modifications that they requested for his IEP (instead adding only one accommodation).

"He hasn't made progress," Dana said, flipping through the IEP pages. "How can they justify giving him *less*?"

Marcus nodded grimly. "This isn't working for Jalen. We need to fight this."

Jalen was also displaying difficulties at home with behavior while the school said he was doing fine in his classes with minor behavioral incidents. Jalen's parents tried to tell the school that he was keeping in his frustration and anxiety during the day and releasing it when he got home. After several tense emails and a contentious IEP meeting that ended without agreement, Dana reached out to the state's parent advocacy center, where a counselor suggested mediation (i.e., a meeting that was supported by a neutral third-party mediator).

"Mediation is less adversarial than a due process hearing," the counselor explained. "It gives you a chance to work with the school in a structured, neutral environment." With apprehension, the Greenes agreed and since they were not happy, they made a request for mediation to occur.

Note: Both the mediation and due process scenarios are based on the same student, family, school, and situation; however, the mediation scenario proves to be a successful endeavor while the due process scenario demonstrates an unsuccessful conclusion to mediation and outlines the next steps (i.e., due process).

These descriptions and the following scenarios offer a general overview and abbreviated example of due process and mediation. Additionally, mediation processes (e.g., specific types of mediation, mediation forms, and specific procedures) and due process processes (e.g., the procedures, burden of proof, timelines, and appeals process) can vary from state to state. As such, individual state-specific resources should be referenced and utilized, as needed.

Part I: Mediation

Preparing for Mediation

The school district's team for the mediation session included Brenda Toller (a veteran special education director), Alicia Lopez (school psychologist), Crystal Johnson (special education teacher), Matt Garcia (general education teacher), and Julia Sanchez (occupational therapist). Brenda had seen several disputes and knew the law well, but she also believed in collaboration. Brenda didn't want this to escalate further. Alicia, Matt, and Julia had previously participated in mediation, but this was the first for Crystal, who was a first-year special education teacher.

The mediator was Ken Ramirez, a soft-spoken, even-tempered professional who had spent fifteen years as a special education lawyer before turning to mediation. Before the session, Ken scheduled phone calls with both parties.

With the Greenes, he was careful to listen, not lead. Dana shared a detailed account of Jalen's struggles, backed by private therapy reports, while Marcus emphasized their exhaustion and sense of being dismissed. "He's not a statistic to us," Marcus said. "He's our boy. We're not being unreasonable."

With Brenda, Ken encouraged openness. "We want to meet their needs, Ken," Brenda explained, "but we also have staffing limits. Still, I think there's room to talk. I just hope they come ready to listen, too."

Ken reminded both sides: "The goal of mediation is not to 'win.' It's to find a solution that works for Jalen."

The Mediation Session

The mediation took place in a conference room within the school district. A rectangular table divided the room, with Ken at the head, Dana and

Marcus on one side, and Brenda, along with the other school district personnel, on the other.

Ken began with ground rules: confidentiality, respect, and no interruptions. "I'm not here to take sides," he said. "I'm here to help you talk and listen. The outcome is up to you."

Dana started. "Jalen thrives when he has structure and predictability. Lately, he's melting down almost daily. We've had to pick him up early from school three times in the last month."

Marcus added, "We're not asking for gold-plated services. We just want support that matches his needs. We've submitted documentation from his private occupational therapist, Leah Nwosu."

Brenda and the other school district personnel listened quietly. Then Brenda responded. "We hear your concerns. We know Jalen is a bright and capable student. But we've also seen him make progress. His classroom teachers feel he's handling transitions more independently."

Dana shook her head. "That's not what we have seen. He holds it together at school, then falls apart at home. That's not progress—it's stress. He is bottling it all up and then can't do simple things at home, let alone homework."

Ken interjected. "This seems like a good moment to shift from positions to interests. Can each side tell me: what are you most hoping to achieve for Jalen in the next six months?"

Brenda said, "We want him to access the curriculum without becoming overwhelmed. We want to support his growth sustainably."

Marcus replied, "We want him to be happy. To feel safe. To learn how to manage the world without feeling like he's constantly failing or that things are falling apart."

Ken nodded. "It sounds like you all care about Jalen's well-being. Maybe there's a shared interest there."

The group discussed a recent sensory assessment that the parents had privately funded. Alicia had not seen it. "I'm open to reviewing it," she said, looking surprised. "That could help us better understand what triggers his stress."

Feeling that the school was hearing her, Dana offered a suggestion. "What if we try a trial period with an aide for six weeks, and we will see how it goes."

Brenda didn't immediately object. "That could be possible. I would also like to collect some additional data before adding the aide, so we can see how he does with and without the aide. I would also have to speak with HR about staffing, so we won't be able to have the aide start immediately. We could collect data over this time and then meet again to review."

Alicia added, "We could build in check-ins to review his behavior logs and sensory needs."

Dana emphasized, "I do not want those check-ins to be with just the teachers. I would like updates sent home at the end of each week." Crystal added that she could send these updates home. Dana and Marcus agreed to collect data with and without the aide.

Momentum was building, and the team continued to work through the areas of dispute.

End of Session

By the end of the session, they had outlined a tentative agreement:

- A six-week trial (three weeks with and without an aide) during which time data collection will occur on Jalen's behavior, time on task, and time engaged in group activities
- Continued OT services at two sessions per week
- Weekly written communication between the teacher and parents
- A meeting after the trial period with data from the aide, teacher, and occupational therapy

Ken facilitated a summary of the plan, and both parties agreed to draft a formal amendment to the IEP.

"Today didn't solve everything," Dana said to her husband as they packed up. "But it's a start. And it feels like someone finally heard us."

The Follow-Up

Six weeks later, the team reconvened to review all the data collected and obtain information on how Jalen had been doing at home. The data showed that before the aide worked with Jalen, Jalen engaged in some instances of challenging behavior, but they were inconsistent. In some of his classes and with some transitions, there were no instances of challenging behaviors, but in other classes and the transitions before those classes, there were challenging behaviors.

After implementation of the aide, there was a decrease in the challenging behaviors during the periods when they previously occurred. Feedback from the aide and teachers also indicated that Jalen was able to participate more in group work and was more focused in the classes where previously he had displayed challenging behavior. The aide did say, however, that in some of Jalen's classes, she didn't need to do much. Jalen did not display challenging behaviors and was very engaged in the class. She indicated that he sometimes had difficulty expressing what he needed, but the teachers were able to find other ways to support him.

"I think we underestimated how much that one-on-one support could change things in some of his classes, but it seems as though he is doing well without support in some classes," Alicia said.

Brenda spoke frankly. "I agree. I was skeptical, but the data speaks volumes. I think, however, we need to be mindful that Jalen is doing well in many of his classes. I want to continue his independence in those settings."

Dana smiled. "I am so glad to hear that he didn't need support in some of his classes. We didn't know that."

Marcus added, "We want to build his independence, too, but are concerned about those other class periods."

Brenda replied, "I think we are on the same page. What if we put an aide in place for those periods in which Jalen has displayed the highest rate of challenging behavior? That way, we can support his independence in the other classes and work toward the best ways to support Jalen in the classes and transitions that are difficult?" Dana and Marcus glanced at each other and nodded. "We think that's great."

Questions:

1. Describe Jalen. What needs does Jalen have?
2. Briefly explain the concept of mediation (in schools).
3. What led to the need for mediation?
4. How did the mediator support both sides?
5. What was the agreed-upon plan?
6. What was the final decision by the team on how to proceed with the aide? How does that differ from the original positions of both the school and the parents?

Challenge: Find the mediation resources for your state. Create an audio reflection (at least five minutes long) on the following:

1 How those resources describe mediation and the role of the mediator
2 How those resources did or did not align with what occurred in this scenario
3 What you think the mediator could have done differently or in addition

Part II: Due Process

As previously discussed, this scenario depicts a mediation session that didn't lead to a successful outcome and resulted in a due process hearing. It includes the same general information as the mediation scenario (see above). The scenario below begins partway through the mediation session after having discussed some of the conflicts and possible solutions.

Mediation

Dana Greene sat stiffly in the gray conference room, arms folded, eyes locked on the district's special education director, Brenda Toller. The air was filled with things unsaid. Across from her sat Brenda and the other school district personnel. Ken Ramirez, the neutral mediator, watched them all with measured calm.

Mediation had been suggested after the IEP meeting stalled. The Greenes had hoped to resolve their concerns: Jalen's sudden drop in occupational therapy, his need for a one-on-one aide, the need for accommodations and modifications, and the school's lack of responsiveness. However, from the start, the mediation session had felt off.

"We've reviewed the private OT information you provided," Brenda said. "But we're confident our current IEP meets Jalen's needs as required by law."

Dana bristled. "You mean the IEP that reduced his support after he started falling apart? That one?"

Ken tried to intervene. "Maybe we could identify shared goals first. What does everyone want for Jalen in the next six months?"

Marcus spoke up. "We want him to stay in school all day without meltdowns and not come home and fall apart... to feel safe, and we want data-driven support, not assumptions."

Alicia replied, "But we haven't seen consistent issues at school. He's not demonstrating a level of need that would warrant a full-time aide."

Dana raised her voice. "That's because he holds it together until he gets home! Then we're left managing the fallout."

Despite Ken's best efforts, neither side budged. After three hours, the mediation ended with no agreement.

"I think we need to take this further," Marcus said to Dana quietly as they walked out.

Due Process Complaint Filing

The Greenes filed their due process complaint the next week. It alleged that the district failed to provide free appropriate public education by reducing Jalen's occupational therapy (OT), refusing additional necessary accommodations and modifications, and refusing a one-on-one aide, despite evidence of regression (i.e., going backward in skills).

They worked with a special education attorney named Rachel Gross, who came highly recommended by the local advocacy center. "She's tough, but she's fair," their advocate had said. "And she knows her way around due process hearings."

Rachel began building their case, gathering the following evidence:

1. Reports from Jalen's private OT, including information that suggested that Jalen needed supports with transitions and within the classroom
2. All previous IEPs and comprehensive evaluations/evaluation reports
3. Emails to and from the school, including the emails from Jalen's parents asking for more support and expressing concerns with Jalen's behaviors and the responses from the school indicating he did not engage in challenging behaviors at school, or if he did, they were minimal incidents
4. Video clips of Jalen's post-school meltdowns, including yelling, crying, screaming, pushing his parents, throwing himself on the floor, and negative verbal statements (e.g., "I hate school")
5. A timeline of IEP meetings and service changes, including when Jalen's services began until his last IEP where there were reductions in OT.

Meanwhile, the district retained legal counsel, as well. Brenda was frustrated. "We're doing everything within reason," she told the school's attorney. "They just won't accept that kids with ASD can still succeed without one-on-one aides."

The state assigned a hearing officer, Judith Palmer, a seasoned former special education teacher turned legal arbitrator. Judith scheduled a pre-hearing conference. Both sides submitted pre-hearing disclosures, which listed witnesses and included documents. Tension was rising.

Due Process Hearing

The hearing took place over two days. The following is a partial synopsis of the testimony that was given:

- The first morning, Rachel gave the Greenes' opening statement: "We will demonstrate that Jalen's IEP fails to meet his unique needs and is resulting in emotional harm and academic stagnation."
- The school district's attorney countered: "The IEP reflects appropriate goals and accommodations based on school data and professional assessments."
- Dana and Marcus testified first. "After the OT was reduced, Jalen started chewing his shirt collars again," Dana said. "He began resisting going to school. His anxiety increased." Marcus added, "He would sob in the car after school. He couldn't tell us what was wrong, but we knew."
- They presented a data chart showing Jalen's school incidents reported by the district versus incidents observed and recorded at home. A sample of this data is included below.
- Their private occupational therapist, Leah Nwosu, testified via video. "Jalen demonstrates sensory-seeking behavior and anxiety indicators that are not being addressed in his current plan," she explained. "Without consistent OT and transitional support, his ability to function in the classroom is compromised."
- The district cross-examined Leah. "You're not affiliated with the school, correct?" Brenda's lawyer asked. "No," Leah responded. The lawyer further questioned, "And you observed Jalen in a clinical setting (separate setting), not a classroom?" Leah responded, "Yes, but sensory integration issues manifest across settings."
- Then the school presented its case. Alicia (the school psychologist), the occupational therapist, Jalen's special education teacher, and Jalen's general education teacher all testified.

Table 17.1 Incident Chart of Jalen's Challenging Behavior at School and at Home

Date of Occurrence	School	Home
9/3		Crying, screaming
9/4		Crying
9/5	Refused to leave classroom to go to next class	Crying, screaming, negative verbal statements, throwing himself on the floor
9/6		
9/9	Didn't join in group activity	Crying, screaming, negative verbal statements, pushed dad
9/10		Crying, negative verbal statements
9/11		Crying, throwing himself on the floor
9/12		Crying, screaming, negative verbal statements
9/13		Screaming, throwing himself on the floor
9/16	Didn't join in group activity	
9/17		Crying, screaming, negative verbal statements, throwing himself on the floor
9/18		Screaming, throwing himself on the floor
9/21		
9/22		Screaming
9/23		Screaming, negative verbal statements
9/24		Crying, screaming, negative verbal statements, throwing himself on the floor
9/25	Refused to leave classroom to go to next class	Crying, screaming, negative verbal statements

- "We've seen growth," Alicia said. "Jalen is staying regulated most days and does well in most of his classes. We use flexible seating and positive behavior reinforcement."

- ○ The teacher, Matt Garcia, added: "He works independently during center-time. We have one aide in the room who checks on all students."
- Rachel, representing the Greenes, cross-examined. "Is that the same as a dedicated aide?" "No," Matt replied. Rachel continued, "So, when Jalen shows early signs of dysregulation, is anyone specifically monitoring him?" Matt indicated, "Well… not one-on-one, no."
- The district wrapped up its case, emphasizing that a one-on-one aide could reduce Jalen's independence and wasn't medically or educationally necessary, according to their team.

The hearing officer thanked both sides and adjourned. "You'll receive a written decision within thirty days."

Waiting

The month dragged on. Dana checked the mail obsessively. Marcus reread their closing statement. Rachel remained cautiously optimistic. "It's not guaranteed," she warned. "But you presented a strong case… especially with the evidence that you provided, which demonstrated the contrast in challenging behavior between the home and school settings."

Meanwhile, Jalen's behavior at school worsened. For example, one day, he locked himself in the school bathroom, in response to the loud noises of a fire drill. The school called Dana to pick him up. "This is what we were trying to prevent; I'll be there to pick him up soon," Dana replied in a tearful voice.

The Decision

The decision finally arrived.

Findings of Fact

The facts within the hearing include the following:

- The reduction in OT services occurred without an updated evaluation or mastery of IEP goals.

- Evidence showed Jalen exhibited significant dysregulation at home, which was not accounted for in the school's assessment.
- The current classroom support did not include individualized adult assistance.
- The district provided some data (teacher reports) that Jalen did not engage in challenging behavior across all parts of his day.

Conclusion and Order

The hearing officer ruled in favor of the Greenes and provided the following order.

- The school must provide one-to-one support through a dedicated paraprofessional for Jalen during transitions and group activities.
- OT services are to continue twice weekly, with data collection every month.
- The district is to reimburse the Greenes for the cost of the private OT evaluation and legal counsel.
- A revised IEP must be provided to the Greenes within ten business days.

Dana cried when she read it. Marcus sat in silence, stunned but relieved. "It's not about winning," he said eventually. "It's about knowing we did right by him."

Implementation and Follow-Up

The district complied, albeit reluctantly. Brenda arranged for an aide, and a revised IEP was developed with the hearing officer's findings as the foundation.

They held a follow-up IEP meeting, in which they all agreed to the revisions. During the meeting, there was no open hostility, but the atmosphere was tense.

Once the new IEP was implemented, everyone began to notice positive changes in Jalen. Ms. Lopez, the new aide, bonded quickly with Jalen. She learned his cues and intervened early when needed. OT sessions became structured, focusing on self-regulation strategies.

Over the next three months, Jalen stopped chewing his shirts. He began using a "feelings chart" to express himself. His meltdowns decreased dramatically. As a result, the Greenes agreed to reduce the support the aide provided in Jalen's most successful classes.

One day, he asked to stay after school for a math club. "He's thriving," Dana told Rachel during a follow-up call. "We're still cautious, but it feels like we're on the right path."

Reflections and Impacts

Due process had taken a toll, financially, emotionally, and even relationally. Dana and Marcus had deliberated over every step in the process, often losing sleep, and this impacted the quality of their family life and time. Further, the school district had spent money defending a case it ultimately lost. Brenda later admitted to a colleague, "We probably should've done more earlier. But due process isn't the best way to resolve these things; it's just what happens when communication breaks down."

Rachel, the attorney, often told families, "Mediation is cheaper, faster, and less divisive, but sometimes, you need the power of legal accountability to be heard." For the Greenes, the decision validated their concerns, but it didn't erase the stress they'd endured. And yet, on a warm spring afternoon, Jalen ran up the front steps after school and hugged his mom. "I stayed all day," he said proudly. "I didn't even cry once."

Questions:

1. What is due process in schools?
2. What disagreement led to the due process request by the Greenes?
3. What parts of due process do you think are supportive? Not supportive?
4. What would be your concerns if you had to testify as a teacher?
5. What impact did due process have on the Greenes? On the district?

Challenge: Interview an educational professional (e.g., teacher, therapist, principal, school psychologist) who has participated in due process on their experience with the process, their thoughts about the process, and any challenges that they experienced during the process. Write a reflection on your interview.

Least Restrictive Environment and Team Decision Making

Tara S. Guerriero, PhD

Preparing for the Upcoming IEP Meeting

Colin turned to his wife, Angie, and said, "There are so many options for his education. How will we know what is right for Sam?" Angie replied, "I don't know; I just hope that they listen to us and take our opinions into consideration." Their son Sam was ten years old and had recently been diagnosed with a learning disability in the areas of reading and writing. Angie and Colin Penny had read a lot about learning disabilities and were happy that they finally understood what was happening with Sam's learning.

They were preparing for their upcoming IEP meeting at Sam's school and they wanted to be as ready as possible to make sure that Sam would get the education that he needed to help him learn. They had several friends whose kids had IEPs, and some had good experiences while others had bad experiences with the whole process. They just wanted the best for Sam and wanted to be as prepared as possible to make sure that would happen.

The Concept of Least Restrictive Environment (LRE)

They were able to find their state's IEP form online, and they began to look through the different aspects of it. Through their research, they felt like most of it made sense to them. They understood the present levels, the goals, the concept of specially designed instruction, and the types of support. However, the concept of LRE seemed much more complex and a little bit confusing. As they read more and more about it, they kept coming across the term "inclusion." Inclusion is the concept that students of all ability levels can be educated together. From what they gathered, there were differing opinions on whether full inclusion was the best option for all students.

Luckily, Angie's sister, Emma, was a special education teacher. She helped them to better understand the concept of LRE. She told them that one of the big decisions that the team would make when developing the IEP was to determine Sam's least restrictive environment. She explained that the Individuals with Disabilities Education Act (IDEA), the primary special education law, requires that all students with disabilities be educated with students without disabilities to the maximum extent that is appropriate. Emma went on to explain that depending on the student, different types of placements could be appropriate. She explained the following types of placements in order from the least restrictive settings to the most restrictive settings (Center for Parent Information & Resources, 2022; Iris Center, n.d.):

- **Full Inclusion in the general education classroom:** With this option, students are fully included in the general education classroom with supplementary aids and supports. Students receive the special education services that are outlined in their IEP, but that support happens in the general education classroom.
- **Part-time or full-time education in a special education classroom:** If deemed appropriate by the IEP team, students can receive part or all of their education in a special education classroom. For some, this might mean spending the majority of the school day in the general education classroom with a specific amount of time per day in a special education setting (e.g., thirty minutes per day in a learning support classroom). For others, it might mean spending the majority or entire school day in a special education classroom.
- **Specialized school:** There are a number of specialized schools that serve students with a variety of disabilities in a setting outside of the neighborhood public school. Special schools aim to educate students with specific educational needs.
- **Homebound, Hospital, or Residential facility:** Based on the student's needs, it may be deemed appropriate that they be educated in their home, in a hospital setting, or in a residential facility for individuals with disabilities.

Emma explained that determining the least restrictive environment is such a complex decision with many factors that need to be considered. What is considered appropriate for one child might not be appropriate for another child. It is up to the team to determine what is the best option for each student. She said that options like a specialized school or more restrictive placement wouldn't be appropriate for Sam.

Angie and Colin spent some time reading about the different types of placements to better understand the options. They agreed that Sam should stay in his regular school; he didn't need a more restrictive environment in their opinion. During the days leading up to the meeting, the Pennys spent a lot of time talking to Sam about his learning, what he thought helped him the most, and what types of things were the easiest or most difficult for him. They also asked him his thoughts about where he would learn best to get a feel for what would make him the most comfortable. He said that there were several kids in the class that got extra help and that some of them left the classroom for help while others stayed in the classroom. He talked about how much he loved being in the classroom with his friends, but he also said that it was really embarrassing for him when the teacher came over to help him. He felt like everyone was looking at him, and it made it harder for him to learn. He shared that he thought that he learned better with just a few kids as opposed to the whole class when he was working on something that was hard for him. They told him that they would talk to the school about his opinions and see what would be best for him.

The IEP Meeting

On the day of the meeting, even though the Pennys were nervous, they immediately felt at ease when they got to the school and Sam's teacher was there to greet them. She assured them that they would work together to do the best that they could for Sam. The team included Sam's teacher, a special education teacher, the principal, the school psychologist, and Angie and Colin. As they progressed through the different parts of the IEP, the Pennys really began to feel like part of the team. The team discussed that Sam would receive learning support in the areas of reading and writing; his learning support would be delivered by the special education teacher.

The school indicated that they would need to determine where he would learn best. When the topic of LRE came up, the Pennys felt prepared to talk about the placement with the rest of the IEP team. They all agreed that Sam should spend the majority of the day in the general education classroom with his peers. Once that was determined, the school explained that his learning support services could be delivered by the special education teacher in the general education classroom or in a special education classroom. They went through the pros and cons of full inclusion in the general education classroom with learning support as compared to learning support in a special education classroom (more specifically the learning support classroom). They wanted to make sure that they really thought about how Sam learned best. The Pennys shared what Sam had said about learning in the classroom. His teacher said that she had noticed something similar. She also noticed that he seemed to get distracted when he was really trying to concentrate and there was a lot going on in the classroom. Based on what they knew about Sam and his learning, they all agreed that his least restrictive environment was the general education classroom for the majority of the day with some time in the learning support room to focus on reading and writing. Once they finished fully going through the IEP, they all signed the document, and the school said that Sam's services would begin as soon as possible.

Concluding Thoughts

On the way home, Angie said, "That was a lot easier than I thought it would be. They really wanted to hear our thoughts. This is going to be a good thing for Sam."

Colin answered, "I'm happy that we were prepared for the meeting; it really helped when we were talking about the different options. I bet what Emma said is really true; figuring out the LRE must be such a hard decision to make for a lot of kids depending on what they need."

Overall, the Pennys had a good first IEP meeting experience and were grateful that they had been prepared to help make decisions with the team.

Questions:

1 How did the Pennys prepare for Sam's IEP meeting?
2 What is the least restrictive environment (LRE)? Describe the different options for LRE.
3 The Pennys went into the meeting feeling prepared because they felt like they understood the process. All parents/guardians have different levels of experience and knowledge of the IEP process.

How can the school help to prepare the parents/guardians for what will happen in the meeting so that they can best collaborate with the team?
4 What did the teacher do to help Angie and Colin feel at ease? Why was this a good approach?
5 Discuss Sam's LRE. What factors contributed to the team's decision regarding LRE?

Challenge: For each of the following case studies, describe the child's LRE and discuss why it may have been beneficial for the student: Darius (assistive technology #1 case study, chapter 1, p. 4), Allie (deaf-blindness case study, chapter 13, p. 98), and Lauren (traumatic brain injury case study, chapter 16, p. 131).

Challenge: Investigate the history of inclusive practices. Make a list of the pros and cons of inclusion. Discuss why LRE is such an important aspect of a child's IEP.

Section 504 of the Rehabilitation Act of 1973

Mary A. Houser, EdD, and Tara S. Guerriero, PhD

A Section 504 plan or Section 504 service agreement, sometimes referred to as a "504 plan," is a document that ensures students with disabilities have equal access to educational opportunities. They play a critical role in providing accessibility to general education for these students. They are the result of Section 504 of the Rehabilitation Act of 1973, a federal law that protects against discrimination based on disability in any program or activity that receives federal funding.

Students with disabilities who have 504 plans are typically educated in the general education setting and do not require specially designed instruction (instruction specific to a particular student) provided by special education services (under IDEA); however, they do require some assistance. Students with 504 plans often receive accommodations such as preferential seating, extended time on tests, assistive technology, and alternative assignments. These plans can also provide related services such as occupational therapy or speech therapy. It is important to know that 504 plans can vary from district to district and from state to state. State and local school districts are permitted to adjust their policies if they comply with federal guidelines. Federal law provides eligibility criteria for such plans, but states and local school districts may interpret these in their own way.

Not all students with disabilities require special education to be successful at school, Marco thought to himself. *Some students with disabilities can be successful in general education if they receive appropriate support through 504 plans. How can we best explain this to parents so they can understand?*

Teamwork: Marco and Ryan's Parent Meeting

Marco is a veteran general education teacher who has spent a good part of his teaching career working with students with disabilities who have 504 plans in the general education setting. He has worked as a high school English teacher for the past ten years. Marco and his friend, Ryan, a special education teacher, were asked to speak to a district-wide parent group whose children have recently received or will be receiving 504 plans as part of their education. The children of these parents vary in age range and by disability category. Some of the parents' children are elementary students with attention deficit hyperactivity disorder (ADHD) or autism spectrum disorder. Others are middle schoolers with sensory impairments, learning disabilities, and ADHD. There are even a handful of high school students who had IEPs in middle school and previously received special education services but are now able to be included in general education with accommodations as directed by their 504 plans. All of these families have one thing in common: they are new to 504 plans and how these plans will offer them accessibility to the general education curriculum.

District administrators value both Marco and Ryan's expertise as classroom teachers and asked them to talk to this parent group about the purpose of 504 plans, what is included in them, and how they differ from IEPs and special education. They were also asked to talk briefly about how 504 plans came to be and why they are instrumental in providing equal access to general education. Marco and Ryan spent some time organizing their thoughts and developing a presentation to share with the families.

"What is the most important message we want to convey to parents about 504 plans?" Ryan asked Marco.

"Well," Marco responded. "I think it is important to discuss the differences between 504 plans and special education services. A lot of times, parents confuse the two of them."

"Right," Ryan responded. "Why don't you discuss how students with disabilities are educated in public schools and how it is decided whether a student needs an IEP or a 504 plan? Then, I can explain to parents what a 504 plan is all about and how it is implemented in a general education setting."

"Sounds like a plan! That should work!" Marco exclaimed.

Both teachers sat down and mapped out how they would present these concepts to the parents at the upcoming meeting. Together, they determined the key points each of them wanted to discuss so that they had a full understanding of how their children with disabilities would be supported in the general education setting at school.

The parent meeting was only about a week away. Ryan and Marco went over their presentation, ensuring that their information was both clear and understandable to parents, and they did not miss any important points. They had their principal review the presentation just in case. On the evening of the meeting, Ryan and Marco got to school early and organized their presentation materials. They stood by the doors, welcomed the interested parents, and made small talk about their school.

Once everyone was seated, the teachers looked around and noticed there were probably twenty to twenty-five parents in the room. Ryan and Marco then began the meeting by introducing themselves and their roles at school. Ryan started by describing the purpose of the presentation—to explain 504 plans—and how they are implemented. He stated that Marco would begin by giving an overview of disabilities in public schools and how a decision is made about whether a student with a disability requires a 504 plan or special education services (under IDEA).

The Individuals with Disabilities Education Act (IDEA)

Marco began the presentation by discussing the various disability categories under the Individuals with Disabilities Education Act (IDEA). He briefly explained each of the disabilities (e.g., intellectual disability, other health impairment, learning disability) and some of their characteristics. He then moved on to the core concepts of IDEA (e.g., FAPE, LRE, zero reject) and emphasized that all children with disabilities have a place in the public school system. Marco mentioned that the type of support they require, however, does differ and is dependent on the individual child. He stated that typically, a child with a disability will either receive special education services under IDEA or a 504 plan.

Since he was the special educator, he summarized the eligibility process for special education, which included a comprehensive evaluation and the determination of whether the student had a disability that negatively impacts their educational performance. Marco further communicated that the child must benefit from specially designed instruction to help them learn in order for them to receive special education services under IDEA.

Lastly, he spent a few minutes discussing the IEP. Marco explained that children with disabilities who do not qualify for special education services might be eligible for a 504 plan. He stated that 504 plans are not considered special education, but they do support students with disabilities. Marco then handed the presentation over to Ryan.

Section 504 Plans/Service Delivery

Ryan continued with his discussion of 504 plans. He began by stating that 504 plans are a general education service provided to students with disabilities. Ryan highlighted that the purpose of the 504 plans is to "level the playing field" between students with disabilities and their neurotypical peers in general education. He discussed different ways 504 plans make general education more accessible to students. Ryan explained that oftentimes, children with disabilities just need accommodations in the general classroom to be successful.

Ryan reiterated Marco's comment that 504 plans are available to students with disabilities who do not qualify for special education services. Ryan mentioned they are governed by Section 504 of the Rehabilitation Act of 1973 and not by the IDEA. In essence, he elaborated, this is an anti-discrimination law. Ryan shared that it is the general education teacher and staff who are primarily responsible for a 504 plan's implementation. He told parents that for students to be eligible for a 504 plan, there are generally three criteria that must be met:

1. Have a physical or mental impairment that substantially limits one or more major life activities; or
2. Have a record of such an impairment; or
3. Be regarded as having such an impairment.

(U.S. Department of Education OCO, 2025, para. 5)

Ryan spent time discussing the three criteria and what they meant. After all, sometimes terminology can be confusing to parents. He provided the parents with examples of how a physical or mental impairment (aka their child's disability) can limit one's major life activities, such as walking, breathing, seeing, caring for oneself, and performing manual tasks (U.S. Department of Education OCO, 2025).

Ryan then went into detail about how students with disabilities can be effectively served in the general education setting with accommodations. He spoke about accommodations and how these are at the center of a student's 504 plan. Ryan told parents that accommodations are adaptations used to support a child's disability and help them to be more successful without changing the content that the student is learning or the expectations. He revealed the different types of accommodations, such as presentation accommodations, setting accommodations, response accommodations, and testing accommodations. To help parents understand accommodations better, Ryan provided them with a simple list of accommodation examples and explained each of them:

- **Presentation accommodation:** text-to-speech software; note-taking assistance; increased font size
- **Setting accommodation:** preferential seating; study carrel; the use of fidgets
- **Response accommodation:** oral response; scribe/note-taker; typing instead of handwriting
- **Testing accommodations:** extended time; frequent breaks; testing in a distraction-free environment

He emphasized that accommodations are individualized to the student based on their disability and support needs. Ryan expressed that different disabilities often require different types of accommodations. To illustrate, he stated that a student with a learning disability might benefit from extended time on tests and being provided with a study guide or review sheets for a test, whereas a student with a hearing impairment would likely benefit from having captioning provided for videos used in class and having teachers obtain the student's attention before they speak. These accommodations are quite different and serve different purposes when supporting students.

Component of a Section 504 Plan

Ryan proceeded to discuss the contents of 504 plans with the parent group. Ryan specified that 504 plans are typically less formal and shorter in length than IEPs. The format may also vary quite a bit across schools and districts. He outlined the following components of the 504 plan itself:

- **Student information:** basic demographic information such as name, address, and the school currently attended
- **Services:** various services a child might need (e.g., support services or health-related services) and the person at school who is responsible for their implementation
- **Evaluation information:** medical records, classwork examples, direct and indirect observations, and test results
- **Accommodations:** one or more presentation accommodation, setting accommodation, response accommodation, and/or testing accommodation
- **Description of the concern and diagnosed disability:** detailed information about the student's challenges (e.g., attention difficulties, organization difficulties, or sensory challenges) and the diagnosed disability
- **How disability affects major life functions and rationale for a 504 service plan:** description of how the individual student's disability inhibits their ability to be successful in the general education setting without support

It took Ryan some time to go over each component of the 504 plan. As he went through each component, without revealing their identities, Ryan used examples of children with disabilities he had taught in the past with 504 plans and what their plans consisted of. Lastly, Ryan mentioned that if parents do not agree with their child's 504 plan, they should set up a meeting to talk to the school about their concerns. He revealed to parents that there is a procedure for handling disputes and dispute resolution regarding 504 plans with the school district and explained mediation and due process to them.

Ryan and Marco were pleased with their presentation. They left a few minutes at the end of the hour so that parents could ask questions. Not surprisingly, parents had several questions about the 504 plans. Here are some of the questions parents asked:

1. Will there be other students with 504 plans in my child's class?
2. If my child is unsuccessful with a 504 plan, can he receive special education services?
3. My child has ADHD. Will his general education teacher allow him to get up and move around the classroom when he needs to?

As the meeting came to a close, Ryan and Marco told parents that school personnel will be available to them to respond to their questions and provide progress updates on their child. All in all, the parents seemed satisfied with the information they received and left the meeting that evening with increased confidence that their child would be supported at school. They also had a much better understanding of the differences between special education services provided through an IEP and accommodations provided through a 504 plan.

Questions:

1. What is a 504 plan? What law is this plan a result of?
2. Why might a child with a disability receive a 504 plan and not an IEP/special education services?
3. What educational placement is a student with a 504 plan typically educated in? General education classroom or special education classroom?
4. List the four types of accommodations found in a 504 plan and provide an example of each.
5. Summarize the different components of a 504 plan.
6. If you were a parent attending this meeting, what question(s) might you have about your child receiving a 504 plan?
7. Max (visual impairment case study, chapter 13, p. 107) and Gia (hearing impairment case study, chapter 13, p. 104) both receive 504 plans for their disabilities. Discuss their accommodations and how these have helped them succeed at school.

Challenge: Interview the parent(s)/guardian(s) of a pre-K through grade 12 student who currently has a 504 plan. Create a list of interview questions that address the child's disability, reasons they were provided a 504 plan, the accommodations they currently receive, and their success in the general education setting resulting from their 504 plan.

References

Center for Parent Information and Resources (April, 2022): *Considering LRE in placement decisions.* https://www.parentcenterhub.org/placement-lre/

Every Student Succeeds Act (n.d.). *Assessments under Title I, Part A & Title I, Part B: Summary of final regulations.* https://www.ed.gov/sites/ed/files/policy/elsec/leg/essa/essaassessmentfactsheet1207.pdf

IRIS Center (n.d.). *Information brief: Least restrictive environment (LRE).* https://iris.peabody.vanderbilt.edu/wp-content/uploads/pdf_info_briefs/IRIS_least_restrictive_environment_info_brief.pdf

Office for Dispute Resolution (2021). *Your guide to special education mediation.* Pennsylvania Department of Education. https://odr-pa.org/wp-content/uploads/medguide.pdf

Pennsylvania Department of Education (PDE). (2025). *Accommodations guidelines: 2025 PSSA and Keystone exams.* https://www.pa.gov/content/dam/copapwp-pagov/en/education/documents/instruction/assessment-and-accountability/pssa/accommodations/accommodations%20guidelines%20for%20pssa%20and%20keystone%20exams.pdf

U.S. Department of Education – Office of Communications and Outreach (OCO). (2025, January 13). *Frequently asked questions: Section 504 free appropriate public education (FAPE).* https://www.ed.gov/laws-and-policy/civil-rights-laws/disability-discrimination/frequently-asked-questions-section-504-free-appropriate-public-education-fape

18

Individualized Education Programs (IEPs)

This chapter includes several case studies related to the topic of individualized education programs (IEPs):

- Annual Goals, Present Levels, and Progress Monitoring
- Case Management
- IEP Meetings
  - IEP Meetings #1: First-year teacher
  - IEP Meetings #2: Veteran teacher
- Specially Designed Instruction (SDI)
  - Specially Designed Instruction #1
  - Specially Designed Instruction #2
- Transition (Secondary)

An IEP is a blueprint of the educational program of a child with a disability detailing how they will receive their special education and related services. It is a legal document that is created by an IEP team (aka multidisciplinary team). An IEP team typically includes the parent(s)/guardian(s), a special education teacher (or other special education representative), a general education teacher, an administrator (e.g., principal, assistant principal), a school psychologist (or other professional who can interpret and explain the test results), a local education agency (LEA) representative, and related service personnel, as needed (e.g., physical therapist, occupational therapist, speech therapist/pathologist, audiologist). It is valid for one calendar year, and a new IEP is developed annually (if the student continues to be eligible for special education services).

The formatting and order of an IEP can vary from state to state; however, all IEPs have several mandatory components. Every IEP includes the student's present levels of academic achievement and functional performance (PLAAFP), annual goals, special education and related services, justification for the extent of participation/nonparticipation in the general education classroom, transition services (if appropriate), specially designed instruction, accommodations and modifications, educational placement, and participation in state and local assessments. All of these components will vary from student to student depending on each student's unique strengths and challenges. An IEP is a critical document for special education teachers, general education teachers, related service providers, parent(s)/guardian(s) and the student to understand an appropriate educational program for the student with special needs. Additionally, it serves as a roadmap for the implementation of the student's educational program.

Special education teachers have many responsibilities related to IEPs for students with disabilities. For example, they often lead IEP meetings where they provide valuable insight and information to parents, interpret educational test results, make IEP recommendations, collaborate with other education professionals, coordinate the compilation of the written IEP document, advocate for students with disabilities, and implement specially designed instruction in a variety of educational placements. A general education teacher is also a member of the IEP team and provides insight into the general education curriculum. In addition, the general education teacher is responsible for knowing and implementing the services and supports that a child with a disability will need to be successful, while in their classroom. The related service providers often work directly with students with disabilities providing therapeutic services and/or provide consultative services to teachers.

This chapter examines the following topics related to IEPs:

1 **Annual Goals, Present Levels, and Progress Monitoring:** In this case study, a special education professional is preparing to give a workshop for new special education teachers based on the concepts of annual goals, present levels, and progress monitoring.
2 **Case Management:** In this case study, the duties related to case management of a third-year special education teacher are examined. It includes a discussion of the students on his caseload, his teaching

responsibilities, and his case management responsibilities. The development and implementation of IEPs is an integral component of case management.

3. **IEP Meetings (2):** In these case studies, the IEP meeting experiences of both a first-year special education teacher and a veteran special education teacher are explored. It reveals how years of teaching can influence the IEP meeting process.
4. **Specially Designed Instruction (2):** In these case studies, the authors delve into the process associated with interpreting, implementing, and updating the "Specially Designed Instruction" (SDI) section of the IEP.
5. **Transition (Secondary):** In this case study, the secondary transition process is detailed. Concepts such as transition assessment and transition services are highlighted.

Annual Goals, Present Levels, and Progress Monitoring

Tara S. Guerriero, PhD

Caroline was busy preparing for an upcoming professional development workshop that she was going to be giving to a group of brand-new special educators. The topic of the workshop is *annual goals and progress monitoring*. She thought to herself, *annual goals are such an important part of a student's IEP; they guide the IEP and set the tone for what the student will focus on for the year*. She thought that it might be beneficial for her if she first developed a set of questions that she had as a new teacher and that other new teachers might have when thinking about annual goals. She thought of it almost like a list of frequently asked questions (FAQs). This would help her to organize her ideas and ensure that she covers everything that she wants to cover. The following was her initial list of important questions:

- What is an annual goal?
  - An annual goal is a skill or behavior that can be reasonably accomplished by the student within a twelve-month period of time or calendar year.

- In certain instances, it might be appropriate for goals to be written for a period that is shorter than twelve months.
- How do you determine what areas of achievement should be represented in the annual goals?
  - Annual goals can be academic, social, behavioral, and/or functional, in scope.
  - Goals should be included in all areas of need for a student.
  - Closely examining the student's present levels in all areas is key in considering the student's current level of skills and determining what is important for the student to focus on.
- How many goals should be included?
  - There isn't a specific number of goals that should be included in an IEP. The focus, rather, is on making sure that all the important areas of need are included.
- How can you project what a student will be able to accomplish in twelve months?
  - It can feel daunting to project out a full year and determine what a child should be able to do twelve months later.
  - In addition to using the present levels to help determine what to focus on, present levels serve as the starting point or baseline for instruction. Knowing a student's starting point is a critical part of thinking about what might be able to be accomplished in a year.
  - If it is a student's first IEP, the team will evaluate and consider all the data and information that has been collected for the comprehensive evaluation that was used to determine eligibility for services. Based on that information, they will try to determine how much the student can accomplish in a year.
  - If the student already has been receiving services, there may be more specific information to help with determining what might be a realistic expectation for the year. The team will analyze the progress toward the previous goals, often through progress monitoring data, to better understand how quickly the child has been able to progress. Progress monitoring is when a student's skills are evaluated at regular intervals (e.g., weekly, biweekly, monthly) to determine how the student has progressed in skill development as well as how quickly progress has been made.
- How are goals written? What is included in a goal?

- While goals are only a sentence or two in length, it is important that they contain a specific set of information.
  - Goals must be clearly written, measurable, and observable. The goal must include specific language to indicate the skill or behavior that the student will demonstrate. Further, the goal must be written in such a way that the student's performance can accurately be measured through data collection.
  - Goals must be time-bound, meaning they need to indicate when the goal will be accomplished.
- How are goals used to guide instruction?
  - Once the goals are determined, the IEP team can decide on the specially designed instruction and adaptations that will be used to help the student to accomplish the goal.
- How is progress toward goals monitored throughout the year?
  - As was previously mentioned, it is important to consistently evaluate a student's performance to measure ongoing growth over the course of the year to ensure that the student is progressing toward the annual goal.

After looking at her list of questions, Caroline feels like she has a good start in thinking about what will need to be included in her workshop. Annual goals are such an important part of a student's instructional program, and she wants to make sure that she covers as much as possible to help the new teachers. As she starts to prepare her materials and talking points, she knows that she will include much more content, including many examples of how to use progress monitoring data to establish present levels, which can then be used to develop goals. Participants will also spend time writing goals. This workshop is shaping up to be beneficial; she wishes that she had a similar workshop when she first started teaching.

Questions:

1. What is an annual goal?
2. What does the term "present levels" mean?
3. Explain the concept of progress monitoring.
4. What period of time do most annual goals cover?
5. How are annual goals used to guide instruction?

Challenge: Consider the following goal: *By (date), Caroline will solve three-digit by three-digit addition problems that require regrouping with 90 percent accuracy on four out of five consecutive trials.* Describe the process that you might use to measure progress toward this goal.

Case Management

Alyssa Blasko, PhD, BCBA and Colleen E. Commisso, PhD

Andrew McHuttin is in his third year as a learning support teacher at Rosedale Elementary School. As a learning support teacher, in addition to his lunch and preparation period, Andrew teaches four classes within his resource classroom that focus on teaching reading, and he also co-teaches one science and one social studies class within a general education classroom. In the classes that focus on reading, Andrew is responsible for developing lessons, creating activities, grading, communicating with the parents (as needed), and collecting data on the students' reading skills. Within the courses that he co-teaches, Andrew is responsible for implementing student accommodations, adapting materials, creating study guides, creating guided notes, teaching parts of lessons, grading, and planning lessons with the general education teacher.

In addition to his teaching responsibilities, Andrew is also responsible for a special education caseload that includes twenty first- and second-grade students with a variety of identified disabilities and levels of support needed. His caseload consists of the following students:

Table 18.1 Andrew's Caseload

Student Name	Disability Category	Time in General Education
Kevin Aldridge	Specific Learning Disability	100%
Isabel Brenner	Other Health Impairments: ADHD	80%
Ethan Callahan	Specific Learning Disability	70%
Samuel Corwin	Specific Learning Disability	80%

Frank Corwin	Specific Learning Disability	100%
Reagan Drayton	Emotional Disturbance	100%
Preston Elway	Specific Learning Disability	70%
Nicholas Fenwick	Specific Learning Disability	60%
David Halberg	Other Health Impairments: ADHD	100%
Carly Hollis	Emotional Disturbance	80%
Tobais Langford	Emotional Disturbance	60%
Angelina Marlow	Specific Learning Disability	60%
Hector Navarro	Other Health Impairments: ADHD	100%
Gustavo Rivas	Other Health Impairments: ADHD	100%
Javi Serrano	Specific Learning Disability	80%
Matthew Stanton	Other Health Impairments: ADHD	90%
Quinn Throne	Specific Learning Disability	70%
Larissa Voss	Specific Learning Disability	70%
Oscar Whitaker	Other Health Impairments: ADHD	80%
Bethany Winslow	Specific Learning Disability	100%

Andrew's caseload has seven students who are fully included in the general education classroom. These are students with whom Andrew collaborates alongside the general education teacher to ensure their support, as he does not directly teach them. The other fourteen students are included for less than 90 percent of the day in general education and Andrew teaches each of them for at least a portion of every day.

Andrew's Teaching and Case Management Responsibilities

As both a teacher and caseload manager, Andrew has a wide range of responsibilities to balance.

Andrew is proud of himself for finding some level of balance with his job responsibilities. He credits this balance to having a formal schedule to manage his teaching responsibilities, case management, parent communication, service to the school community, collaboration with others, and staff management. The execution of this lengthy list of responsibilities would not be possible without Andrew's Monday morning

Table 18.2 Andrew's Teaching and Case Management Responsibilities

	Teaching Responsibilities	Case Management Responsibilities
Ongoing/Daily	<ul><li>Lesson/activity development</li><li>Provide instruction</li><li>Grading</li><li>Providing accommodations and modifications for students</li><li>Creating study guides and guided notes</li><li>Responding to parent requests/questions for students in classes or in co-taught classes</li><li>Collaborating with general education teachers that he co-teaches with</li></ul>	<ul><li>Writing legal paperwork (i.e., IEPs, RRs, NOREPs, invitations to meetings)</li><li>Responding to parent requests/questions about students on caseload</li><li>Responding to other teacher requests/questions about students on caseload</li><li>Ensuring all students on his caseload are receiving their required accommodations/modifications</li><li>Ensuring that all data toward his caseload students' IEP goals is being collected</li><li>Collaborating with related service providers (e.g., occupational therapy, speech and language)</li><li>Responding to students in need that requested a break to access their caseload manager</li></ul>
Weekly/Biweekly	<ul><li>Collecting data for students' IEP goals in his classes that are measured weekly/biweekly</li></ul>	<ul><li>Collecting data for students IEP goals that are measured weekly/biweekly</li><li>Checking caseload students' grades including missing work</li><li>Providing email updates to parents if included as an accommodation in the students' IEP</li></ul>
Monthly	<ul><li>Collecting data for students' IEP goals in his classes that are measured monthly</li><li>Attend special education department meetings</li><li>Attend general education department meetings for co-taught subjects</li><li>Attend faculty meetings</li></ul>	<ul><li>Collecting data for students' IEP goals that are measured monthly</li></ul>

Quarterly	• Complete quarter grades for his classes • Support general education teacher to complete quarter grades for co-taught courses	• Complete progress monitoring reports • Send progress monitoring reports to parents
Yearly		• Holding IEP meetings for each student on his caseload • Providing accommodations for standardized assessments

ritual, where he arrives at school early and checks his special education case management spreadsheet to determine what tasks and student paperwork he needs to prioritize. From this spreadsheet check, Andrew proactively makes any changes or revisions to tasks and keeps all due dates at the front of his mind.

Caseload Changes

In addition to the tasks above, Andrew must be flexible and ready for changes to his caseload. As his students' needs (e.g., IEP goals) change, his responsibilities also must be updated. This cycle is continuous. Further, students may be added or removed from his caseload (e.g., moving in or out of the school). When new students are added, Andrew's responsibilities include the following:

- Reviewing any available paperwork
- Building initial rapport with the student
- Building a plan for the student's first day or two of school before they have an official schedule
- Determining an appropriate schedule for the student based on their needs and previous classes
- Contacting the parent(s)/guardian(s)
- Holding an IEP meeting

Impact

Andrew has become increasingly worried about managing the teaching and caseload responsibilities in his packed schedule. He is feeling overwhelmed and is unsure of what to do. He decides to reach out to another special education teacher in his school who has been a special educator for ten years and was a friend from college. Andrew hopes to learn a few tricks for reducing stress and improving his caseload workflow.

Questions:

1. Reflect on Andrew's responsibilities. What might be challenging about having a caseload of students with varying strengths and needs as well as widely different schedules?
2. Consider this:
   a) If you are a future general education teacher, what responsibilities of a special education caseload manager are you also a part of? What is your role in these responsibilities?
   b) If you are a future special education teacher, explain how do you think you could balance/organize the numerous teaching and caseload responsibilities?
3. Andrew was asked to join the school events committee that will help plan all the community-building events each school year (e.g., back-to-school carnival, holiday dance, end-of-school-year field trips). If Andrew agrees, he would need to attend a meeting once a month and complete some tasks in between meetings to help organize events. Andrew's students are extremely excited for him to join the committee as committee members' students get first access to the events, and Andrew can ensure the events are inclusion-focused.
4. Explain the pros and cons of him joining the committee. Be sure to take into consideration his current teaching and case management responsibilities.

Challenge: Teachers (general educators, special educators, and specialists) have a lot of responsibilities that come with their job. They often take work home at the end of school day to ensure that they are able to accomplish all of their responsibilities. Write an argument that would convince a teacher to create a work–life balance and ensure that they engage in self-care.

IEP Meetings

IEP Meeting #1: First-Year Teacher

Mary A. Houser, EdD

Carson's First IEP Meeting

I am so nervous. I only attended one IEP meeting during my student teaching experience, Carson thought to himself. *Now, I am going to oversee running them!* Carson was a first-year special education teacher at an elementary school in central Pennsylvania. He recently graduated from a state university and got his first special education teaching job, teaching students in grades K–2 with intellectual disabilities in a self-contained classroom. *What if I screw things up? What if I make mistakes during the IEP meeting?*

His first IEP meeting was at the end of October. Markeith was the student who was the subject of the IEP meeting. He is six years old and was diagnosed with fetal alcohol syndrome (FAS) at birth (Note: Markeith was introduced in the multiple disabilities #1 case study, chapter 10, p. 72). This resulted in an intellectual disability and aphasia. As such, he was placed in Carson's self-contained special education classroom. Markeith lives with his brothers and his adoptive mother, Sunshine. Little is known about the biological mother except that she was unable to provide for her children. There is no information known about Markeith's father.

Sunshine adopted the brothers when they were very young. Sunshine has done more than just take care of the boys' basic needs; she has genuinely cared for them and wants them to have a good life. She and the boys spend a lot of time together riding bikes, reading books, and dancing to 1980s music in the living room. They live in a two-bedroom home, and the boys all share one bedroom. Meals are basic, and there are never any of the "extras" that some children have, like trendy clothes or the latest iPhones, but Markeith and his brothers always have fun and feel loved.

Preparing for the IEP Meeting

The invitation letter to attend the IEP meeting was sent to Sunshine, and she informed the school that she could attend the IEP meeting. Carson followed up, reaching out to her by sending a parent questionnaire home to complete in preparation for the meeting. The questionnaire included questions such as these:

- Describe your child's strengths and talents.
- What are your dreams for your child?
- In what areas does your child need to improve?

Carson wanted to gather as much information as he could before the meeting. This would be the first time he would meet Sunshine and discuss Markeith, because she was unable to attend the Back to School Night in September. He was hoping the parent questionnaire would give him a little insight into her hopes and dreams for Markeith.

Carson spent considerable time preparing Markeith's new IEP before the meeting. About two weeks before the meeting, he made sure all Markeith's formal assessments had been completed, and the results were available to discuss. He also double-checked the meeting room reservation, made copies of the new IEP for all the IEP team members, ensured he had class coverage, and gathered notepaper, pens, and water bottles for all the invitees. There was a lot to remember!

About one week before the meeting, Carson reviewed Markeith's drafted IEP. He created graphs and charts depicting Markeith's progress and reviewed his current supports. In addition, Carson gathered work samples to support the discussion. Carson knew he had to be very organized to be successful, so he also created a checklist that he would bring into the meeting so that he would not forget to address anything. On this checklist, he included reminders such as to review the agenda, discuss Markeith's PLAAFP, discuss annual goals, determine accommodations and modifications, discuss progress monitoring, determine schedule of special education services, determine educational placement, get consent, and obtain proper signatures.

The IEP Meeting

The day of the meeting finally arrived. The IEP members filed into an empty meeting room at the school, and all the stakeholders took their seats. Carson passed out a draft copy of Markeith's new annual IEP to the team members. Carson felt anxious but knew he had done everything he could to make the meeting successful. He started the meeting by introducing himself and welcoming the other IEP team members to the meeting. He then asked Sunshine to introduce herself. Carson gave her a copy of the procedural safeguards notice to review her rights as Markeith's mother. This handbook summarizes the rights of parents whose children receive or may receive special education services. After this, Carson had the other IEP team members introduce themselves and explain their roles. The IEP team members consisted of Carson, a general education teacher, a speech and language pathologist (SLP), a physical therapist (PT), an occupational therapist (OT), a school psychologist, and an assistant principal. Most importantly, the IEP team included Sunshine, the parent.

Carson continued the meeting and briefly discussed Markeith's multiple disabilities and how they affect his school performance. He then provided the team with a meeting agenda. As he discussed the order of the meeting with everyone, Carson remembered learning that it was important to always start by making positive statements about a child's performance before discussing any challenges. This is something he had learned in one of his teacher preparation classes. He also remembered that he did not want to use a lot of educational jargon with Sunshine when discussing progress, since she would likely have trouble understanding these unfamiliar terms. Furthermore, Carson also wanted to make sure that she clearly understood the results of Markeith's recent assessments, because oftentimes parents need assistance in understanding assessment results. He took a deep breath and continued.

Carson then proceeded to review all sections of the IEP. He began with Markeith's PLAAFP, referring to a summary created by the IEP team. This summary indicates Markeith's strengths and challenges at the time of the IEP meeting. Carson began by stating that Markeith was a six-year-old boy with an intellectual disability and aphasia. He continued to explain his global deficits in reading, writing, and mathematics. He broke down each subject and provided specific examples of his current performance. To illustrate, Carson discussed Markeith's deficits in letter writing abilities, ability to read sight words, and identifying his numbers. From this, Carson shared new annual goals in each of these areas. Here are a few examples:

- By the end of the IEP cycle, Markeith will accurately and legibly trace all uppercase and lowercase letters with 80 percent accuracy, as determined by teacher observation.

- By the end of the IEP cycle, given a list of high-frequency sight words, Markeith will accurately read aloud five sight words in four out of five consecutive opportunities, as assessed by teacher observation.
- By the end of the IEP cycle, Markeith will be able to independently wash his hands (according to steps on the task analysis) 80 percent of the time, as assessed by teacher observation.

In addition to learning functional academics, Markeith also had several important daily living skills that he will need to learn over the next year. Carson stated that Markeith would receive direct instruction for most of his learning tasks, both the functional academics and the activities of daily living. He briefly explained to Sunshine how direct instruction differs from other types of instruction. He then described the daily living skills they would be working on over the next year, such as personal hygiene and getting dressed.

Carson indicated that Markeith would be given a task analysis for more complex skills, such as shoe tying and toileting. He emphasized the need for using visuals when instructing Markeith, and lots of repetition and practice to acquire these skills. Carson informed the team that the more hands-on application Markeith received in the classroom, the more likely he would be to achieve his annual goals.

Carson further discussed the need for clear and consistent behavioral expectations. He mentioned that he should be given choices whenever possible. Carson spoke about a reinforcement system that would be put in place to keep Markeith interested and motivated to learn. This would be a First–Then board where Markeith would be expected to complete a less desirable task to receive a preferred item or activity. To illustrate, first, Markeith would practice his sight words, then he would be allowed to take a five-minute break to play a game on one of the class iPads.

Carson then turned to Markeith's related service personnel (SLP, OT, and PT) to share their updates on his progress and to discuss new annual goals for him. Markeith's speech and language pathologist spoke about Markeith's current skill level. She mentioned that Markeith has difficulties swallowing and how this could be addressed in therapy. She also told the team that Markeith's aphasia is a disability that makes it difficult to understand what he is saying. Moving forward, speech therapy would target his swallowing and aphasia. He will also be working on following simple one-step directions. Lastly, the SLP discussed the possibility of him using an alternative augmentative communication (AAC) device to support his language development. She indicated that he would need to receive an AAC assessment as a first step to determine his assistive technology needs.

After the speech and language pathologist spoke, his occupational therapist provided progress updates. He spoke about Markeith needing to strengthen his fine motor skills to complete functional tasks such as buttoning and zipping his clothing. The OT explained that fine motor skills are central to many everyday tasks he will need to complete. He recommended activities that would strengthen his ability to cut, color, and write. He, too, shared new annual OT goals for Markeith.

Lastly, Markeith's physical therapist (PT) provided updates on his progress. She spoke about the balance issues that Markeith was experiencing. At the current time, Markeith was not able to stand on one foot and jump. The PT talked about strengthening his balance through play-based activities such as hopscotch and using a balance beam. The PT also discussed with the team how a lack of balance can have a significant impact on Markeith's development, which can lead to clumsiness and uncoordinated movements. He shared Markeith's new IEP goals for the next year.

Carson moved on to discuss Markeith's participation in state and local assessments. He mentioned that taking the PSSA (Pennsylvania System of School Assessment), even with accommodations, was not a feasible choice due to Markeith's cognitive impairment. Instead, Carson suggested that he participate in an alternate assessment—the PASA (Pennsylvania Alternate System of Assessment). The team then discussed that Markeith would take alternate assessments for any local assessments.

Carson continued to discuss progress monitoring. Progress monitoring occurs when a student's performance is regularly collected and analyzed to determine progress toward their annual goals. Carson informed Sunshine that she should be updated on Markeith's progress regularly. He added that progress monitoring can take on many forms, such as direct observations or gathering information from others in the form of interviews and checklists. Sunshine seemed pleased to know this information.

After they had gone through all the sections of the IEP, it was time to discuss Markeith's educational placement. Due to his significant support needs, it was agreed that Markeith would remain in his current self-contained setting for 80 percent or more of the school day. The team discussed that at the current time, this would be Markeith's least restrictive environment. Carson completed the justification statement portion of the IEP that indicates why inclusion with his typical peers would not be appropriate for Markeith at this time.

The IEP meeting lasted about an hour. In a successful conclusion to the meeting, all participants agreed to the conditions of the draft IEP and signed off on it. Carson thanked everyone for attending the meeting, and the meeting came to an end. Carson was pleased with the outcome of the meeting and that he did not forget to address any important issues about Markeith's progress.

Carson's Reflection

As he lay in bed that evening, reflecting on his day, Carson thought about what he would do differently at his next IEP meeting. He thought perhaps he should have given Sunshine more time to express her desires and any concerns she might have had. Carson thought maybe he was too concerned about getting through the information on the IEP and not attentive enough to her need to share information. He also thought he might have spent a little too much time reporting on some sections of the IEP, while not spending enough time on others. He pondered how he would adjust his timing at his next meeting. Carson thought to himself how important it was to consider each of these students as individuals and to plan accordingly. After all, their individualized education is at the center of all their learning. He closed his eyes and drifted off to sleep.

Questions:

1. Describe Carson's feelings about running his first IEP meeting. Would you have felt the same if it were your first IEP meeting? Why or why not?
2. What did Carson prepare about two weeks before the IEP meeting?
3. Who is Markeith? What do we know about Markeith as a student with disabilities?
4. Who were the members of Markeith's IEP team?
5. Discuss the specially designed instruction (SDI) in Markeith's new annual IEP.

6   What related services did Markeith get during school?
7   Discuss why Markeith does not take the regular state and local assessments like other children his age.
8   At the end of the day, Carson reflected on his first IEP meeting experience. What did he decide to do differently next time? Explain.

Challenge: In a small group, brainstorm your goals and concerns about running your first IEP meeting as a special education teacher. Be prepared to share your ideas with the rest of the class.

IEP Meeting #2: Veteran Teacher

Brittany Severino, EdD

Ms. Sheer takes a deep breath, pauses for a second as she is slightly nervous, and says, "Good afternoon, everyone, thank you for attending Rahul's IEP meeting today." Ms. Sheer has facilitated numerous IEP meetings over the course of her career as a secondary special education teacher; however, this one was different because there were so many participants, and a translator also attended the meeting. Nine individuals were sitting around the large conference table, which was the most that Ms. Sheer had invited to an IEP meeting.

Rahul Mookerjee is a seventeen-year-old student on Ms. Sheer's caseload, diagnosed with autism spectrum disorder (ASD), who excels in math but exhibits some difficulty in reading, writing, and social skills (Note: Rahul was introduced in the ASD #1 case study, chapter 3, p. 22). Rahul's parents, Mr. and Mrs. Mookerjee, are not fully fluent in English and speak Hindi as their primary language. An interpreter, Amrita, is present as part of Rahul's IEP meeting team to help provide translation. Additionally, Mr. and Mrs. Mookerjee have an advocate whom they invited to Rahul's IEP meeting to help them navigate the meeting and create a new IEP for their son. An educational advocate is someone well-versed and knowledgeable about the special education process and services to help families. They also help provide a different perspective for the IEP team to consider, as they are not an employee of the school. Rahul's IEP team also includes the assistant principal serving as the local education agency representative, Rahul's general education geometry teacher, Rahul's school counselor, Ms. Sheer, and most importantly, Rahul.

Navigating IEP Meeting Dynamics with an Interpreter

Ms. Sheer has all the IEP team members introduce themselves, provide their signatures to acknowledge their attendance, provide Mr. and Mrs. Mookerjee with a copy of the procedural safeguards notice, and then begin to review the agenda for the IEP meeting.

Ms. Sheer says, "We are going to review a new draft IEP for Rahul to help him finish this academic year and transition into twelfth grade. First, we will review Rahul's current grades and the progress he has made on his IEP goals in the Present Levels of Functional Performance and Academic Achievement. Then—"

Amrita interjects and politely reminds Ms. Sheer that only a few sentences can be interpreted at a time, and to try and utilize user-friendly explanations when discussing special education terminology.

Ms. Sheer apologizes and restates, "We will review Rahul's draft IEP, which is this document that has all of Rahul's support and services at school. We will start by discussing how the current school year is going for Rahul." Ms. Sheer pauses to provide time for Amrita to translate and makes sure she continues to engage in appropriate eye contact with Mr. and Mrs. Mookerjee to ensure they feel a part of a mutual conversation.

Responding to Advocate Questions: Working Collaboratively

Ms. Sheer asks Rahul how the school year is going, including his favorite and least favorite classes. Rahul responds, "It's going okay. I like going to geometry the best since I'm good at math. I like being in our classroom to see my best friend Maximo, but I wish I could attend more classes with everyone else."

Mr. Turner, Rahul's geometry teacher, shares input on how Rahul is performing in his class. "Rahul is doing well! He currently has a B+, 89 percent, that I anticipate could bump up to an A before the marking period is over." Mr. Turner waits for Amrita to interpret that input, and further explains, "Rahul has demonstrated consistent performance on quizzes and tests. Rahul has exhibited some difficulty working with others in class on projects or group assignments."

The family's advocate, Lori, reminds the IEP team that social skills are an area of need for Rahul and asks, "What current accommodations or modifications are being provided to help Rahul in geometry with tasks that require group work?" Ms. Sheer's heart begins to race as she feels nervous to respond. She understands Lori's role is to support Rahul and his family but wants to make sure she properly explains his support and services.

Ms. Sheer clarifies, "Rahul is made aware of any group assignments or activities before the class session begins. Mr. Turner will also let him know who his group members are, and he will be provided a specific role within the group, with a clear list of tasks he is required to complete."

Lori asks, "Do we think it could be appropriate for Rahul to be exempt from group work or the option to complete the assignment independently?"

Ms. Sheer explains how, even though social skills are an area of need for Rahul, it is something important for him to practice as he will need to collaborate with others in a college or work environment. Mr. and Mrs. Mookerjee agree and share how they would like Rahul to be more comfortable talking to other people. Ms. Sheer suggests having Rahul work on role-play scenarios in the autistic support classroom that involve working with others on group assignments and having Rahul create a small card with reminders or strategies that he can use in his classes when he becomes nervous to socialize.

Lori remarks, "I think that's great! Rahul can practice the skill in an environment where he feels safe but then create a resource to help him practice it in other classes. I'm glad we were able to think that problem through collaboratively."

Student Advocacy: Keeping Least Restrictive Environment in Mind

Rahul reminds his IEP team that he would like to engage in more classes than geometry, electives, and lunch with his grade-level peers. Mr. and Mrs. Mookerjee identify that they are hesitant because they don't want Rahul in classes that are too hard or for him to potentially fail a class and impact his grade point average (GPA).

Lori asks, "Can any push-in special education services be provided to help Rahul be successful in participating in more grade-level courses?"

Mr. Corbett, the assistant principal, explains how the special education services and school schedules are currently implemented in a pull-out model. However, the IEP team can discuss whether Rahul could be successful with specific modifications in those courses or with the potential support of an instructional assistant who could provide more one-on-one check-ins for Rahul and other students in class.

Rahul interjects, "I don't want an adult with me in the classes. I don't need a babysitter."

Ms. Sheer assured Rahul that he would not be assigned a one-on-one instructional assistant. Instead, she proposed making a change to Rahul's schedule for the second half of the school year, as the school operates on a block schedule, for Rahul to participate in the general education social studies course in the spring. Rahul would have accommodations and modifications added to his IEP to support him with reading and writing tasks in the course.

Additionally, the team would check in to see how Rahul is doing in the course with this support to determine whether more is needed and to continue or add additional general education courses to Rahul's twelfth-grade schedule.

Lori comments, "I think that's best that we make these schedule changes one at a time to ensure Rahul feels comfortable and is set up for success in them."

Rahul shares, "I'm excited to be with my friends for another class. Nervous. But mostly excited."

Discussing Transition Planning at the IEP Meeting

Ms. Sheer announces, "We will now move on to discussing transition services, or planning for what Rahul wants to do after he graduates from high school." Ms. Sheer asks Mr. and Mrs. Mookerjee what their vision is for their son after he graduates. Amrita helps translate the questions as well as the responses.

Mr. and Mrs. Mookerjee think it would be best for Rahul to stay in high school after turning eighteen years old. They plan for him to continue living home with the family and are interested in having him attend the local community college as a part-time student.

Ms. Sheer then asks Rahul what he wants to do after he graduates from high school. Rahul responds, "I don't want to graduate after my younger brother. That doesn't make sense. I like computers a lot. I want to start working now to earn money so I can have an apartment one day."

Ms. Sheer reinforces that Rahul's vision for himself is important and that it has some similarities with his parents, but some areas the IEP team might need to discuss. Ms. Sheer asks Rahul if he has any interest in attending the county's vocational high school, which offers half-day programming in a variety of career fields.

Rahul responds, "Does that mean I can't go to college?"

Ms. Sheer explains that they have several programs related to computer programming or IT security that would give Rahul hands-on experience before going to college, and he could possibly start earning college credit, as the vocational high school has an agreement with the local community college.

Rahul shares, "Maybe, that could be cool."

The IEP team decides that Rahul will tour the vocational high school to decide whether he wants to attend for twelfth grade. Additionally, if Rahul enjoys it and wants to continue, he could primarily attend the vocational high school after he completes twelfth grade or turns eighteen until he ages out or decides to fully transition into the community college setting. His twelfth-grade experiences, including his exploration of the vocational high school, could help Rahul determine if he's ready to graduate after twelfth grade or if he would like additional time in high school or vocational high school before transitioning to the local community college.

Ms. Sheer asks Mr. and Mrs. Mookerjee if they've heard of the Office of Vocational Rehabilitation (OVR). They both shake their heads side to side in confusion, indicating no. Ms. Sheer further explains how OVR is a federal agency that can help provide support services to adults with various disabilities in life after high school. Ms. Sheer provides Mr. and Mrs. Mookerjee with a handout providing an overview of OVR and how to apply for services.

Ms. Sheer adds, "Lori, if you can help Mr. and Mrs. Mookerjee apply and follow up with OVR, this would be a great support for Rahul. This way, I could invite them to his IEP meeting next year, and we will have additional input on the possibilities for Rahul after he graduates from high school." Lori thanks Ms. Sheer for this information and agrees that this is an appropriate next step.

The IEP meeting wraps up with Ms. Sheer asking if there are any additional questions about Rahul's current special education services. Mr. and Mrs. Mookerjee share, "No, we are proud of the progress Rahul is making and what will be next." Lori comments, "This was a very productive IEP meeting. Thank you for listening to the parents' input."

Ms. Sheer thanks everyone for attending and helps escort Mr. and Mrs. Mookerjee, Lori, and Amrita to the front office to sign out. Ms. Sheer returns to her desk with a smile on her face, "Well, that went better than expected!"

Questions:

1. What is an educational advocate? How can they support students and families?
2. When preparing for another IEP meeting with an interpreter, what are some helpful tips for Ms. Sheer to keep in mind from Rahul's meeting? What else could Ms. Sheer do to ensure that a family whose primary language isn't English can fully participate and understand the complexities of an IEP meeting?
3. Did all IEP team members equally contribute? If not, when or how could specific IEP team members participate or lead certain sections of Rahul's meeting?
4. Ms. Sheer notes how Rahul's IEP meeting went better than expected since this was her first time working with this many team members, including an interpreter. Why do you think she says that?
5. How does Ms. Sheer respond to questions and help all IEP team members work collaboratively?

Challenge: The Office of Vocational Rehabilitation services helps provide support services for adults with disabilities after they graduate from high school. Find the office for your state and locate or create a handout that can be provided to secondary-aged students during their IEP meeting. Describe how you would discuss this handout with families, especially those who do not speak fluent English.

Challenge: Create a list of accommodations and modifications that could help Rahul with reading and writing assignments in his new general education social studies class next marking period.

Specially Designed Instruction (SDI)

Specially Designed Instruction (SDI) #1

Ashlee M. Brown, PhD, BCBA, LBS

Background and Context

Mr. Hewitt felt confident as he completed the classroom setup for his second year of teaching at Stenton Middle School, which served children in seventh and eighth grades. He decided to set up his room a week early, before the first day for faculty, so he could focus his efforts those first few days of the school year on preparing content for his students.

Mr. Hewitt looked around his well-designed seventh-grade English classroom in late August with satisfaction and energy. He was ready to enter his second year, feeling much more adept at tackling the curriculum and classroom management. He had established some strong relationships with his peers, including his mentor teacher, and was significantly more fluent in the professional expectations. His first year was tough, for sure, but he had grown so much, and he was grateful to learn he would remain in the same grade, subject, and even the same classroom this year. This is a win!

Mr. Hewitt is passionate about transferring a love for literature and writing to his students. He enjoys selecting engaging texts and challenging his students to dig deep for meaning. And the writing! He has always loved to write, and now he takes great pleasure in reading his students' submissions—especially poetry. A few of his students from last year were quite skilled, and this led him to develop and become the faculty adviser for the school's latest club, Poetry Corner.

He wondered about his students this year—who would they be? What challenges would they have? What strengths will they bring? He checked his email one more time to see if class lists had possibly come through—nothing yet. Nonetheless, despite the many challenges, he was ready for the new school year to begin. He gave his classroom one final look, offered himself a nod of approval, and shut his classroom door. When he returned next week, the school year would be in full swing!

In what felt like the blink of an eye, the first day for faculty arrived. Mr. Hewitt and his peers showed up early, coffee in hand, eager to catch up with one another and to hear from the principal, Mr. Lemek, as part of his annual "opening day speech." Mr. Lemek did not disappoint with this year's talk. He was truly a leader who could inspire his team to work hard on behalf of students. This year, the school will be focusing on implementing the school-wide positive behavior support plan with greater fidelity, as well as analyzing placement decisions for children with disabilities to increase the amount of time spent in general education to the greatest extent possible. "Excellent targets!" thought Mr. Hewitt. He had some coursework in his undergraduate program on special education, and while not his particular area of expertise, he enjoyed supporting children with disabilities in his classroom. He had a way of inspiring a love for literature despite learning challenges.

The Challenge

Shortly after Mr. Lemek's opening speech, class lists were finally shared via email. Mr. Hewitt and his peers darted to their classrooms to open their email and review this year's rosters.

"Another great group!" said Mr. Hewitt as he scrolled on through. He knew a few of the students from a "Visit Day" the school hosted last spring. One student did catch his eye, however. Anna Jones, a twelve-year-old, incoming seventh-grade student with a specific learning disability (SLD) in reading and writing with a deficit in visual perception (Note: Anna was introduced in the learning disabilities case study, chapter 9, p. 65). He knew he would have to pull and review Anna's IEP immediately. Anna was slated to spend most of her day in general education but would receive intensive support in a learning support classroom for one period, totaling forty-five minutes, per day.

Since Anna would be new to Stenton Middle School, Mr. Hewitt didn't have immediate access to her previous learning support teacher. However, Anna would join the seventh-grade learning support caseload of Ms. Grath, who was quite skilled in supporting children with learning disabilities. Mr. Hewitt decided to walk down to Ms. Grath's classroom to see if she had a few minutes to discuss.

As he arrived, Ms. Grath was sitting at the small group table in her classroom, surrounded by IEPs. Her glasses sat on the tip of her nose as she studied one intently. "Knock, knock," said Mr. Hewitt, "do you have a minute?" Ms. Grath looked up with a smile on her face and a warm reply, "Hello there, Mr. Hewitt! I sure do, come on in."

Ms. Grath and Mr. Hewitt briefly reviewed Anna's IEP together, and Ms. Grath explained the nature of Anna's learning disability and her current instructional level. Mr. Hewitt left the room feeling much more confident in being able to effectively support Anna in his English class. He knew he had a lot more reading to do, however, and prep work for Anna's arrival.

That evening, Mr. Hewitt conducted another review of Anna's IEP. This time, he was particularly interested in the SDI that Anna was to receive. Specially designed instruction, or SDI, includes all of the adaptations to content, methodology, and delivery of instruction so that Anna can access the seventh-grade general education curriculum. As he reviewed these adaptations, his earlier confidence quickly faded. Was it just him, or were the SDIs outlined in Anna's IEP far too general and vague? Here are a few examples:

- Provide modified reading materials
- Use of assistive technology
- Offer extended time
- Utilize graphic organizers
- Pre-teach concepts

Unsure of how to translate these accommodations into his daily classroom practice, Mr. Hewitt feels unprepared and anxious. He wondered how anyone could implement Anna's IEP effectively. Is this how you write and develop SDI? He attempts to think back to his special education coursework—SDI, SDI, SDI. Unfortunately, it didn't come to him. Mr. Hewitt reflects on how he will proceed. Ultimately, he decides that he is still a new teacher, and he doesn't want to appear as though he cannot handle supporting a child with a disability in his classroom. He will interpret the SDI as best he can in the first few weeks of school and ask for guidance if needed.

A Valiant Effort

The first two weeks of the school year fly by, as they always do. Mr. Hewitt enjoys meeting his new students, setting expectations, and getting moving with the curriculum. Anna, he learns, is a dedicated and hardworking student. It is evident that she truly wants to do well in school. She has many friends and is kind to others. Mr. Hewitt works to support Anna the best he can. He attempts to implement the SDI in the following ways:

- Giving Anna more time on reading and writing assignments in the classroom, as well as homework
- Allowing her to use a laptop for written work
- Allowing her to work with a partner for peer editing

Despite these efforts, Mr. Hewitt has noticed that Anna still struggles with reading grade-level texts, and she has recently become visibly frustrated during independent reading and essay writing activities. Her written work often lacks structure, and she has begun to avoid assignments that require extended written responses. Anna's mother recently noticed her frustration, too, and emailed Mr. Hewitt in hopes of discussing these observations. Mr. Hewitt is a bit taken aback by the email. However, he can certainly see that his efforts in the classroom are insufficient in meeting Anna's needs. Before responding, he makes another visit to Ms. Grath. Mr. Hewitt learned last school year that talking things through with a colleague and obtaining additional perspective often yields a better outcome, and he isn't shy when it comes to asking for help.

Much to his relief, Ms. Grath shares the same concerns. She has also been experiencing difficulty supporting Anna in her classroom. The SDIs outlined in Anna's IEP are challenging to implement due to their lack of specificity. She meant to discuss this with Mr. Hewitt the previous week, but her many start-of-the-school-year tasks interfered. Ms. Grath explains to Mr. Hewitt that SDI should be written with a level of specificity so that it can be implemented in any program with ease. If Anna were to move to a new school district tomorrow, the receiving school should not have questions about how to implement Anna's IEP.

Ms. Grath also admits that she just recently finalized her student support schedule, and she should be supporting Mr. Hewitt during Anna's time in his classroom to ensure proper delivery of her SDI. She reminds Mr. Hewitt that SDI can include adapted materials, activities, techniques or strategies, assessments, curriculum, and so on. Ms. Grath shares that she will contact Anna's parents, as well as the building's supervisor of special education, to schedule an IEP meeting on behalf of Anna.

"An IEP meeting? Now? But her IEP due date isn't until the spring," says Mr. Hewitt. Ms. Grath explains that an IEP meeting can occur at any time and can be initiated by the school or the parent. Ms. Grath was resurfacing information that Mr. Hewitt indeed learned in his coursework several years back. It was all coming back now!

A Team Approach

Within a week, Anna's IEP team came together on her behalf to discuss her current program and to discuss any changes that may need to occur to ensure her success. This also allowed the team an opportunity to discuss Anna's transition to middle school, her many strengths, and, specifically, her areas of need. Anna joined the meeting, as well, to share what she loved about school and to report on what helps her and what is challenging for her.

Anna and her parents were able to share information from previous school years that shed great light on the contingencies and strategies that allow Anna to be successful in the classroom. For instance, Anna thrives when given support to help organize her thoughts; she often uses speech-to-text to "get her ideas out" and help to organize her ideas. Then, she can transfer those ideas into a graphic organizer like a visual mind map, which without this process would be too difficult for her given her visual perception difficulties. As a result of her use of speech-to-text software, she has become fluent in her use of technology, and she is able to use various software programs both at school and at home to assist in her completion of homework. Another strategy that has helped her with both her reading and writing has been to focus on learning orthographic patterns (e.g., *-tion*, *-ing*, *-dis*, *-ight*), which she was able to visualize as a whole rather focus on each individual letter, which was more difficult for her.

This strategy also helped her with her word choice when writing. Anna also shared that she often used audiobooks when she was learning so that she could understand the ideas but used written books when working on improving reading. Mr. Hewitt, having attended only a few IEP meetings in the past, was impressed at the level of collaboration that occurred during Anna's meeting. It was thought that the IEP team was truly developing her program as a cohesive unit with all members providing helpful input and joining in on productive conversations. He learned so much and attributed much of the success to Anna and her parents' ability to describe her needs and the supports that allow her to be successful.

Mr. Hewitt left Anna's IEP meeting armed with very specific strategies and supports he can utilize to effectively craft Anna's educational program. The team also formally decided that Ms. Grath would co-teach Mr. Hewitt's English class daily to seamlessly support Anna in both her general and special education classrooms. Anna's updated, more specific SDI included the following:

- **Reading Instruction and Modified Reading Materials:**
    - Provide Anna with audiobooks or text-to-speech versions of novels and reading passages longer than three paragraphs
    - Use high-interest, low-readability books for independent reading assignments
    - Pre-teach key vocabulary before reading a text
    - Practice using orthographic patterns to assist in reading text
- **Assistive Technology:**
    - Utilize speech-to-text software for developing her ideas for writing assignments longer than three paragraphs
    - Use apps such as Read&Write for Google Chrome that support reading and writing accessibility
    - Use computer to write assignments longer than three paragraphs, rather than handwriting
- **Extended Time:**
    - Ensure Anna receives time-and-a-half for in-class essays and quizzes
    - Break long assignments into smaller, manageable chunks with separate due dates
- **Graphic Organizers:**
    - Provide templates for narrative structures, essay outlines, and character analysis
    - Allow Anna to brainstorm using visual mind maps or apps, such as Popplet
    - Provide a grammar self-checklist for essays or writing assignments longer than three paragraphs
- **Alternate Assessments:**
    - Allow Anna the choice to demonstrate understanding through oral presentations, video summaries, or illustrated storyboards instead of traditional essays that are five paragraphs or longer

- Use rubrics that emphasize content understanding over grammar and spelling

Success and Conclusion

Over the next few weeks, Mr. Hewitt and Ms. Grath begin to incorporate these strategies, and they are blown away by Anna's academic success, as well as the incredible increase in her confidence. A few examples of implementation of these efforts follow:

- During a unit on *The Giver*, Anna listens to the audiobook while following along with a print copy that includes vocabulary support in the margins.
- For the final assessment, she creates a visual storyboard and gives a verbal explanation of key themes, which Mr. Hewitt assesses using a differentiated rubric.
- She begins to use graphic organizers routinely and successfully outlines her first multi-paragraph essay using voice-to-text support.

Mr. Hewitt feels empowered by the collaboration and guidance he has received from Ms. Grath, the special education supervisor, and Anna's parents. He reflects on his growth through his experience with Anna this year, and he wonders who has grown more! Anna's success in the first trimester of the school year allowed her to reduce her time in the learning support classroom to one period per week. Mr. Hewitt had no idea at the opening of the school year that he would contribute to the principal's goal of increasing the amount of time children with disabilities spend in the general education classroom at Stenton Middle School. Both Anna and Mr. Hewitt ended the school year labeling it as "the best year yet!"

Questions:

1. What is specially designed instruction (SDI)?
2. How might you interpret the original list of SDI provided in Anna's IEP? Choose one of the listed items and describe what you think that it means.
3. Discuss why SDI must be written into IEPs with a high level of specificity.

4 The implementation of SDI should be overseen by a special education teacher and/or related service personnel. How did the team accomplish this in Anna's case?

Challenge: Examine the principles of the Individuals with Disabilities Education Act (IDEA) and indicate which main principle of the IDEA aligns with Stenton Middle School's initiative to increase the amount of time their students with disabilities spend in general education.

Challenge: Research evidence-based strategies for children with learning disabilities. Then, brainstorm additional SDI recommendations you might make on Anna's behalf keeping in mind that she has difficulties with visual perception.

Specially Designed Instruction (SDI) #2

Colleen E. Commisso, PhD, and Alyssa Blasko, PhD, BCBA

Mr. Calderone sat quietly at his desk after dismissal. The room smelled faintly of glue sticks and markers, a typical end to a full day in first grade. Mr. Calderone keeps an organized binder with all his students' accommodations in his desk for easy access during lesson planning. He reached into his accommodations binder and removed the accommodations list for Matthew. The list included the following:

- Reminders of expected behaviors
- Use of a daily point card for expected behaviors, including discussion of points earned and behaviors displayed at the end of each period
- Check-ins with caseload manager at the beginning and end of the day
- Use of reinforcements if a designated number of points are earned on the point card
- Access to the emotional support classroom as needed
- Use of a break/help card
- Preferential seating near the main instructional area

- Chunking of assignments into smaller components (e.g., ten math problems into two sets of five)
- Verbal specific praise when the help or break card is utilized
- Verbal specific praise when the student is engaging in appropriate behaviors
- Positive behavior support plan (this was attached as a separate document)
- Ability to take any tests or quizzes in the emotional support classroom
- Ability to have all items on tests/quizzes/assignments/activities read aloud
- Rephrasing of questions/directions/unknown vocabulary words (unless vocabulary is being assessed)

He reached into the green behavior folder sitting on his desk and pulled out Matthew's point card for the day. Matthew's point card is a part of his accommodation: "use of a daily point card for expected behaviors including discussion of points earned and behaviors displayed at the end of each period." He did the math and Matthew earned 57 out of 60 points.

Matthew chose the animal video today and sat at his desk after pack-up and quietly giggled at penguins sliding on ice for five whole minutes. Mr. Calderone smiled as he slipped the card back into the folder. Then he stood, grabbed it, and made his way to room 102, Miss K's classroom. He knocked softly. Miss K looked up from her desk, where she was sorting sticker charts. "Hi! Come on in, Mr. Calderone." He stepped inside and gave a small wave.

"Hey. Got a few minutes?"

"Always," she said, gesturing to the blue chair across from her.

He handed her the folder and sat down. "Wanted to talk about Matthew." Miss K's expression was instantly focused, but open, too. "Okay. What's going on?"

Mr. Calderone took a breath. "He's doing well. Like, well."

Miss K's eyebrows lifted slightly, not in alarm, but curiosity. "Tell me more," she said, flipping open the folder.

Mr. Calderone leaned forward. "So you know he's been using the behavior point card since October. He has a morning check-in with you, and then the card goes from class to class, and at the end of each block, we review how he followed the rules and give him points."

Table 18.3 Matt's Point Card with Earned Daily Points

Matt's Point Card

Class	Behavior Goals			Points Earned	Point Criteria	Reinforcement
	Raise My Hand	Use My Break	Use My Help Card			
Homeroom	2	2	2	6	0 = I did not meet my goal and needed more than three teacher prompts	If I earn <u>51</u> or more points, I get to pick: Prize from the prize box
Math	2	2	1	5		Watch one animal video
Science	2	2	2	6	1 = I partially met my behavior goal and needed 2–3 teacher prompts	Play with dinosaurs for five minutes
Reading	2	2	2	6		
Writing	2	2	2	6		
Lunch	2	2	2	6	2 = I met my behavior goal with one or less teacher prompts.	
Recess	2	2	2	6		
Social Studies	2	2	1	5		
Specials	1	2	2	5		
Homeroom	2	2	2	6		
			Total Points Earned	57/60 = 95%		

Notes: Matt had a great day. He used his break card when he was frustrated in math class and was observed being kind to others at recess! Matt picked a video about penguins to watch at the end of the day. Way to Go, Matt!

"Right," Miss K nodded. "And he also uses his 'help/break' card."

"Exactly. Well, over the past six weeks, his scores have been consistent. He's earning above 85 percent of his points nearly every day. He's starting to internalize the rules. You can *see* him catching himself before talking to his peers. He has also started to use his card without needing reminders, and I have also seen him taking deep breaths."

Miss K looked at today's chart and nodded. "Over 90 percent again."

"Right," Mr. Calderone said. "And I've noticed something else. He doesn't seem as interested in the prize at the end. Today, I asked what he wanted, and he shrugged and said, 'I guess I'll do the penguin one again.' It seems like the prize doesn't matter as much."

Miss K smiled. "That's a great sign. He's not needing the externalizing reinforcer as much; engaging in the appropriate behavior is becoming intrinsically motivating."

"Oh, that's great!" Mr. Calderone said.

He further added, "So, I was wondering if there is a way for us to change what we are doing, or should we keep going since it is working? I don't want to mess anything up."

Miss K flipped through a few of Matthew's old behavior charts. "He's come a long way. In September, he couldn't go ten minutes without a redirection. And now he's leading the line-up, helping other kids clean up, raising his hand to ask for help."

"I've noticed," Mr. Calderone said. "He's proud of himself, and he has been doing a great job!"

Miss K was quiet for a moment, thinking. "Let's put something together to fade the point chart. When I say fading, I mean that we should reduce the frequency/intensity of use to begin phasing it out. I'd like to write up a modified intervention plan—maybe a two-week trial where we reduce point checks but keep morning check-ins and still reflect at the end of the day. We could have you give him his earned points after every two periods instead of at the end of every period. What do you think of that?"

"That's reasonable," Mr. Calderone said, nodding slowly. "He's shown he can be successful with support. Now we will see how he does with a lower number of times reviewing the rules and providing points."

"Okay, sounds great. I appreciate you being flexible, we never want to completely remove interventions. Instead, we want to fade them or slowly reduce them. Let's touch base after the two-week trial and discuss the data that we have. Does that work for you?"

"That works for me," said Mr. Calderone. "Do you want me to talk to him tomorrow, or do you want to do that?"

Miss K responded, "I will talk to Matthew tomorrow morning during our morning check-in. I want to make sure that he knows this is a good thing."

"Okay, I can tell him that I'm proud of him also, and it is because he is doing *so well*."

"Yes," Miss K said. "We frame this as a *step up*, not a removal."

"Also, quick question, could we also still keep the help/break card, I think it is still helpful?" asked Mr. Calderone. "Definitely," Miss K replied. "That's still his safety net. Even if we're reducing point monitoring, he still needs a voice, and for Matthew, the card *is* his voice."

Mr. Calderone also asked, "Do you think we could change any of his other accommodations? For the most part, he has been working right through all the assignments, and I have not needed to break them into chunks."

Miss K reached for a notepad. "So, let's wait to remove/change any other accommodations since we are going to be changing his point card. I do not want to change too much at the same time, to make sure we know if the change in the point card is working. This is what I'm thinking: After two weeks of reducing the number of times he gets feedback on his point card from you, if he is doing well, we can discuss changing other accommodations.

"I will also touch base with his parents to let them know what we are planning. We would need to revise his IEP if we are going to remove any other accommodation(s) and make additional changes to his point card system. Does that work for you?"

"Sounds good," Mr. Calderone responded.

They sat quietly for a moment, thinking. Miss K looked thoughtful. "Do you think he could get to a place where he doesn't need the intervention at all?"

"I do," Mr. Calderone said, with no hesitation. "Not tomorrow. But soon. He's already building habits. If we keep reinforcing the right things, I think he can get there."

Miss K smiled. "That would be amazing. And of course, if he ever needs to go back to more frequent supports, we'll be there."

"Always," Mr. Calderone agreed.

Miss K turned her notepad toward him. "All right. I'll write up the intervention modification tonight. We can tell him the plan and celebrate why we're trying it."

"Yes," Mr. Calderone said. "He deserves to hear he's doing well from both of us."

As he stood to leave, he glanced once more at the folder in Miss K's hand. "That card, 'Help' on one side, 'Break' on the other—that thing changed everything. It was such a small tool, but it gave him so much power."

Miss K nodded. "He just needed a way to tell us what he needed without getting in trouble for it."

"He's learning how to do that now," Mr. Calderone said. "He's learning to say, 'I need something'—before it becomes a meltdown."

"And that's the whole goal," Miss K replied. "Emotional support isn't about fixing kids. It's about teaching them how to ask for help before they explode."

Mr. Calderone opened the door. "Thanks, Miss K."

"Anytime."

As he walked back to his classroom, the hallway felt just a little brighter. Tomorrow, they would tell Matthew about his new plan. They'd tell him that he was growing, and because of all the work he'd done, he'd earned a new level of independence. It wouldn't be perfect; there would be hard days, maybe even regressions. But Matthew would know that his teachers believed in him enough to give him more room to grow. And sometimes, the most powerful kind of support is knowing when to take one small step back so a student can take one giant step forward.

Questions:

1 Why did Mr. Calderone think that the use of the point card that was being used with Matthew could be changed?
2 What does Miss K mean when she says that Matthew's break/help card "*is his voice*"?
3 Pretend you are Miss K or Mr. Calderone and share how you would describe the change above to Matthew.
4 Describe the connection between Matthew's profile needs, accommodations, and point card.

Challenge: Research ways teachers can determine what to use for reinforcements/rewards with students. List at least four methods. What are the pros and cons of these methods?

Challenge: Choose one of the methods that you researched in the first challenge question that would be appropriate for Mr. Calderone or Miss K to use with Matthew. Explain why it would be beneficial for Matthew.

Transition (Secondary)

Brittany Severino, EdD

What Is Transition Planning?

The Individuals with Disabilities Education Act (IDEA) requires transition planning for students who receive special education services. Transition is the process of going from one grade, age, or type of service to another. Transitions occur throughout a student's pre-K through grade-12 education. Special education teachers and the IEP teams need to consider and plan for how a student can successfully transition from early intervention services to elementary school, from elementary school to middle school, and from middle school to high school. One of the most important aspects of transition planning is secondary transition, focusing on preparing a student for life upon graduation from high school or completion of their secondary schooling.

IDEA (2004) requires secondary transition planning to begin at sixteen years of age, or younger, for any student receiving special education services. Each state has set its age requirement based on IDEA, ranging from twelve to sixteen years old (Suk et al., 2020). Secondary transition planning has three specific domains, including post-secondary education or training, employment, and independent living skills. Transition planning begins with administering formal and informal types of transition assessments to determine a student's strengths, preferences, interests, and needs (SPINs) as well as developing their IEP.

Transition planning must be documented in a student's "Transition Services" or "Transition Grid" section of their IEP to include post-secondary goals, courses of study, services, and activities. Additionally, the IEP team should also use this information to guide the remaining sections of the IEP to create cohesive programming that ensures the student is best supported to accomplish their post-secondary transition plans.

Secondary Transition in Practice: Mr. Brodie

Mr. Scott Brodie has started his first full-time job as a high school special education teacher. Mr. Brodie worked as a long-term substitute (LTS) last year, as a fourth-grade learning support teacher, after he obtained his special education certification (pre-K through grade 12). However, a full-time position opened at the school district's high school, for which Mr. Brodie applied and was selected for the position. He is now a learning support and autistic support teacher with a caseload of twenty students, ranging from ninth to twelfth grade, who identify for special education services, under IDEA, with a "Specific Learning Disability" (SLD), "Other Health Impairment" (OHI), or "Autism."

Mr. Brodie is very confident in his abilities to manage his caseload and conduct his IEP meetings. He was responsible for a similar-sized caseload last year when he worked as an LTS. However, Mr. Brodie has realized there is a new aspect to his role that he is not as familiar with—transition planning. Mr. Brodie took one transition course as part of his teacher preparation program. Mr. Brodie works in New York, which requires transition planning to begin at fourteen years of age and qualifies all the students on his new caseload.

Mr. Brodie is preparing for an upcoming IEP meeting that he has for a student on his caseload, Alexandra (Alex) Peters (Note: Alex was introduced in the OHI case study, chapter 11, p. 81) Alex is sixteen years old and qualifies for special education services due to OHI with a medical diagnosis of epilepsy. Mr. Brodie talks to his mentor teacher, who has been a high school special education teacher for ten years, and who reminds him that transition planning should guide the IEP for all secondary-aged students.

Once a student graduates from high school, they are no longer covered under IDEA (2004) or have an IEP. However, they can be eligible for reasonable accommodations in post-secondary education or training and employment under the Americans with Disabilities Act (ADA) and Section 504 of the Rehabilitation Act of 1973. Mr. Brodie wants to ensure that his students are set up to achieve their transition plans and understand what accommodations or supports they can advocate for themselves after they graduate.

Getting Started: Conducting Transition Assessments

Mr. Brodie begins preparing for Alex's upcoming IEP meeting by engaging her in a transition planning approach referred to as person-centered planning. Person-centered planning ensures that Alex is in control of guiding what she wants to do after she graduates from high school, and that her wishes are not misinterpreted by any IEP team members. To ensure Mr. Brodie has a clear vision of Alex's aspirations, he wants to gather information regarding Alex's SPINs to guide the development of her IEP. Mr. Brodie calls Alex down from advisory so they can meet and discuss one-on-one.

Mr. Brodie printed out a transition planning inventory as an assessment tool to help Alex brainstorm information. This assessment included statements about further education and training, employment, daily living, leisure activities, community participation, self-determination, communication, and relationship skills for Alex to respond to using a five-point Likert scale (0–Strongly Disagree to 5–Strongly Agree, with the option for "I Don't Know"). Additionally, the assessment included several open-ended questions for Alex to respond to, including items like "If you plan on working, what jobs are you considering?" Mr. Brodie encouraged Alex to try her best in answering each item based on her own opinion, and that it was okay to leave any items blank. Mr. Brodie helped provide read-aloud or clarification as needed.

During Mr. Brodie's prep period later that day, he began to analyze the results of Alex's completed transition planning inventory to determine her SPINs. He documented and summarized this information in the PLAAFP of Alex's draft IEP. Mr. Brodie included the following information based on Alex's results:

- **Strengths:** Alex identified as agreeing or strongly agreeing to several areas she feels independent with including daily living skills (e.g., personal grooming and hygiene, cleaning, managing money); managing her health (especially her epilepsy diagnosis); and leisure activities (e.g., participating in indoor and outdoor activities for fun).
- **Preferences**: Alex reported enjoying getting to work with other people and tasks that require working on the computer or using technology.

- **Interests**: Alex has recently become a part of the school's yearbook and newspaper clubs, which has sparked an interest in possibly pursuing a career related to these areas.
- **Needs**: Alex gave herself low ratings (strongly disagree or disagree) or does not yet feel independent with skills such as communication (e.g., initiating or engaging in conversation with peers); relationship (e.g., maintaining friendships, meetings new friends); and self-determination skills (e.g., self-esteem, confidence, and making decisions about her future).

Planning for the Future: Transition Services or "Grid"

The next day, Mr. Brodie began the transition services section of Alex's IEP, which he remembered was referred to as the "grid" in his educator preparation courses based on the table format. The information he found out about Alex yesterday, which is summarized in the PLAAFP, would be valuable in helping Mr. Brodie design *post-secondary goals* (what Alex wants to do for education, employment, and independent living after graduation), services (special education services that will help support Alex), and activities (tasks or experiences that will help prepare Alex) based on her SPINs.

Additionally, Mr. Brodie wanted to engage in backward planning, another transition planning approach, since Alex is a junior and has at least another year of high school. Using this approach, Mr. Brodie wants to consider Alex's desired post-secondary outcomes and work backward to determine what steps should be taken during both her junior and senior years to achieve those outcomes. He will determine what Alex could work on this year and also make sure that she can continue to grow and expand on these skills until graduation.

Based on the information that Alex provided, Mr. Brodie drafted post-secondary goals. He remembers that post-secondary goals are written very differently from annual IEP goals. They should address two main components, including: when the goal will happen, and what the student will be doing or completing. Mr. Brodie drafts the following post-secondary goals for Alex:

- **Post-Secondary Education and Training**: Upon graduation from high school, Alex will attend a four-year college or university.

- **Employment:** Upon graduation from high school, Alex will obtain competitive employment in the field of journalism or marketing.
- **Independent Living Skills:** Upon graduation from high school, Alex will live with a roommate in on-campus housing.

However, Mr. Brodie knows it is important for Alex's post-secondary goals to be connected to her annual IEP goals. Alex's annual IEP goals should be based on her identified areas of need for special education services that Mr. Brodie is responsible for collecting progress monitoring data on. If Alex improves in these areas, it will ultimately help her be better prepared for obtaining her post-secondary goals of going to college, getting a full-time competitively employed position, and moving out to live with a roommate.

Mr. Brodie remembers that there is some information in the "Transition Services" or "grid" section of the IEP that can be similar for each post-secondary goal, but there is also information that needs to be different. For all three post-secondary goals, Alex is participating in all general education classes as her *course of study*. Alex is currently in Honors American Literature, Honors Algebra II, Chemistry, World History, Health/Physical Education, and Spanish II, which put her on track with typical college requirements. Additionally, Alex is in Creative Writing as an elective class that is connected to her extracurricular activities and career interests. Lastly, Alex receives one period per day of learning support services from Mr. Brodie for support in her areas of need. This will be included as the required *service* (at least one) for each of Alex's post-secondary goals.

Mr. Brodie remembers that each post-secondary goal needs to have at least two *activities*. These activities are assignments, scenarios, resources, community experiences, or other items that members of the IEP team can use to support Alex in accomplishing the elements of her new annual IEP. These activities also need to be varied for each post-secondary goal and changed annually. Mr. Brodie reviews Alex's old IEPs to identify the activities that she completed during her ninth and tenth grade school years, and drafts the following new activities for each post-secondary goal:

- **Post-Secondary Education and Training:**
  - Alex will research three colleges or universities that she is interested in applying to next year as a twelfth-grade student.

- ○ Alex will write a college essay that she can use as part of her college application.
- **Employment:**
  - ○ Alex will update her résumé and create a cover letter to apply for jobs.
  - ○ Alex will complete a one-day internship at a local newspaper or marketing company to learn about possible positions she is interested in pursuing.
- **Independent Living Skills:**
  - ○ Alex will practice conflict resolution strategies by discussing real-life or hypothetical scenarios she could encounter while living on a college campus and with a roommate.
  - ○ Alex will create a resource that she can use each semester with her roommate, friends, or professors on symptoms of her epilepsy and proper medical steps in case of an episode.

Mr. Brodie will work on accomplishing the remaining sections of Alex's IEP later this week during his prep periods. He wants to make sure he considers what special education supports, especially accommodations, will help Alex now in her high school classes and could be applied in her future college courses, too. Mr. Brodie is still adjusting to his secondary transition planning responsibilities, but so far, loves it! He finds it exciting to help the students on his caseload figure out what they want to do after they graduate from high school.

Questions:

1. How would you define transition planning in your own words? What three domains does it include?
2. What section(s) of a secondary-aged student's IEP include or are based on transition planning? What kinds of accommodations might Mr. Brodie include in Alex's IEP based on her profile, and might be accepted by the Office of Disability Services at a college or university?
3. How would you describe the person-centered and backward planning transition approaches Mr. Brodie used?
4. How many services and activities should be included with each post-secondary transition goal?

5 What other IEP team members should Mr. Brodie obtain transition-related information from to support Alex? What kinds of questions could he ask those IEP team members?

Challenge: Rahul Mookerjee (introduced in the ASD #1 case study, chapter 3, p. 22) was introduced during part I. How might transition planning look different for Rahul based on his strengths, preferences, interests, and needs (SPINs)? Download a copy of the IEP template from your state's Department of Education website or another resource. Complete Section III, Transition Services or "Grid" to create Rahul's post-secondary goals, courses of study, services, and activities based on this information.

Challenge: Research your state's transition guidelines. At what age is transition planning required in your state (the state you will be certified to teach in and/or plan to teach in)?

References

Individuals with Disabilities Education Act, 20 U.S.C. § 1400 (2004)

Suk, A. L., Martin, J. E., McConnell, A. E., & Biles, T. L. (2020). States decrease their required secondary transition planning age: Federal policy must change. *Journal of Disability Policy Studies, 31*(2), 112–18.

19

Early Intervention (EI) and Individualized Family Service Plans (IFSPs)

This chapter includes several case studies related to the topic of early intervention (EI) and individualized family service plans (IFSPs), which are the following:

- Diagnostic Process
- Early Childhood Special Education Service Delivery
- Family Response to a Disability Diagnosis

Early intervention (EI) services are designed to support young children ages birth to five with developmental delays or disabilities. The purpose of most EI services is to prepare young children for school entry by improving existing skills and adaptive behaviors in the developmental domains: physical and movement development, social-emotional development, cognitive development, and language development. Early intervention services assist with developmental screenings and diagnosis, family trainings, and therapies (e.g., OT, SLP, PT).

This chapter examines the following aspects of EI and IFSPs:

1. **Diagnostic Process:** In this case study, the process of receiving an initial disability diagnosis is described for a young child displaying developmental delays. It chronicles the early intervention evaluation process and the roles of the various educational professionals on the early intervention team.

2. **Early Childhood Special Education Service Delivery:** In this case study, a first-year teacher explores her roles and responsibilities as an early childhood special education teacher with her new class of students with disabilities ages three to five.
3. **Family Response to a Disability Diagnosis:** In this case study, a single parent is receiving a disability diagnosis for her toddler. It details the mother's concerns for her child, the process for receiving early intervention services, and the opportunities provided to the child by obtaining an IFSP and early intervention services.

Diagnostic Process

Dawn R. Patterson, EdD

Evaluation Background/History

Tyrese is the only boy sandwiched between his two sisters (Note: Tyrese was introduced in the intellectual disabilities case study, chapter 8, p. 59). Tyrese was conceived through artificial insemination from a sperm donor profile selection by his two mothers. For the first two years of his life, Tyrese's development aligned with his older sister, and he met all his developmental milestones. Four weeks after his second birthday, Tyrese experienced a stroke due to a blockage in the vertebral arteries. The doctors informed his mothers that due to the lack of oxygen and nutrients to his brain, there was damage, and that Tyrese may experience delays. The doctors informed his mothers to watch him closely for the next several weeks and months. The doctors reassured Tyrese's mothers that at each of the follow-up appointments, he would receive a thorough examination, including full reports of their observations of him. He had many different appointments during this time including seeing an optometrist and an audiologist; there were no concerns in either of these areas. After the third follow-up appointment, approximately twelve weeks after the stroke, the doctors noted that Tyrese was not regaining many of the previously acquired skills and that his milestones were not being met according to his chronological age. The doctors recommended that his mothers contact their local school district and request a comprehensive evaluation.

The initial request for the evaluation was made by his mothers when Tyrese was two years and five months old. The Department of Human Services made contact and scheduled an appointment for his mothers to sign paperwork permitting the evaluation process to begin. The assessment was scheduled fourteen days after the initial referral. The assessment was scheduled with a multidisciplinary team of professionals, and the *Transdisciplinary Play-Based Assessment* (Linder, 2008) was used.

Preliminary Evaluation Description

On the day of the evaluation, there was a speech-language pathologist, an occupational therapist, a physical therapist, a certified early interventionist, and a school psychologist. Tyrese's mothers were present, and they brought copies of his comprehensive medical file, which included pre-post stroke and stroke specific information. The assessment space resembled a two-year-old's daycare classroom. There were toys available for Tyrese to play with as he desired. The space included an assortment of blocks, vehicles, pretend play and dress-up area, assorted puzzles, beads of various sizes to string, shape sorters, paint, crayons, markers, two pairs of safety scissors, paper on the table, and a painting easel with many of the same utensils. There were balls, mats, and blocks to build with or climb over, and a fenced-in playground just outside the classroom. There were books, magnifying glasses, magnets, insect figurines, sensory bottles, and other tools.

Evaluation Description

Early Interventionist

The evaluation began from the moment Tyrese and his two mothers arrived. The two mothers were asked to sit at a table off to the side while each member of the interdisciplinary team took turns sitting on the floor following Tyrese's lead. Initially, the team observed Tyrese's reactions to the environment and how easily he separated from his mom, which was scored in the social-emotional development category of the assessment. He was also observed removing his jacket and the assistance that was provided to him. This was scored in the sensorimotor category as daily life and self-care were assessed. The early interventionist was sitting on the floor in the middle of the assessment space, ready to welcome Tyrese and follow his lead. Tyrese immediately walked to the blocks and began taking the wooden blocks out of the storage bin to begin building; he did not acknowledge the adult sitting on the floor. The early interventionist, Ms. P, immediately repositioned herself close to Tyrese and the blocks and followed along with Tyrese's plan to build a house. Ms. P began building the neighbor's house. Tyrese turned to look at Ms. P, smiled, pointed to the neighbor's house, stating "M," then pointed to the house that he was building, stating "My hou." As this was occurring, the speech-language pathologist and occupational therapist sitting at the table were using their TPBA-2 scoring guide to record everything in the categories of communication, social-emotional, sensorimotor, and cognitive for the assessment.

Tyrese sees the bin of vehicles on the shelves and drives the trains around the carpet. Ms. P imitates his actions, making the "toot, toot" sound of a train. Tyrese states, "too." Ms. P drives her train through the neighborhood, and Tyrese states, "No, loud," and covers his ears with his train in his left hand. Ms. P states, "the people are sleeping, ssshhh" while making the quiet gesture. Tyrese looks around the room. After a few moments, he states, "man" as he looks at Ms. P. Ms. P states, "Mr. N" as she points in the direction of the speech-language pathologist. Tyrese states, "No, man," as he continues to look around the room and finds the storage bin of people. He pulls a male figurine from the bin and places it on the train. Ms. P states, "The man is driving the train, toot-toot." Tyrese glances up at Ms. P's face, smiles, and states, "too." Ms. P and Tyrese play in this manner for about fifteen more minutes, and then Mr. N switches adult roles with Ms. P as Tyrese explores the science-like area, the play kitchen area, the fine motor area, and the puzzles.

Speech-Language Pathologist

While Mr. N is with Tyrese, he tries to gain more specific information about Tyrese's communication. While the two are stringing large beads side-by-side, Mr. N knocks over the bucket of beads. He waits for Tyrese's reaction. Initially, Tyrese drops his string with his single bead on it, leans forward from his crossed leg position, and scatters the beads around with his hands, with his eyebrows scowling. Mr. N picks up a single bead and places it into the bin, with a hollow plop sound. Tyrese is unresponsive.

Mr. N repeats this action two more times, saying nothing. Tyrese becomes less interested in scattering the beads and pauses momentarily. Mr. N then states, "Give me a bead, please." Tyrese picks up a square bead and hands it to Mr. N, who then asks three more times before Tyrese begins to help Mr. N put most of the beads back into the bucket.

Approximately fifteen minutes after Mr. N is spending time with Tyrese, another thirty-month-old boy enters the assessment space and goes directly to the pretend play area and finds doctor dress-up clothes. Tyrese does not notice the boy, Max, until he walks up to Tyrese in his doctor attire holding the end of the stethoscope, asking, "Are you ok?" Tyrese turns around to face Max expressionless, stating, "Ye." Tyrese tries to take the stethoscope from Max's ears, but Max states, "No, I check." Mr. N pats the floor for Tyrese to lie down and states, "Max wants to check your heart." Tyrese lies on the floor and pretends to be the patient. After Max checks his heart, Tyrese quickly sits up and states, "My tur." Max gives Tyrese the stethoscope and immediately plays patient while Tyrese imitates Max's actions. Mr. N makes the thump-thump sound of the heart, and Tyrese smiles. Tyrese removes the stethoscope, drops it to the floor, and returns to the blocks and cars. Max gets up and removes his lab coat and goes to the table with the paint and markers.

Occupational Therapist (Part I)

Max uses the thick-handled paintbrush and blue paint to make a picture. Max turns to Tyrese and states, "Come paint" with an arm gesture. Tyrese immediately joins Max. Now the occupational therapist, Ms. Didi, serves as the adult mediator, and Mr. N resumes his data collection role. Tyrese picks up the paintbrush with the ball grip with his right hand and puts it in the green paint. He uses only his right hand and paints over the entire paper. Midway through, Ms. Didi assists by holding the paper still for Tyrese. When he is finished, he states, "par." Ms. Didi states, "You painted a picture of the park, and Max painted the sky." Both boys smile.

Ms. Didi gets another sheet of paper for each of the boys. She removes the paint and puts the bucket of markers to the left of Max. Max immediately selects a marker and begins drawing, while Tyrese tries to reach across and lean into Max's space to get a marker. "Hey!" Max responds, and Tyrese gets out of his chair to walk around Max to get a red marker from the bucket. Tyrese sits back in his chair, removes the lid with his right hand, and uses a palmar grasp to draw a picture of his house. He reaches again for a different color marker, and Ms. Didi states, "Marker, please." Tyrese says, "pupuh." Max hands Tyrese a green marker. "No! Pupuh," asserts Tyrese. Max hands Tyrese a blue marker. "No! Pupuh," states Tyrese. This time, Ms. Didi helps Max hand the correct color (purple) to Tyrese.

Tyrese smiles, removes the lid with his left hand, and draws something that resembles two big people and a smaller person. Ms. Didi points to the house and asks, "What is this?" Tyrese responds, "My hou." Ms. Didi points to each of the figures, again asking, "And this?" Tyrese states, "Mum." Tyrese touches the next figure, "Mommy," and then the next, "Nini." Ms. Didi confirms Tyrese's response and states, "Tyrese, you drew a picture of your house with your two moms and your sister." Tyrese looks up to Ms. Didi with a grin. Max leans over, looks at Tyrese's picture, and says, "Pretty picture. See mine." Ms. Didi comments about Max's picture of a blue colored-in rectangle and the person in the pool, "Max is swimming in the pool," while Tyrese looks at it.

Physical Therapist

Ms. Didi says, "Let's go to the playground," and both boys jump up and run to the door. They both stop and wait for Ms. Didi. The two boys run to the play set. Tyrese climbs the stairs to the slide, placing two feet on one step before stepping up to the next step. The physical therapist, Ms. Katie, Ms. Didi, Mr. N, and Ms. P are all taking careful notes. When Tyrese reaches the slide, he sits and waits for Max; together, the boys slide down, with Max behind Tyrese. The boys repeat this several times, because Max ascends the stairs a little faster than Tyrese, he sometimes sneaks in an extra slide down. Tyrese states, "Go!" and smiles at Max.

Tyrese spots a ball across the playground, he points to it, says "Ba," and looks back at Max to make sure that he is following him. Tyrese stands on his right foot and kicks the ball toward Max. Max runs after it, picks it up, and throws it underhand, saying "Catch it" to Tyrese. Tyrese closes both his arms to catch the ball, but he is too early, and it falls to the ground. Tyrese kicks it again, this time with his right foot. Max throws it again; this time the ball hits his stomach, and then Tyrese closes his arms to catch the ball. During this time, Tyrese does not attempt to throw the ball to Max. The two boys are laughing together. They run around the playground and play on all the equipment. Tyrese sits on the swing and walks his feet forward to try to get himself swinging. He looks at Ms. Didi. He tries some more. He looks at Ms. Didi. This time she asks, "Would you like a push?" She walks toward him, pulls him back in the swing, and says, "Ready… set…" and Tyrese shouts "GO!"

Occupational Therapist (Part II)

After they have been in the playground for about twenty minutes, Ms. Didi informs them that it is time to go back inside. Both boys continue to play, and Ms. Didi repeats herself. Max comes running toward Ms. Didi, but Tyrese looks at Ms. Didi and climbs the stairs to the slide again. He slides down and slowly walks to the door.

Ms. Didi tells them that they need to wash their hands, and then they will have a snack. Once inside, the two boys go to the sink. Tyrese needs help turning the water on, getting the soap, and washing thoroughly. He forgets to turn the water off but knows how to get the towel and dry his hands. Tyrese pulls the chair away from the table and sits in front of one of the napkins set at the table. The boys have a choice of banana, apple, or plain mini rice cakes. Tyrese points, and says, "nana," Ms. Didi places the entire banana on his napkin. Max asks for the rice cakes. Again, Ms. Didi places the entire closed bag of rice cakes on Max's napkin. Max picks up the bag and asks for help. Ms. Didi takes out a few rice cakes and places them on Max's napkin and keeps the bag in front of her.

Tyrese sits in his chair and watches. Both boys have free access to their water bottles in front of them. Ms. Didi adds a cup of applesauce to the choices and asks Tyrese, "What do you want?" Tyrese picks up his banana and reaches it toward Ms. Didi and says "nana." Ms. Didi asks, "Do you need help?" Tyrese nods, and Ms. Didi breaks the banana open and hands it back to Tyrese, where he easily peels it, bites, and chews the banana. Tyrese eats the rest of the banana and drinks his water independently. After the two boys finish eating, the parents tell them, "Time to go."

As the school psychologist is escorting Tyrese and his two moms out, she informs them that the interdisciplinary team will meet and discuss the assessment, and then each professional will write their section of the assessment. The parents will receive an invitation within the next two weeks to return for another meeting. At that time, the results of the assessment will be discussed, and if it is determined that Tyrese is eligible for early intervention, the team will develop an IFSP. The meeting was scheduled on the fortieth day from the initial referral.

Questions:

Please refer to the following information when responding to the questions below:

- There are five developmental domains:
  - Cognitive
  - Physical Development, including vision and hearing
  - Communication
  - Social and Emotional
  - Adaptive Behavior
- The TPBA-2 scores in the following areas:
  - Sensorimotor
  - Vision
  - Emotional and Social
  - Communication
  - Hearing Screening and Visual Modifications
  - Cognitive

1. Why did the transdisciplinary team not assess vision or hearing?
2. Select one of the developmental domains and identify three different times from the case study when information from the domain was collected. Describe how this fits into the domain and how it was assessed.
3. Why was Max included in the assessment? Explain your reasoning using at least three examples from the case study.
4. Adaptive behavior is defined as the practical, everyday skills a person needs to be effective and independent in their environment. The TPBA-2 does not have a specific scoring section for adaptive behavior, but were there times during the case study that adaptive behavior abilities were evident? If you think so, describe them.

Challenge: The case study contains segments of the assessment time. How could more cognitive information be gathered? Research ways to evaluate cognitive development during an EI assessment. Create an infographic using Canva or Piktochart that describes the methods. When developing the infographic, include images of specific materials to target cognitive abilities with a video narration to explain the information that you have discovered.

Early Childhood Special Education Service Delivery

Ashlee M. Brown, PhD, BCBA, LBS

Background and Context

Rosa was thrilled to have recently graduated with her undergraduate degree in early and special education from ACB University. She knew very early on during her undergraduate program that she wanted to become a special education teacher. It took her some time and multiple field placement experiences, however, to recognize that her strengths were in working with the youngest population. Thus, when she was offered a full-time early childhood special education teaching position, she leaped at the opportunity! Throughout her initial onboarding experience, she was full of energy and enthusiasm to get moving with her student caseload. Ultimately, she would be assigned to serve a total of seven children in a full-time, self-contained early childhood special education classroom. The classroom was housed in a building that served children with disabilities, ages three to five, across the county. There were a total of eighteen classrooms in the building and approximately 150 students. Most of the students received county or district-provided transportation. The children on Rosa's caseload had a variety of disabilities, including autism, developmental delay, and orthopedic impairment. Several classrooms in the building served a wide array of disability categories, while other classrooms were disability-specific, autism support classrooms, for instance.

Upon assignment of her caseload, Rosa began reviewing her students' individualized education programs (IEPs), communicating with families, and preparing paperwork, specifically data sheets that aligned with their varied IEP goals. Rosa also purchased a wide array of decorative items for her classroom, as well as various activities that she thought might engage her students. She prepared for her first day by touring the building, setting up the physical design of her classroom, and meeting the various related service personnel, including the speech and language pathologist (SLP), occupational therapist (OT), and physical therapist (PT) assigned to her students. Rosa was quite grateful that the SLP, OT, and PT assigned to her classroom were seasoned service providers and had been in the field for many years. They each gave her their schedule of pull-out related service sessions for her students. The schedule was a bit overwhelming to wade through, but nothing Rosa couldn't handle. She also made time to connect with the paraprofessional assigned to her classroom, who had also worked at the program for quite some time.

As the first day of school rapidly approached, Rosa armed herself with a Pinterest board full of sensory-friendly activity ideas. She created a "cozy corner," softened the lighting in her classroom, and posted visual schedules. She re-read every IEP, color-coded her lesson plans, and even rehearsed her morning routine aloud. Needless to say, Rosa felt ready when, finally, her first official day with her students arrived. Rosa's reality check, however, walked in with her students.

The Reality Check

At 8:10 a.m., four-year-old Mason arrived. Mason has autism, is nonverbal, and full of energy. Within minutes, he was throwing puzzle pieces across the room and screaming when Rosa gently tried to guide him toward the sensory table. She scrambled to redirect him, remembering something about "first-then" boards, but where had she put them?

By 8:20 a.m., another student, three-year-old Michael, entered the classroom using his walker and being supported by a building-wide paraprofessional (Note: Michael was introduced in the orthopedic impairment case study, chapter 12, p. 87). Michael had cerebral palsy and a significant orthopedic impairment. Michael also had minimal verbal language and was crying upon arrival. As the building-wide paraprofessional left the classroom to support other children in the bus area, Rosa realized she did not know how to communicate with Michael. She also realized she had minimal knowledge of cerebral palsy (CP). "In what class did we discuss CP?" she quietly questioned herself.

At 8:45 a.m., two students were crying. One had stripped off their shoes and was hiding under a table. Another student, four-year-old Jaden, had bolted out the classroom door, and Rosa chased him down the hallway, desperate to keep him safe. Her paraprofessional looked equally overwhelmed. This new group of students had tremendous needs.

At 9 a.m., Rosa had planned to begin Circle Time, but the beautiful visual icons structuring her Circle Time were now missing. Gathering the students on the carpet took up much of her Circle Time allotment. The rest of the morning was a blur of diaper changes, meltdowns, misunderstood communication attempts, and Rosa's rising panic. By lunchtime, she had barely touched her carefully planned lessons. She sat on the floor next to Michael, who had finally calmed down in the reading corner, and she felt tears welling up in her eyes.

"I thought I was ready," she whispered to herself. "I'm not sure I can do this."

Later that day, the SLP popped in and reassured Rosa that the first days are always the hardest. The OT helped her adjust a student's seating for better support. Her paraprofessional, seeing the exhaustion in Rosa's face, stayed late to clean up and talk through the day.

Rosa drove home in silence, her confidence shaken, but something inside her remained steady. She knew tomorrow wouldn't be perfect either, but she also knew she wasn't alone. And most importantly, the children deserved her best, even if her best, for now, meant simply showing up again tomorrow. She reflected on sound advice given to her months ago by one of her favorite professors: "It takes a village" and "Use your resources." Rosa knew she had to rely on her team. What was that called again? It took some digging through old coursework textbooks and notes, but eventually she found what she was looking for—"Ah-ha! *Transdisciplinary Practice!*"

The Proposal

The next morning, Rosa spoke to her related service team, alongside her paraprofessional, and she scheduled a team meeting for later that day. At the team meeting, Rosa spoke with enthusiasm about some of what she had previously learned through her coursework in transdisciplinary practice and embedded instruction. Transdisciplinary practice is a shift from the previously relied upon interdisciplinary model, where team members work relatively collaboratively yet within their own "lane" and within their specialization. This may mean a special education teacher supports cognitive development, while the SLP enriches language development. Alternatively, in a transdisciplinary model, team members seek to achieve shared roles and expertise to result in holistic student support. This is often best achieved through an embedded-instruction-type approach, where instruction and service delivery occur within naturally occurring routines and activities in the classroom versus in separate, or segregated activities or locations. This would mean that the team would be forced to pivot from traditional, pull-out related service sessions to push-in support that provides services within typical classroom routines and activities.

Initially, the team was hesitant to agree to this type of shift in pedagogy. After all, the related service team had been working in this field for a long time, and the traditional approach had worked well for them. Their schedules for the school year were already developed and approved by their supervisors, and they had recently shared this information with families. With that said, the team had heard whispers of new service delivery models emerging, and they were impressed by Rosa's enthusiasm, willingness, and flexibility. She approached this conversation with genuine intentions, helpful information, and positivity. It also took great courage for a first-year teacher to propose such a significant shift in the service delivery model—and to seasoned professionals! The team agreed to do some of their own research and to consider the proposal. For the next few days, Rosa did what she could to reduce the chaos in her classroom and to support her students in learning the classroom routine. She arrived early in the morning to prepare for the day, meticulously crafting plans A, B, and C. She also stayed late, engaged in thoughtful reflection of what went well and the reasons behind the things that went wrong.

A Way Forward

By the end of week 2, Rosa had managed to get through five full minutes of a Circle Time activity—a true triumph! Nonetheless, there was significantly more progress to be made. By this time, the related service personnel were able to chat with their respective supervisors, who expressed enthusiasm for the new model Rosa proposed. It turns out the school's leadership team had been having similar conversations, and they decided to utilize Rosa's classroom as a "pilot" for the embedded instruction and transdisciplinary approach. The rollout began with a group meeting led by the various supervisors, as well as the assignment of an online module on embedded instruction through the CONNECT Modules, *The Center to Mobilize Early Childhood Knowledge*, through the Division of Early Childhood (DEC), a subdivision of the Council for Exceptional Children (CEC). Then, the real planning and implementation began.

To begin, the team decided to formally meet for a "weekly huddle" on Monday mornings before student arrival, and again for a "weekly debrief" on Friday afternoons after the students had been dismissed. This would offer an opportunity for the team to routinely collaborate on the implementation of services and interventions for the students in Rosa's classroom. They would prioritize areas or goals to address for each student and develop concrete action plans to achieve those goals. Then, at the end of the week, they would reflect as a team on areas of growth and areas for greater attention or improvement.

The team then turned to each student's IEP, and they developed, based on student goals and service delivery frequencies, a schedule and mode of support that would allow them to achieve functional outcomes for their students. For instance, the SLP decided to push into the classroom to support multiple students with basic "requesting" goals during snack time. This offered a natural and highly motivating opportunity for the SLP and Rosa to address the need for increased communication of their students through a typical daily activity and routine. The occupational therapist would also support during this time, as it allowed for a very natural opportunity to support students with fine motor needs via opening of the various snack bags and containers, as well as effectively using utensils. The physical therapist would join the class during transitions throughout the building, as the safe and successful navigation of hallways, stairways, the playground, and so on, was a functional way to develop and strengthen gross motor skills.

The team used an electronic shared document to outline their schedules and the target skills being addressed for each student during each classroom routine and activity. Rosa was responsible for the master schedule, as well as the overarching development of each activity. Knowing her limits, she continuously probed her team for valuable input:

- How might I increase the opportunities for children to respond during this art activity?

- What developmentally appropriate sounds should I target for approximation during Circle Time?
- Are there strategies or adaptations I can use to increase independence during this cut/paste activity?
- How can I embed movement into this social activity?

From Vision to Victory

Over time, the transfer of knowledge across team members was apparent, as was student progress. The consistent, intimate collaboration of the team allowed for the swift implementation of communication strategies, including the use of high-tech augmentative and alternative communication (AAC) systems for Mason and Michael. It came as no surprise that, as their communication skills increased, their challenging behavior decreased. The use of an icon-based communication system (ICBS) allowed Jaden to request a "walk" via visual representation, rather than eloping unexpectedly down the hallway. The consistent and strategic use of Michael's walker, a plan developed by his PT and implemented by the full team, increased Michael's strength and independence in the classroom. Michael's parents observed the difference at home, too, and they were sharing news of his rapid progress with their peers. It wasn't long before other parents and staff members were asking questions about this new model of service delivery.

At the end of the year, Rosa and her team were responsible for presenting data regarding student progress to their supervisory team. This information would assist the supervisory team in making strategic decisions about the model they would employ moving forward. The school year was not perfect by any means, and the journey was filled with a myriad of challenges. There were many areas for continued improvement, but ultimately, the students made significant growth, as did the school-based team. The data told a story not just of student progress, but of a team that grew stronger and more capable through their work as a collective whole.

Questions:

1 What is a transdisciplinary model in early intervention? What are the benefits?

2 Why do you think teams often tend to rely on an interdisciplinary approach versus a transdisciplinary approach?
3 What do you think is meant by "functional outcomes"?
4 Advocating for additional resources or the use of newer, evidence-based practices can be extremely challenging for new teachers. Rosa used a bold approach. What other strategies could early teachers use to garner interest in updating service delivery models?
5 How can new teachers build resilience when their first days or weeks don't go as planned?
6 How might Rosa and the school-based team have included Michael's family in their shift to a transdisciplinary and embedded instruction approach to increase parental engagement and support the generalization of skills across settings?
7 What resources could Rosa have relied on, aside from her team, to learn more about cerebral palsy, given that this diagnosis was relatively new to her?

Challenge: Interview a supervisor at a local early childhood special education program about their chosen service delivery model. How does it compare to and contrast from the model discussed in this case study?

Challenge: Develop an example of embedded instruction in a preschool special education classroom.

Challenge: Discuss how an embedded instruction model could also effectively support a child with a disability in a typical early childhood education (ECE) program.

Family Response to a Disability Diagnosis

Mary A. Houser, EdD

"Just slow down and tell me what the doctor said today. Everything is going to be all right, Mom," Leila said to her mother as she spoke with her on the phone. "I know this is coming as a surprise to you, but we will get through this as a family."

Leila was the oldest of five children, and Molly always felt like she could confide in her daughter about her struggles. She leaned on Leila more than ever this past year, since her husband passed away. Leila was only twenty years old, but she was wise beyond her years and had a wonderfully calming nature about her. "Yes, you did have him when you were older in life, but a lot of parents have children in their early forties," Leila said.

After she hung up the phone, Molly sat quietly on the sofa, looking at Jimmy in his playpen. To her, Jimmy had always been her perfect little two-year-old boy. He was the youngest of the five children. Today, the doctor told her Jimmy's language development was delayed, and so were his cognitive skills. He stated that by the age of two, Jimmy should have many single words and should be starting to spontaneously put two words together. He was not doing this.

Molly knew Jimmy wasn't talking like her other children did, but his siblings always jumped in and talked for him, so she did not notice his delay. She thought to herself that there were times when Jimmy would look at her as if he did not understand what she was saying to him. Molly also said that it was unusual that Jimmy did not follow simple directions, enjoy looking at picture books, or imitate his siblings like the others did when they were his age.

The doctor also mentioned that his eye-hand coordination was weak. Molly remembered that Jimmy had problems holding a crayon when he wanted to color and had difficulties holding onto a ball. The doctor recommended she take him to a developmental pediatrician for an evaluation. With her face in her hands, Molly let out a deep sigh. Having a house full of children and a full-time job was a lot for any parent to handle. It was even more for a single parent, who just lost her husband, to handle. Perhaps Molly just overlooked things because it was easier than taking on one more thing.

Evaluation by a Developmental Pediatrician

Over the next month, Molly had Jimmy evaluated by a developmental pediatrician, and he received the diagnosis of a developmental delay. The developmental pediatrician recommended that she contact early intervention services in her local school district. He provided her with the necessary contact information to reach out to them and concluded their visit. The next week, Molly contacted her county's early intervention office and made an initial appointment to discuss Jimmy with them. Shortly after, she phoned Leila and asked if she would go with her to attend the upcoming meeting for moral support. Leila agreed. The night before the meeting, Molly told Leila she had spent the last couple of weeks researching Jimmy's diagnosis to learn more about it. She told Leila that learning more about it had consumed her, and she spent all of her free time trying to learn as much as she could.

Early Intervention Information Meeting

The next week, Molly and Leila went to their neighborhood elementary school, which houses its county's early intervention program on its campus. There, they met with a case manager for what is called an information session. Molly told the case manager about Jimmy's developmental problems, their recent visit to the developmental pediatrician, and the diagnosis he received. As they sat at the table, Leila could feel Molly's leg shaking next to hers. Leila carefully reached under the table and put her hand on her mother's knee. Molly needed her support. The case manager listened closely to Molly talk about her son. She asked pointed questions about Molly's pregnancy and Jimmy's developmental history. They talked about Jimmy's interest in socializing with other children and his play skills.

After the case manager gathered all the necessary information, they scheduled an appointment, which was Jimmy's early intervention evaluation. This would consist of a play-based assessment and some direct observations of Jimmy. The case manager explained that Molly would have to give consent before the evaluation could be conducted. Before she left, the case manager gave Molly the Vineland Adaptive Rating Scale to complete at home before their next visit. This was a checklist that reports a child's daily living skills, as interpreted by the parent or caregiver. The results of this would later be factored into Jimmy's early intervention programming.

The ride home in the car from the meeting was quiet. Molly felt okay about the meeting and believed the school district wanted to help them. Leila turned to Molly and said, "That was not too bad, Mom. I think they want to help us." Molly smiled a little and nodded her head. Molly was afraid, however. There seemed to be so much coming at her at once. How would she go about sharing the news about Jimmy with her other children? Her parents? Some of her children were still young and would not understand what was happening with him.

Neither of her parents saw anything wrong with Jimmy's development, and Molly was doubtful they would be supportive of him receiving early intervention. Molly's parents were the "wait and see" type and had commented that "children grow out of things, give them time," whenever one of her children displayed something out of the ordinary.

Molly did not want to wait any longer to help Jimmy. She had been told by the developmental pediatrician how important receiving early intervention services were for children with Jimmy's kind of problems. Molly was also fearful about Jimmy's long-term prognosis. Her mind began to race. Would he grow up to live on his own, complete high school, and have a job to support himself? What worried her most, however, was who would care for him once she was no longer alive. Molly knew Jimmy had brothers and sisters, but she felt strongly that she did not want to burden them with the responsibility of caring for Jimmy throughout his adult years.

Early Intervention Evaluation

Within a couple of weeks, Molly took Jimmy to his early intervention evaluation. The evaluation was just like the case manager explained it would be. They discussed Jimmy's progress in meeting his developmental milestones and asked about any concerns Molly had about his development. They spent ample time observing Jimmy both in a free play setting and a structured play environment. During free play, he mostly wandered around the room and picked up a toy or two but would throw it down after only a moment. It was as if he did not know what he was supposed to do. The structured play was a little better. He was given a place setting with some plastic utensils. He briefly pretended to feed himself but lost his grip on the spoon and then gave up.

The team also examined him interacting with Molly and the team members. They talked about the impact that her husband's death had on Jimmy and how the family was doing now that he was gone. At the end of the evaluation, the case manager told Molly she would be in touch to schedule a meeting to discuss the results of today's evaluation. After this, Molly took Jimmy's hand, and together they left the school building.

Molly was anxious about attending the next meeting to discuss the evaluation results. All of this was so brand new to her and overwhelming. It was times like these that Molly missed having her husband by her side.

About a week later, Molly received the results of the evaluation from the early intervention team. There were many different scores on the report, which she did not understand, and she found it difficult to make sense of the report. Molly was glad they would be meeting to discuss the evaluation results.

Early Intervention Evaluation Results

When Molly arrived on the day of the meeting, she tried to remain confident that everything would work out. Even though Leila could not attend the meeting with her, she remembered the words that she said when she first phoned Leila with the news about Jimmy from the developmental pediatrician. She repeated it quietly to herself, "Everything is going to be all right. Everything is going to be all right."

When she walked into the meeting room, there were several school personnel waiting to greet her. Molly felt intimidated by the number of educators attending the meeting. She did not expect there to be so many. Fortunately, everyone was friendly and helpful. The meeting began with the IFSP team introducing themselves to Molly. There was the case manager, an occupational therapist, a speech and language therapist, an early intervention teacher, and an early intervention official from the county. Molly was so nervous that she could not remember any of their names. The case manager continued the meeting by stating that Molly's input in the meeting would be critical to Jimmy's success because she could best explain his strengths and needs. The case manager also stated that parent education and support are an important part of early intervention services, and that the team was there to provide her with guidance, resources, and support to nurture Jimmy during his early years. This made Molly feel better and allowed her to relax somewhat as the meeting continued.

The Individualized Family Service Plan (IFSP)

The case manager went on to discuss concerns that Molly had noted about Jimmy's development and stated that the results of his early intervention assessment indicated that Jimmy qualified for early intervention services. This meant Jimmy would have an IFSP, which was a plan specifically designed for him that details the early intervention services that he will receive to aid in his development and the support provided to his family.

The team discussed the results of the Vineland Adaptive Behavior Rating Scale Molly had provided, and the developmental pediatrician's report. The various related service personnel (e.g., speech and language pathologist and occupational therapist) discussed Jimmy's strengths and challenges, and how they planned to work with Jimmy to improve his skills by creating specific goals for him. An early intervention teacher spoke to Molly about the curriculum that was used in her classroom, where Jimmy would be placed, and about how excited the other children in his class would be to have him there. Each of the related personnel highlighted some of the annual goals Jimmy would work toward based on the results of the evaluation. To illustrate, the speech and language pathologist discussed working on Jimmy following simple commands and identifying parts of the body. The occupational therapist mentioned that an annual goal for Jimmy will be to work on his eye-hand coordination with activities such as stringing beads and stacking cups. Molly did her best to understand everything the professionals said, but she found it hard to remember everything. At times during the meeting, she felt herself getting teary-eyed as the reality of his disability was becoming more apparent. Molly asked how she would receive updates on Jimmy's progress and what would happen with his programming moving forward. The team assured her that she would be informed of Jimmy's progress regularly and that any time she had a question or a concern about how he was doing in school, she could reach out to them. They also mentioned that, at a minimum, they would be meeting together as a team annually to review his progress and create new annual goals for him.

As the meeting came to an end, Molly signed Jimmy's IFSP, acknowledging her role on the IFSP team and indicating consent for Jimmy's early intervention services to begin. The members of the IFSP team assured Molly that Jimmy's attending their program was the right choice for him. They wanted her to feel good about the program and services they provided for children with developmental disabilities.

That evening, Molly and Leila had supper alone together. Molly was emotionally exhausted but hopeful about Jimmy starting early intervention services. She explained today's meeting in detail to Leila, telling her as much as she could remember about the results of the early intervention evaluation and next steps. Leila comforted her and told her she had made the right decision about taking Jimmy to a developmental pediatrician and following through with the early intervention services. Molly decided she would tell her other children the next day about Jimmy's new school. She also decided it was best to let her parents know soon about her decision to have Jimmy begin early intervention. She looked at Leila and said, "Everything is going to be all right, Leila." Leila smiled, "Yes, it is, Mom."

Questions:

1 What diagnosis did Jimmy receive from the developmental pediatrician? What did he recommend Molly do next after receiving the diagnosis?
2 Explain Molly's emotions as a new parent of a child with a disability and beginning her son's educational programming. Provide examples.
3 Who is Leila? Discuss the relationship she has with Molly and why she was instrumental in Molly's successful meetings with both Jimmy's doctors and early intervention services.
4 Who was on Jimmy's IFSP team? What type of information did they provide to Molly at the meeting?
5 Compare Jimmy and Hao's (developmental delay case study, chapter 5, p. 37) developmental challenges. In what ways are they similar? Different?
6 Discuss the different family structures that Jimmy and Michael (orthopedic impairment case study, chapter 12, p. 87) experience. In your opinion, how might a two-parent family differ from a one-parent family when raising a child with a disability?
7 List two takeaways you learned about families and the IFSP/early intervention process.

Challenge: Create a list of interview questions for interviewing an early intervention classroom teacher. Be sure the questions include specifics about the early intervention classroom, the students served, the curriculum, the related service professionals, and the relationships the early intervention classroom teacher has with the parents/families of the children with disabilities they serve.

Reference

Linder, T. (2008). *Transdisciplinary play-based assessment* (2nd ed.). Paul H. Brookes Publishing Company.

20

Collaboration and Inclusive Practices

This chapter includes several case studies related to the topic of *Collaboration and Inclusive Practices*, which are the following:

- Co-Teaching and Consultation
- Home-School Collaboration
- Paraprofessionals
- Teaching Across Student Populations

Collaboration and inclusive practices are at the forefront of teaching students with disabilities and those with additional learning needs. Collaboration occurs when educators work together toward a common goal or purpose. For example, collaboration can occur when the special educator works with other special education teachers, general education teachers, related service personnel, and parents to ensure quality education for their students. Inclusive practices are also highly regarded in today's public schools. Inclusive practices in education are about respecting all students' cultures, disabilities, and differences to ensure that everyone is valued and accommodated regardless of their diverse backgrounds and learning needs, so that all students can belong and learn together in the classroom.

This chapter examines the following aspects of collaboration and inclusive practices:

1 **Co-Teaching and Consultation:** In this case study, a first-year general education teacher learns that he will be co-teaching with

a veteran special education teacher. It focuses on their interactions and planning for their first year together in a co-taught inclusive general education classroom. It explores the six co-teaching models that are often found to be effective.

2. **Home-School Collaboration:** In this case study, two young teachers (a special education teacher and a general education teacher) explore how to strengthen their existing home-school collaboration with their students' families through a professional development opportunity.

3. **Paraprofessionals:** In this case study, a teacher preparation student begins a part-time job as a paraprofessional in a neighborhood school and gets some hands-on experience learning the daily ins and outs of being a special education support staff by effectively collaborating with the teacher of record.

4. **Teaching Across Student Populations:** In this case study, a middle school teacher learns how to be a more culturally responsive teacher as he transitions a fifth grader from elementary school to middle school in a New Mexico public school.

Co-Teaching and Consultation

Colleen E. Commisso, PhD

When Anthony Gallo first stepped into the brick-lined hallways of Lincoln High School, he carried with him a mix of nerves and quiet excitement. Even though Anthony did his student teaching in this school, this was now real, he was no longer a student learning from a seasoned educator; he was now the *teacher*.

It was late August, and Anthony was arriving at the high school to start the first of two days of in-service before the first day of school. As he unlocked the door to his classroom and turned on the lights, he looked around his new classroom. He spent the last two days inventorying supplies, making seating charts, hanging up the daily schedule, putting first-day-of-school documents on his homeroom students' desks, and pinning up various biology-themed posters.

Sitting down at his laptop to check the schedule for the day, there was a knock on the open door. A woman stood on the threshold, holding a coffee in one hand and a clipboard in the other.

"You must be Anthony," she said with a warm, no-nonsense tone. "I'm Tessa Morgan—your co-teacher."

Anthony blinked, unsure how to respond. "Co-teacher?"

"Yep. I'm the special education teacher assigned to your inclusion classes. I'll be in your second and third periods. We'll be working with several students who have individualized education programs (IEPs), some with learning disabilities, others with autism, emotional disturbance, or attention deficit hyperactivity disorder (ADHD). I'm here to make sure they have the support they need to access the curriculum."

"Oh, right, of course," Anthony said, recovering. "Sorry, no one told me that any of my classes were co-taught."

Tessa grinned. "No problem, you wouldn't have known; my schedule was just changed. It will be great! I'll see you later!"

Tessa walked down the hallway, leaving Anthony confused and unsure of this new teaching arrangement. Anthony wanted to touch base with Tessa later in the day, but the rest of the day consisted of meeting after meeting, and much new information. Anthony's head was spinning. By 3 p.m., Anthony was exhausted. When he stopped by Tessa's room at 3:15 p.m., her door was already closed, and the light was off.

Initial Conversations

On the second day of in-service, all the teachers had time in their classrooms to prepare for the next day, and during that time, Anthony walked down the hallway to find Tessa. Tessa was busy typing on her computer when Anthony knocked on her open door. Tessa quickly looked up and welcomed him into her classroom.

Anthony entered the room carrying his laptop and the class rosters for the periods that Tessa said she would be in his classroom. He wanted to know more about the students who had IEPs in those periods that would be co-taught. Over the next hour, Tessa talked about the students in the two shared periods while Anthony wrote down notes and asked questions. Out of the fifty-five students across the two periods, almost half of the students had IEPs.

Tessa explained that most of the students had specific learning disabilities, and many had difficulties reading text and/or understanding what text means. She also said that a few students had internalizing or externalizing behavior challenges. One student, specifically, had very high levels of anxiety and difficulties with forming attachments with teachers. She explained that Anthony would need to give the student space until she was comfortable in the class and with him. Some of the students who engaged in externalizing behaviors would sometimes refuse to do work, talk to their peers, and call out in class.

Another student was deaf and had a cochlear implant. Tessa explained that an interpreter would also be coming to class to support this student. Three students had autism. Tessa explained that the students were very different. One student was very strong academically, but had difficulties with social skills, asking for help, and transitioning from one activity to another. She said that the other two students had difficulties with academics and social skills. Anthony then asked about a few students who had other health impairments (OHI) listed as their disability category. He indicated that he knew that label could be used for students who have ADHD. Tessa confirmed this and indicated that all the students with OHI in this class have ADHD.

At the end of the hour, Anthony was feeling overwhelmed. He had pages of notes about the students and did not know where to begin with the information provided. Tessa reassured him, stressing, "This is why these classes are co-taught. I am here to support you and the students. We will do this as a team."

Anthony also wanted to talk to her about how she had worked previously with other co-teachers. Tessa explained that for some years, she had a shared planning time with the general education teachers, while in other years she did not. Unfortunately, Tessa and Anthony did not have a common time to plan, but they decided that they would touch base before/after class and set up other times to meet.

Tessa shared with Anthony that when she had co-taught before, there were sometimes difficulties with differences in how they responded to challenging behaviors in the classroom. She described that one time the teacher she worked with was too friendly with the students. They did not have clear expectations and joked around with the students when they were not following the rules. She felt as though she and the teacher were never on the same page. Anthony confirmed that he wanted to talk about behavior as well. He handed her a copy of his class syllabus that included his behavioral expectations; he wanted to make sure that they were "on the same page." Tessa said that she was glad that he had some general behavioral expectations.

Beginning of the School Year

In those first few weeks, Anthony learned that Tessa was the kind of person who could both calm a chaotic classroom and challenge experienced teachers, all in the same sentence. She had quiet authority, a way of speaking to students that made them listen without feeling scolded. Tessa learned that Anthony was a fun-loving teacher who brought interesting examples to enhance the content. She also learned that he worked very hard to develop activities and labs that would be engaging for the students. Although they learned a great deal from each other, working collaboratively was bumpy. Anthony felt as though they could not "get in a groove." Anthony was uncomfortable with having another teacher in the classroom and was worried that if he made a mistake, it would be viewed negatively; he felt as though he was constantly being observed.

Getting to Know Each Other

One day after class, Tessa pulled him aside. "Hey," she said, not unkindly. "That was solid content. But Jamal and Ayesha, both on my caseload, were lost by slide seven. Jamal was doodling on his paper, and Ayesha looked confused and told me this later in the day."

Anthony frowned. "Too fast?"

"Way too fast. I was able to redirect them to the video that you started playing, but they missed some of the notes. I will follow up with them, but how about I create some guided notes for the students so they can listen more and know what the most important information is for the day?"

Anthony responded, "You'd do that?"

She smiled. "That's what I'm here for." Anthony had to learn to adjust his teaching pace for these classes compared to his other periods.

Over the next few weeks, Anthony began to not only become more comfortable with how the students learned best but also learned more about what type of supports Tessa could provide. During lab days, Anthony led the full-group setup, while Tessa floated among students needing extra help with reading or understanding directions. On test days, Tessa took the students who needed instructions, had questions, and/or required read-alouds to her classroom so that the accommodation(s) could be fully provided.

Tessa also asked questions during instruction when students seemed confused, so Anthony could restate/reexplain important concepts. At first, this was difficult for Anthony to get used to, but he soon realized that it helped the students hear the information again and provided him with the opportunity to give additional examples. Tessa, who had not co-taught biology before, learned that Anthony had a great deal of knowledge about the concepts and utilized multiple examples, often the weird and unexpected aspects of animals and nature, to help the students remember. These examples helped the students stay engaged and interested in the content. Tessa also learned that Anthony liked to utilize hands-on activities, which was also a good teaching strategy to keep students engaged during class.

Learning to Compromise

Even though they both learned about each other, their co-teaching relationship was new, and there were times when they did not agree. For example, one time, there was a student, Jonathan, who did not hand in any labs or homework assignments. At the end of the second quarter, Jonathan went to Anthony and asked what he could do to pull up his grade. Anthony discussed with him that he had multiple chances to hand in the late work, including a few days in class, and it was too late.

Later in the day, Tessa came to Anthony and asked about Jonathan's work. After Anthony explained, Tessa expressed her concerns. She indicated she understands that Jonathan had opportunities to make up the work; however, if he doesn't get any credit for the work, his grade will be so low that he would have almost no chance of passing for the year. She also said that she is afraid that he may display challenging behaviors if he knows he probably will not pass. Anthony said he understood but was also afraid that Jonathan would take advantage of this in future quarters. Tessa said that she does not want that to happen either.

After thinking about the issue over the next day, Anthony approached Tessa with an idea. He said that he was willing to give Jonathan some credit for the missing work so that his quarter grade would not be catastrophic to his final course grade, but he would not offer the same courtesy again. Tessa, someone who always allowed her students to hand in work late for full credit, did not fully agree with this plan, but also understood that this was a change for Anthony, so she compromised.

Mid-Year

As the pair entered the late fall, they seemed to be more comfortable with each other. As the class was about to begin learning about evolution, Anthony emailed Tessa to meet. Anthony was concerned about the level of difficulty within this textbook chapter and wanted to get Tessa's thoughts on how they could work together to support the students. While meeting, Anthony described the content, lessons, and activities he had planned. Tessa listened intently, looking at the materials Anthony showed.

Once he finished talking, Tessa asked, "Would you like to try something different?"

Anthony, unsure what she meant, responded, "Um… I'm open to ideas. What were you thinking?"

Tessa explained, "Up until this point, I have mostly been supporting the students by circulating the classroom and making changes to assignments and activities as needed. This has been great and helpful for the students, but there are also other ways I can provide support in the classroom. We could try to utilize a different co-teaching model."

Anthony responded, "I remember learning about those, but I did not co-teach during student teaching. What were you thinking?"

"Well, there are six in total," she stated. "We have mostly been using one-teach, one-assist (or one-drift), but there are five others. I have to run, but I will send you a link to a great description of the models. You can check them out, and then we can touch base about what models you would like to try."

Anthony said, "Yeah, that works for me. Thanks."

While Tessa packed up her bag, Anthony also had another question for Tessa. He recently got a new student in another one of his classes, Megan, who had a visual impairment. Besides enlarging materials and letting her use her iPad, he did not know how to support her with lab assignments, especially the use of the microscopes.

Tessa did not have an answer, and after looking at the student in the school's database, she noticed that the student was in all general education courses. She did not personally know the student, so she suggested that Anthony reach out to the student's caseload manager for consultative support. She explained that special education teachers not only teach their classes and co-teach but also provide support for students on their caseload on an as-needed basis. After consulting her list of students, she told Anthony that Tom in room 6 was the student's caseload manager. Anthony thanked her and went to see if that special education teacher was still at school.

Consultation Support

Fortunately, Tom was just leaving his classroom when Anthony rounded the corner. Anthony introduced himself and asked if they could chat on their way to the parking lot, but he did not want to bother him. Tom was more than willing to chat, and while walking, Anthony explained the situation with Megan.

Tom listened thoughtfully and when Anthony finished talking, he replied, "Let me email Amanda; I will cc you on the email. She is the vision specialist that supports students who are blind or have visual impairments. She will set up a time to meet with you and discuss what questions you have. Does that work?"

Anthony said, "Yeah, of course, that would be great. I didn't know we had a vision specialist at the school."

Tom responded, "Yeah, Amanda's great; she can consult with you anytime you have a question. She also will stop by on a regular basis to learn from you what is upcoming in your class so she can provide additional supports as needed."

Anthony thanked Tom, and they both headed home for the night.

Co-Teaching Models

After going to the gym, taking a shower, and eating dinner, Anthony jumped on his computer, like he did almost every night, to prepare for the next day. He was interested in looking at more information on co-teaching models and clicked on the link that Tessa provided. The link provided the following information about the co-teaching models:

1 **One Teach, One Assist (or drift):** One teacher teaches while the other circulates the class, supporting individual students, as needed.
2 **One Teach, One Observe:** One teacher teaches while the other teacher observes what is happening in the classroom. The teacher observing could collect data specifically on the students (either the group as a whole or individual students) or on the entire classroom environment.

3. **Alternate Teaching/Alternative Teaching:** One teacher teaches a small group of students (e.g., advanced students who need enrichment, students who are having difficulties and need more support). The other teacher teaches the rest of the class.
4. **Parallel Teaching:** The class is divided into two groups, and each teacher teaches half of the class. The two teachers are teaching the same content but teaching in a different way. For example, if they are teaching a play, one may teach students to read the play and complete a graphic organizer to better understand the characters' traits. The other group may act out the parts of the play and talk through the characters' traits.
5. **Station Teaching:** The lesson content is divided into different parts, and each teacher teaches a station with part of the content while other stations are completed independently. The students rotate through all stations until they visit each station.
6. **Team Teaching:** Both teachers teach the content together, working collaboratively to provide instruction and engage students in learning.

After reading about the different models, Anthony was both excited and a little nervous. He had multiple ideas running through his head, but this was also new; he was not sure how it would go or the best way to plan for the use of these models. He also did not know if Tessa and he would be able to implement these models without a common planning time.

The next day, Anthony stopped by Tessa's room before homeroom and shared his mixed feelings about the co-teaching models. Tessa asked if he would be willing to try just one model for one lesson, and then they could touch base to see what they both thought. Anthony liked this idea. It allowed for a small amount of change without having him feel like his normal process was upended. Anthony and Tessa tried parallel teaching a few days later. Although there were some minor bumps, Anthony liked the small teacher-student ratio. Tessa shared that she was a little unsure about being fully responsible for the content, given that she was not certified in biology but knew she could become more comfortable. Anthony also said that he would be more than happy to answer any questions Tessa had about the content. Tessa thanked Anthony, and they both agreed that they wanted to try additional co-teaching models as the year progressed.

End of Year

By the end of the year, Anthony and Tessa had become closer colleagues. They worked to try various co-teaching models, sharing what they thought worked and did not work following the lessons. Although this trust and ability to be honest was very hard at first, Anthony and Tessa acknowledged when they made steps, even small steps forward. They told each other when they appreciated something; and when there was a concern, they shared that concern without placing blame on the other person. Anthony also felt more comfortable having additional people in his classroom. They developed and strengthened multiple skills, including the following:

- identifying clear roles and responsibilities,
- valuing each other's expertise,
- solving problems together, and
- discussing concerns about students together.

When schedules were being created at the end of the year, Anthony was assigned two co-teaching sections of biology with Tessa. Anthony and Tessa were looking forward to developing more activities and lessons collaboratively and becoming more comfortable with each other.

Questions:

1. Reflect on Anthony's initial feelings upon learning that he was co-teaching. How would you feel if you learned a few days before the start of the school year that you were (a) a general education teacher getting a co-teacher in your classroom and (b) a special education teacher co-teaching in a general education classroom?
2. How did Anthony and Tessa's relationship change throughout the year? Give specific examples.
3. How did consultation and co-teaching occur within this case study? Give specific examples.
4. Compromising or finding a different solution is often important in co-teaching. How did this happen with Anthony and Tessa?
5. What skills, both professionally and personally, did Tessa and Anthony display that made their co-teaching pair strong? Give specific examples.

Challenge: Tessa and Anthony seemed to have similar thought processes on how to respond to off-task behaviors. What challenges could exist if they did not have similar thoughts on responding to challenging behaviors? How could they work through those differences?

Challenge: Research three different checklists or rating scales that can be utilized by co-teaching pairs. Review and discuss the strengths and challenges of those materials.

Challenge: Think more about the different co-teaching models. Choose two different co-teaching models and for each, develop a lesson idea that could be co-taught between Tessa and Anthony.

Home-School Collaboration

Mary A. Houser, EdD

Maggie and Annie: Teacher Friends

Maggie is a second-year special education mathematics teacher at a local high school. She loves her students and her teaching job. She teaches an inclusive general education geometry class for two periods per day and self-contained life skills math classes for the other class periods. Maggie teaches several disability populations, which include students with learning disabilities, other health impairments (e.g., epilepsy), autism spectrum disorder, and intellectual disabilities. She finds working with a wide variety of students challenging and she enjoys finding new ways to teach them.

Over the past year, Maggie became friends with Annie, a general education high school English teacher. The two of them started their teaching careers at the same time and have shared the trials and tribulations of being new teachers together. Maggie is always glad to have Annie just down the hallway to talk to her about her school day. Annie feels the same way and confides in Maggie, too. Having a teaching buddy allows them to feel supported in their new careers.

Home-School Collaboration

One afternoon, Maggie and Annie were in the teachers' lounge eating their lunches, and some veteran teachers at their lunch table were talking about an upcoming professional development day. The topic of the professional development day will be home-school collaboration. The school's administration has scheduled speakers to come and discuss the importance of working with and communicating with parents/caregivers. They will also provide helpful tips and strategies to inform the teachers' current practices.

As they sit there eating their lunches, Maggie tells Annie she is regularly in contact with several of her students' parents/caregivers. She explains that it was not uncommon for special education teachers to have increased parental contact due to some of the challenges students with disabilities present. Annie remarks that she does not have very much contact with her students' parents/guardians. She only communicates with them at back-to-school night; parent-teacher conferences to update them on their child's progress; if their child has a behavioral concern in her classroom; and by sending regular class updates through email. She also says she had never really *collaborated* on anything with them before.

Annie comments that home-school collaboration seems to get less frequent as students advance by grade level. She mentions that when students are in elementary school, there are more opportunities for parents to come to school and get involved. She comments on how parents come to school to read to students, help out in the art room, or attend field trips with the class as an extra set of hands in lower grades. Their conversation continues as they contemplate the strengths and challenges of collaborating with their current parents/caregivers. Maggie tells Annie she has two students who are in the same class with whom she has very different types of home-school collaboration.

Maggie's Home-School Collaboration Experiences

Maggie begins telling Annie about Alex, who is an eleventh-grade student with epilepsy (OHI) in her inclusive geometry class (Note: Alex was introduced in the epilepsy case study, chapter 11, p. 81). Alex recently transferred to their school from the city. She explains Alex's parents have always maintained communication with her teachers since she was diagnosed with epilepsy in elementary school. Maggie mentions that Alex's parents are very interested in her school progress as well as her seizure management at school. Her parents have informed the school that Alex has unique needs due to her health impairment, and they both feel positive communication with the teacher and school allows them to share insights about her academic and physical progress. They remark that regular communication with the school makes it easier to collaborate when they meet for her IEP meetings because they already know each other. Alex's parents state that frequent communication with school personnel allows them to be a better advocate for Alex's needs, such as developing her seizure action plan (SAP), and ensuring she receives her antiepileptic medication during the school day. Lastly, Alex's parents believe that open and honest communication is important in knowing how Alex is doing on a day-to-day basis while at school.

Maggie then tells Annie about another home-school communication relationship she experiences with a different student in the same geometry class: Rahul. Rahul is also an eleventh grader and has an autism spectrum disorder (ASD) (Note: Rahul was introduced in the ASD #1 case study, chapter 3, p. 22). He has a particularly hard time interacting with other students in class during group work. Oftentimes, he sits there and does not say a word. He doesn't participate at all but instead looks around the room as if he is completely distracted. In the meantime, his groupmates are busy trying to complete the assignment because they know they will be receiving a grade for their work. Rahul's lack of attention frustrates his group members, but they never really say anything to him about it.

Maggie states that she knows Rahul can contribute to his group's geometry assignments but refuses to do so. Maggie also indicates that she cannot give him credit for work he is not completing himself, but she does not want to separate him from his groupmates. As a special education teacher, Maggie understands the importance of students with ASD working cooperatively with their typically developing peers. Once this past semester, Maggie tried putting Rahul in a different group with other students to see if that would make a difference, but it did not. Sometimes he gets frustrated during class, too, she tells Annie. He talks under his breath, and it disturbs the students sitting next to him. Maggie knows that Rahul cannot control his verbalizations, and they are likely due to his ASD, but the noise is problematic to the other students' learning at times. Maggie had tried to reach Rahul's parents, but it was difficult to get through to them.

Maggie explains to Annie that both of Rahul's parents are from India and speak Hindi and English fluently. She continues by stating that both parents work full-time, and this makes their weekdays very busy. Maggie is not sure if Rahul has any siblings, but having other children might add to their time constraints. Maggie wonders if there have been any cultural differences that might have created a misunderstanding between them when they met during their school's back-to-school night, but she cannot pinpoint anything. Maggie tells Annie she wants better communication with them. She feels perhaps Rahul's parents could offer suggestions about how to best manage his behavior. Maggie is starting to feel a little desperate about the situation. She admits to feeling stuck in her ability to help Rahul, and that at times she feels defeated by it.

Professional Development Day

The professional development day at school was the following week. Maggie and Annie sit next to each other all day and listen attentively to the speakers. Both are eager to gain some insight into home-school collaboration. The first session discusses the meaning of home-school collaboration and its many benefits. The presenter is a parent whose child had been unsuccessful in school until they began collaborating with their teacher. She tells the staff that home-school collaboration is about creating a partnership between the school/teachers and the parents/caregivers to support a child's academic, social, and behavioral needs.

The parent continues by sharing reasons why home-school collaboration is beneficial. She mentions that a good amount of research has been conducted on this topic. She notes that it can lead to improved student outcomes, students completing homework more consistently, better social skills, increased school attendance, lower drop-out rates, and improved student behavior. She also states it can have a positive impact on students' interactions with peers and adults. Maggie and Annie turned and looked at each other as if they were gaining some valuable insight into today's topic.

Benefits of Home-School Collaboration

The next presenter continued to speak about the benefits of home-school collaboration. Although Maggie and Annie knew the importance of quality communication with their parents/caregivers, they learn some new things. These are their main takeaways:

- At the beginning of the year, ask parents for the best way to communicate with them about their child (e.g., email, text, phone).
- Be consistent when communicating with parents/caregivers. Being inconsistent does not give them an accurate representation of how their child is doing while at school.
- Be sure to communicate what their child has done well at school not just indicate the problems they are having.
- Don't be afraid to ask for input about a student from his parents/caregivers.
- Be specific when discussing school progress with parents/caregivers. For example, when talking about a student's behavior, you could say, "Tommy had great behavior today. He listened carefully to directions and completed class assignments. He did not break any of the class rules."
- Be patient with parents/caregivers. Most of them lead very busy lives with full-time or part-time jobs as well as other responsibilities.
- Realize that parents/caregivers might experience stress when their child is away at school during the day. Be understanding and compassionate.
- Communicate with all parents regularly (regardless of their child's ability and performance); communication can be brief but meaningful if there isn't anything specific to report. Parents/caregivers often appreciate all regular communication.

During their break, Maggie and Annie get coffee together and discuss the information they learned. Maggie asks Annie if she thinks any of the collaboration suggestions mentioned would be helpful when working with her students' parents/caregivers. Annie says she likes the idea of telling parents/caregivers what their child *does* well, and not just what they *do not* do well, when calling home about discipline problems. Annie shares that, as teachers, we are always trying to "fix" student problems but should spend more time recognizing what they do well, too. Maggie agrees. Annie said that she feels bad calling home only to report bad news, and that she is going to make some changes when she communicates with parents/caregivers. Maggie thought that was a smart idea.

Annie then asks Maggie which of the recommendations to improve home-school collaboration she could implement with her students. Maggie takes a moment and thinks about it. She tells Annie she needs to develop more patience with her students' parents. Maggie states that in the past, she has had a hard time understanding why parents don't respond to a phone call home or an email more immediately. She admits that she does not consider the responsibilities that parents/caregivers have daily, as the presenter had mentioned. More importantly, she adds, she had not considered the fact that parents/caregivers might be stressed about how their child is doing. She tells Annie that she, too, would feel concerned if she had a child with a disability who is away at school all day.

Lessons Learned

As the day ended, Maggie and Annie talked about how beneficial the professional development day they attended had been. Annie tells Maggie she has a lot to think about when it comes to how she can become a better partner with her students' parents/caregivers. She states that her next step is going to be to determine the most effective way to reach out to them to start building a relationship. Maggie says her next step is to increase her communication with parents/caregivers and make them feel more a part of their child's high school experience. Both Maggie and Annie gained valuable insight as classroom teachers regarding the importance of a positive relationship between the school and home settings. They are happy they can take a pause in their busy schedules and truly think about ways to better their students' school experiences. Maggie and Annie agree they both are looking forward to their next professional development day.

Questions:

1. What is home-school collaboration? Provide an example of your own.
2. What type of teacher is Maggie? Annie?
3. Discuss the different challenges Maggie had with Alex and Rahul. Explain the different home-school collaborations she had with both of their parents/caregivers.

4 Provide two examples of the benefits of home-school collaboration discussed at the professional development day session.
5 Review the list of takeaways Maggie and Annie learned from the home-school collaboration session. Select two of the items presented that you view as highly important when collaborating with parents/caregivers. Explain why you think they are important.
6 Identify the practical ways that both Maggie and Annie planned to implement some new techniques for improved home-school collaboration. Do you think they will be successful? Why or why not?

Challenge: Create a brief video introducing yourself to your future parents/caregivers. In the video, discuss your desire to help your students reach their potential, and focus on the importance of home-school collaboration and specific ways that you would like to partner with parents/caregivers to achieve specific goals.

Paraprofessionals

Mary A. Houser, EdD

"There is a new program for special education majors at school that sounds amazing," Luke said to his mom. "I could work as a special education paraprofessional and earn credit for my behavior management field course."

Luke attends a state university and is currently enrolled in a special education teacher preparation program. This semester, one of his classes, Behavior Management for Students with Disabilities, has a field component requirement in which special education teacher preparation students complete field hours in classes for students with emotional and behavioral challenges in surrounding school districts. There is a special opportunity for them to become part-time paraprofessionals in the school. These part-time positions allow them to simultaneously gain special education classroom experience and receive credit for their required field hours for their behavior management course, as well as earn an hourly wage. The state university is piloting this program to determine its potential benefits to local school districts that need paraprofessionals while at the same time giving special education teacher preparation students ample hands-on experience in the classroom as well as a paid opportunity.

Luke Applies to Become a Paraprofessional

The next day at school, Luke spoke with his professor about the paraprofessional opportunity. His professor spoke positively about it and encouraged him to apply. His professor then referred Luke to the district's HR department to complete the hiring process. After submitting all the appropriate forms and clearances, Luke interviewed for the job. Luke called his mom that evening, after the interview, and they commented to each other that having a job interview with a school district was a great experience for him. They also discussed that having this paraprofessional experience might be a "foot in the door" for him later when he will be applying for special education teacher positions.

The following week, Luke was hired for the position and began his part-time job as a paraprofessional in Mr. Roberts's eighth-grade class on Monday. By the time Luke joined Mr. Roberts's class, school had already been in session for a month. Luke felt as if he had a lot to learn about how middle school, self-contained, special education classrooms for students with emotional disorders were run. He was also eager to know more about each of the students in class. Luke hoped the content he was learning in his behavior management class would be helpful in his new position. He was optimistic that his paraprofessional job would give him skills that he could later use as a special education classroom teacher.

First Day on the Job

Mr. Roberts smiled as Luke entered the classroom on his first day. He welcomed him and told him how happy he was that Luke was a part of their class. Mr. Roberts introduced Luke to the students in class. As Luke looked around the room, he noticed there were eight students in the class: six boys and two girls. He was told when he was hired that all students in Mr. Robert's class had a diagnosis of emotional disturbance. As Luke looked around at the students in the class, it seemed like just another day to them. They were busy working on an assignment and hardly seemed bothered that someone new was in their class.

Luke took a seat next to one of the students and attempted to make small talk with him. The student answered his questions but did not do much to engage Luke in conversation. Luke wanted the students to like him and want him to work with him. Only time would tell. Mr. Roberts asked Luke to simply observe the students and the class for the first few periods, and they would talk more about his duties during his planning period. The time moved quickly, and before he knew it, a few class periods had gone by, and it was time for Mr. Roberts's planning period.

Responsibilities of a Special Education Paraprofessional

During his planning period, Mr. Roberts sat down with Luke to discuss his responsibilities as a paraprofessional in his classroom. He wanted Luke to have a clear understanding of his role and how he could best serve the students in his class. This is what he told Luke his primary responsibilities would be:

1. **Instructional support:** assisting him with tutoring, adapting instruction, and/or working with students individually or in small groups
2. **Classroom management:** helping him with duties such as organizing classroom materials, supporting student behavior, implementing classroom management procedures, and providing students with positive reinforcement, when appropriate
3. **Non-instructional duties:** monitoring recess, monitoring hallways, and/or providing support in the cafeteria during lunchtime
4. **Role model:** serving as an example of a positive adult who respects all students, parents, and staff members
5. **Data collection and progress monitoring:** assisting him in taking academic and behavioral data

Luke listened carefully as Mr. Roberts discussed each of these responsibilities and asked questions for clarity. Luke was excited to begin his job as a paraprofessional, but he was also a little nervous because he had never had any of these responsibilities before. Mr. Roberts also spent some time explaining to Luke what a paraprofessional is not qualified to do in the classroom setting. He explained to Luke that a paraprofessional may not provide initial instruction, create lesson plans, grade subjective tests, assign grades to students, or assume full responsibility for supervising and planning activities. Mr. Roberts also said that Luke may not act as the classroom teacher should he be absent. He explained that these roles may vary some depending on the state where the paraprofessional works, but this was the case for their state.

Meet Sarah

The next day, Mr. Roberts told Luke he wanted him to start spending some class time working with Sarah, one of the female students in his class (Note: Sarah was introduced in the ED#2 case study, chapter 14 p. 50). Mr. Roberts provided him with a little background information about Sarah, as well as her strengths and challenges. He told Luke that Sarah is introverted and prefers to be alone. Mr. Roberts revealed that she has anxiety that significantly impacts her ability to be productive. He added that Sarah possesses strong academic skills, but the effects of this mental health disability have resulted in her needing to be in a self-contained setting. Mr. Roberts said that his goal was to prepare Sarah for her successful return to general education in an inclusive setting. Mr. Roberts thought that if Luke could work with her on her anxiety and social skills, it might make the transition to inclusive classes easier on her, where the academic and social demands are greater. Luke thought what Mr. Roberts said made sense, but what exactly would he be working on with Sarah? One thing he knew for sure, Luke would have to build rapport with Sarah soon. But how?

Mr. Roberts shared that it was important for Luke to be able to identify the signs of Sarah's anxiety. He stated that Sarah will withdraw from others when she is feeling anxious. This typically happens during large-group and small-group instruction. He added that when Sarah is alone, working by herself, she appears to be the most comfortable. Mr. Roberts asked Luke to keep an eye on Sarah during both of these instructional times, and if he sees her having difficulty concentrating or not participating, to go sit next to her and check in to see if she is feeling anxious. If she is feeling anxious, he should take her back to her seat where he could work with her independently on the lesson until she is ready to return to the group setting. Mr. Roberts emphasized that it is important for Sarah to have a predictable routine when she begins to feel anxious while at the same time continuing to complete her work, as she is able. Mr. Roberts also suggested that Luke work on some relaxation techniques with her, such as deep breathing, if she feels particularly anxious. Mr. Roberts emphasized the importance of being positive with her by reinforcing her for all attempts to try to manage her anxiety. He also said that speaking to her in a calm and quiet voice should help her relax.

Luke went home exhausted from his first day as a special education paraprofessional. He had no idea that the demands of being in the classroom all day would be as all-consuming as they were. Nonetheless, Luke was thrilled about his job in Mr. Roberts's classroom and looked forward to telling his classmates at university about his experiences. He would work one more day in Mr. Roberts's class before he would attend his behavior management course again. Luke called his mom that evening and told her all about his first day at school. As he spoke to his mom, he realized that his vocation truly was working with students with disabilities.

The Next Day

The next morning, Luke walked into Mr. Robert's classroom, and a few of the students in class greeted him. This made Luke feel good. He hung up his coat and briefly spoke to Mr. Roberts about his schedule. Mr. Roberts asked him to stand by the classroom door to monitor the hallway until class began. When the bell rang for class to start, it was time for English language arts (ELA). Luke handed out a worksheet on inferences that the students would be completing during their class period. Mr. Roberts gave a brief review lesson on the topic and broke the students into a few small groups to complete the worksheet together. Mr. Roberts looked at Luke as if to remind him to keep an eye on Sarah for signs of her anxiety. Luke sat down to work with a small group directly across from Sarah's group.

At first, she seemed okay working with her groupmates, but as they started asking her questions, Luke could see her quieting down and retreating into herself. Soon, Sarah was not responding at all to her groupmates' comments or questions. Luke quietly got up and made his way over to her table. He pulled up a chair next to her, greeting the members of the group, and quietly asked her if she was okay. Sarah did not respond. It was like she was frozen. Luke wrote on her paper, "Let's go work at the back table." They both got up and walked to the back of the room and sat down at a kidney-shaped table. Using a calm demeanor,

Luke made small talk with her without putting any real social demands on her. He was trying to establish a connection between them, or at least a little bit of trust. Luke made a few jokes to ease some of her stress.

Sarah did not say very much, but after a minute or two, she began completing her assignment. Luke watched as she completed it, praising her for her correct responses. He even managed to get a smile out of her. When she completed the worksheet, Luke suggested they return to her small group, which they did, and soon after, Mr. Roberts began to get the class's attention.

"Nicely done, everyone!" he exclaimed. "Let's take a look at how you did with these inferences." Mr. Roberts proceeded to call on students who raised their hands to answer a question. Sarah just sat there quietly but did not raise her hand to be called on.

"You got all the answers correct," Luke commented to her. "Why don't you raise your hand?" he suggested. Sheepishly, Sarah raised her hand to answer the next question. Mr. Roberts called on her, and she responded correctly. "See how smart you are," Luke said to her. Sarah grinned.

After class, the students went out to the playground for a break. Luke knew he was responsible for monitoring them while they were outside. As he walked out the back door to the playground, Mr. Roberts touched his arm and commented, "Nice job, Luke. I think Sarah did much better today because of you." Luke looked relieved. "I sure hope so, Mr. Roberts. I just want her to feel better about being here."

Questions:

1. Explain Luke's new job as a paraprofessional. Why might the hiring process and his job as a paraprofessional be a good fit for Luke?
2. Who is Mr. Roberts? In what type of special education classroom does he teach? How many students are in his class?
3. What are some of the duties of a paraprofessional that Mr. Roberts explained to Luke?
4. Mr. Roberts also explained that there were duties he could not perform as a paraprofessional in their state. List three of these.
5. Who is Sarah? Why did she need extra help from Luke?
6. Discuss what Luke did to assist Sarah when she began demonstrating anxiety in her small group. Was he successful?

7 Do you think Luke's part-time job being a special education paraprofessional will give him additional skills that he can use when he becomes a special education teacher? Why or why not?

Challenge: Research the responsibilities of a paraprofessional in your state. Make a comparative list of how their responsibilities are similar and different from the ones indicated in this case study.

Teaching Across Student Populations

Alyssa Blasko, PhD, BCBA

Mr. Gabriel Martinez is a fourth-year learning support teacher at Los Lunas School District. Specifically, Gabriel teaches at Sunset Middle School, a grade 6–8 school of almost eight hundred students. Gabriel is a bilingual teacher and speaks English and Spanish fluently. In his role, Gabriel teaches sixth-grade learning support classes and manages a caseload of twenty-seven students. Despite teaching primarily sixth-grade special education classes, Gabriel keeps each student assigned to his caseload for all three middle school years. Administrators at Sunset Middle School structure caseloads in this manner for consistent, meaningful, and collaborative relationships between teachers and families.

Transition Meetings

In the springtime, Gabriel's teaching responsibilities include helping transition elementary school students to middle school. Gabriel meets with fifth graders and their families transitioning to Sunset Middle School every spring. Gabriel holds these meetings with the students, families, and the fifth-grade special education teachers to achieve a smooth transition to middle school. This is one of the responsibilities that Gabriel loves most! The transition to middle school can seem daunting for students and families, and he is grateful for this opportunity to put some of their fears at ease. The middle school environment has increased demands and challenges that often require conversations with families to determine how to address them proactively. For example, students have a locker where they will independently store their belongings and bring them to each class. Further, students follow a bell schedule and move between classes and teachers.

Regarding Sunset Middle School, one significant difference from elementary school is how special education services are delivered. At Sunset, students receive special education services as a class that meets for one period every day during the electives block. This means that students receiving special education services cannot take an elective (e.g., art, music, robotics) at the school. While the special education support block has shown to be incredibly effective, it's never easy to inform children that they cannot take an elective.

Transition Meeting of Mateo Montoya

One of Gabriel's transition meetings was with Mateo Montoya (a fifth grader), his family, and his current special education teacher (Note: Mateo was introduced in the culturally and linguistically diverse exceptional (CLDE) learners case study, chapter 4, p. 31). Mateo will be an incoming sixth grader on Gabriel's caseload and has a specific learning disability (SLD). Mateo is a bilingual student who is fluent in English and Spanish. Furthermore, Mateo and his family have been living in Los Lunas, outside of Albuquerque, New Mexico, for three generations. In this transition meeting, Gabriel was conflicted about proactively addressing Mateo's family's concerns. Gabriel and the family spoke primarily in English throughout the meeting; however, the parents occasionally switched to Spanish when explaining complex concerns. Gabriel learned the following about Mateo.

- **Strengths:** Mateo's biggest strengths are his creativity and interest in collaborating with peers. He participates in an after-school robotics club, a gamers club, and other creative activities like photography.
- **Middle School Hopes:** Mateo deeply desires to enroll in computer and art classes as his sixth-grade electives. He also wants to participate in the middle school robotics and skateboarding clubs.
- **Special Education Identification and Services:** Mateo has been receiving special education services for just over one school year. He originally received special education services for reading and writing. A few weeks before this meeting, Mateo was exited from

writing services, and his IEP was revised to allow him to receive reading services only.
- **Parental Concerns:** Mateo's parents are concerned about the structure of special education services at Sunset Middle School. As the special education class is during electives, they are worried that losing a potential robotics or art class will isolate Mateo from his general education peers. Further, they worry how removing robotics or art will impact Mateo's school performance, as those are his biggest motivators. The parents' general concerns about transitioning to a much larger school are underlying all these concerns.

As Gabriel sat across the table from Mateo and his parents, he realized he had answers to only *some* of their questions, hopes, and concerns. Mateo remembered the critical advice from his mentor teacher, "It is okay to tell a family that you will do research and get back to them. You do not need to supply an answer on the spot to everything." With that advice in mind, Gabriel provided the following responses and action items.

- **Shadow Day:** Gabriel suggested that the team sign Mateo up for a shadow day at the middle school before the school year ends. Gabriel shared with the family that this is a unique opportunity for fifth graders to walk a day in the life of a current sixth grader. Gabriel will attend the special education and general education classes with a sixth grader on this day. Mateo and his family immediately agreed to the shadow day and completed the signup paperwork at the meeting.
- **Summer Transition Day:** Gabriel shared with the team that the school hosts a summer transition day for all special education students once fall schedules are created. On this transition day, Mateo would take a middle school tour, learn how to open his assigned locker, and walk the routes in the hallway from each class. The school district has not yet sent the invitation home to families, so Mateo's parents did not know this opportunity exists. Mateo was ecstatic that he would get his locker ahead of the first day of school and would look out for the invitation.
- **After-School Clubs:** Gabriel assured Mateo and his family that he could sign up for clubs the first week of school. Mateo smiled from ear to ear and shared how much he could not wait to make new friends and show them his robotics skills.

- **Class Schedule and Electives:** Gabriel approached the conversation about class schedule and electives delicately as he knew in his mind that he did not have all the answers. He did restate to the family that the special education learning support class happens simultaneously as electives. Gabriel shared with the family that he wants to talk to his middle school team and do more research to provide a well-rounded answer and potential options that would best address their concerns for Mateo. Gabriel shared that much of the scheduling occurs with administrators, which prevents him from providing more details or ideas. The family respected Gabriel's response and dedication to finding a potential solution, as this was their biggest concern.

As Gabriel is in his fourth year as a teacher, he is constantly growing and educating himself on how to best support his students. Gabriel met with his mentor teacher, Alexandra, to debrief about Mateo. In the meeting, Alexandra commended Gabriel for how he held the meeting and his responses to the parents. Alexandra highlighted that some of his suggestions were culturally responsive practices and are effective for working with students in Los Lunas Public Schools. Alexandra even challenged Gabriel to take a culturally responsive approach to the rest of the challenges and questions surrounding Mateo's transition to middle school. Gabriel looked confused as he tried to recall what culturally responsive practices were from his teaching preparation program. Alexandra caught on to Gabriel's confusion and asked if he needed more information. Gabriel sighed in relief at her openness to teach him and nodded.

Culturally Responsive Teaching

Alexandra began her mini-lesson on culturally responsive teaching (CRT), and culturally responsive practices. Alexandra shared that Gabriel probably did not realize he was already implementing culturally responsive practices, as they work in a culturally diverse school where most teachers are from the same background as the students. Their "normal" teaching or problem solving is often culturally responsive in their positions. Gabriel learned that CRT has a range of definitions, as many researchers and teams define it differently; however, CRT broadly refers to leveraging a student's background (culture, language, etc.) as a resource in the classroom to create interactive and innovative ways to deliver instruction. She provided some examples from his meeting to prove her point. She explained how Gabriel started transitioning with a family/team meeting where the parents could speak in either Spanish or English to promote participation, which is a core part of the family's involvement in CRT. Alexandra highlighted Gabriel's approach of allowing the parents a voice in the meeting and providing additional resources (e.g., shadow day and summer transition day) to prepare Mateo's parents to be the best advocates for their child.

Alexandra told Gabriel that a large misconception is that culturally responsive teaching is different from good teaching. Gabriel was perplexed by this statement. Alexandra went on to share that *good teaching is culturally responsive*. She elaborated that Gabriel's teaching approach is also culturally responsive. Alexandra gave examples from where she observed Gabriel providing culturally responsive teaching a few weeks ago. She shared how Gabriel holds high expectations for all students in his classroom, utilizes diverse resources in his lessons, and follows a child-centered instructional approach. Alexandra complimented Gabriel for allowing choice, active participation, and hands-on learning opportunities rooted in prior background knowledge, emphasizing that these examples of his teaching are culturally responsive practices. Gabriel was pleased to learn that his current practices align with being a culturally responsive teacher.

Culturally Responsive Teaching and Mateo's Transition to Middle School

Gabriel brought back the conversation to Mateo and the family's concern about having his special education services simultaneously with the electives. Alexandra and Gabriel reviewed Mateo's progress monitoring data to determine where he currently stands in reading skills. Alexandra took her time to read over all the data and brainstormed three potential scenarios for Mateo's situation. Before sharing her scenarios, she reminded Gabriel that Mateo will always have access to the robotics club and any other clubs, regardless of the family's choice.

- **Scenario 1:** Due to Mateo's higher scores, he may be able to participate in the special education class at the start of the year and reevaluate progress in January. Alexandra shared that Mateo may be performing in reading at a rate where his IEP could be revised to receive sufficient accommodations and support in the general education setting to provide adequate progress. In this scenario, Mateo would no longer have to attend the special education class and could attend an elective for the second half of the school year. This scenario would provide him the opportunity to participate in an elective; however, it does not provide access to electives immediately.

- **Scenario 2:** Alexandra shared how middle school is a different challenge and experience for many students transitioning from elementary school. She gave examples of the new demands of managing your books at a locker, knowing your schedule, transitioning from class to class, and learning complex concepts, which can create a situation where Mateo needs the dedicated special education class more than ever. Alexandra suggested they enroll Mateo in the special education class and schedule an IEP team meeting a few weeks into the school year to check in. This scenario would provide the scheduled special education services that Mateo might need as content complexity increases and executive functioning demands are more challenging; however, it does not provide access to electives immediately. This scenario allows Mateo to try middle school with the full scale of support and allows him to have a check-in meeting to share his experience and perspective.
- **Scenario 3:** Alexandra shared how Sunset Middle School has had students who did not attend the special education class every school day, and Mateo could split the class period. She explained how Mateo could attend the special education class three days a week and the elective class two days a week. This scenario would allow access to special education services and highly motivating electives; however, Mateo would have a more challenging workload in balancing both courses.

Gabriel was excited to consider these scenarios and brainstorm other options before meeting with Mateo and his family again. He walked away from his meeting with Alexandra with an overwhelming affirmation that education is not a one-size-fits-all approach. Gabriel now recognizes that incorporating culturally responsive practices makes him a stronger teacher for himself and his students.

Questions:

1. What is a culturally responsive practice? What culturally responsive practices did Gabriel unknowingly incorporate into his initial meeting with Mateo and his family?
2. What were Mateo's parents' most significant concerns with transitioning to middle school? Was Gabriel successful in addressing all their concerns during the meeting?
3. Based on the three scenarios, when considering electives for Mateo, presented in the case study, which scenario would you select? Provide a rationale for your choice.
4. Generate a fourth scenario/option for Mateo that addresses the conflict between the special education class and electives. Provide a rationale for your choice.

Challenge: A core component of culturally responsive practices is incorporating students' backgrounds and interests into the classroom. If Mateo decides to attend Gabriel's special education classroom, how could Gabriel design lessons based on his background and interests? Provide one example of a type of lesson Gabriel can design. Discuss what the lesson might include.

Challenge: Mateo recently completed his shadow day and is more excited than ever about middle school; however, he is still unsure about missing out on electives to accommodate his special education class. Gabriel scheduled a debrief meeting with Gabriel and his family to hear about Mateo's experience. Put yourself in Gabriel's shoes and generate five questions you want to ask Mateo at the start of the meeting to understand his shadow day experience. Your questions should elicit responses from Mateo that cover any of the following topics: rigor of middle school classes, hands-on learning activities in the general education classes, opportunities to use Spanish and English in classes, diverse resources across classes, and special education class reflection. Be sure your questions for Mateo are in student-friendly language.

Index

Bold page numbers indicate tables.

A

Aaron
- alternative assessment and 145
- attention deficit hyperactivity disorder (ADHD) 16–19
- diagnosis 18
- elementary school 17
- Every Student Succeeds Act (ESSA) 145
- individualized education programs (IEPs) 18–19
- learning support 19
- middle school 17–18
- supports for 18–19

academic achievement
- Anna 209
- Darius 6
- Eva 129
- Gabriella 57
- Gia 105
- gifted and talented students 53
- IEPs 182
- intellectual disability 61–2
- Jackson 96
- Jonathan 123, 125
- learning disabilities, students with 65–6
- Markeith 194
- Tyrese 61–2

accommodations 10, 19, 34, 69, 96, 97, 106–7, 110–11, 135–6, 142, 143–5, 153–4, 157, 162, 164, 173, 176–8, **188–9**, 199, 200, 205, 210–11, 214, 217, 272

adaptations 84, 85, 96, 177, 205
adaptive behavior(s) 59, 230
adaptive skills 102
adaptive writing 8
adverse childhood experiences (ACEs) 121
advocates, educational 197, 199
after-school clubs 269
aides, one-on-one 11, 13, **13**

Alex
- epilepsy 82–5
- home-school collaboration 256–7
- other health impairment (OHI) 81–5
- secondary transition planning 216–22

Allie
- deaf-blindness 99–104
- least restrictive environment (LRE) 173

alternate teaching/alternative teaching 253
amblyopia 107–8
American sign language (ASL) 95
Anna, specially designed instruction (SDI) 203–9
annual goals 183–6
articulation disorders 116–19
assessment
- in diagnostic process 225
- Markeith 195
- state testing requirements, ESSA and 143–4

Index

transition planning inventory 218
traumatic brain injury 135
assistive technology
   adaptive writing 8
   assessment for 11
   augmentative and alternative communication (AAC) devices 8
   autism spectrum disorder (ASD) 9–13
   benefits 3
   Chaya 9–13
   classifications 3
   cochlear implants 7–8
   communication 88
   Darius 4–9
   defined 3
   examples 3
   funding 3
   hearing 7–8
   mobility 8
   pencil grips 8
   posterior walkers 8
   slant boards 8
   timers, visual 13
   weighted vests 12–13
athletics, visual impairment and 111–12
attention
   difficulty maintaining 15
   lack of groupwork 257
   Markeith 73
   personal 11
   student's, obtaining 178
   supports helping 19
   traumatic brain injury 131, 135
attention deficit hyperactivity disorder (ADHD)
   Aaron 16–19
   classroom management 10
   defined 15
   diagnosis 18
   early childhood 16–17
   supports for students 18–19
   types of 15

augmentative and alternative communication (AAC) devices 3, 8, 78, 194–5
collaboration, team 236
Picture Exchange Communication System (PECS) 11–12
Proloquo 2Go 27
autism spectrum disorder (ASD)
   assistive technology 9–13
   behavior, communication issues and 27
   Chaya 9–13
   classroom management 10–11
   defined 21
   early childhood 22–3, 26
   early intervention (EI) 26
   one-on-one aides 11, 13
   picture schedules 12
   Proloquo 2Go communication app 27
   Rahul 22–5
   reinforcement of good behavior 28–9
   social skills 24
   support needs 21
   symptoms 21
   timers, visual 13
   token boards 28
   transitions 13
   Trevor 25–9
   weighted vests 12–13

B
behavior(s)
   adaptive 59, 230
   adverse childhood experiences (ACEs) and 122
   annual goals 183–6
   anxious 51
   autism spectrum disorder (ASD) 21
   Check-In, Check-Out 48
   communication difficulties and 27
   due process 155–6, 162–8, **165**

Index

early intervention and 223
emotional disturbance (ED) 45–6, 47–8, 129–30
epilepsy and 82–3
expectations of 248
externalizing behaviors 45, 247–8
home-school collaboration 256, 258, 259
hyperactivity 128–9
impulsivity 19
internalizing behaviors 45–6, 247–8
manifestation determination and 151–4
mediation and 157–62
paraprofessionals and 261, 262, 263
reinforcement of good behavior 28–9, 48, **49,** 194, 204
repetitive 21
specially designed instruction (SDI) 210–15
team collaboration and 236
Vineland Adaptive Rating Scale 239, 242
blindness
   deaf-blindness 93, 98–104
   multiple disabilities and 76
   visual impairment including blindness 93

C

Callie, confidentiality of student's information 146–8
captioned media 97
caseload description 10–11
case management **186–7,** 186–90, **188–9**
case studies
   benefits of for teacher preparation students 2
   Characteristics Matrix xii, xvii, **xviii–xix**
   Crosswalk Table xxi, **xxii–xxiii**
   disability categories covered xi–xii
   language used in 2
   processes and procedures covered xii
   purpose xi
   questions related to xii–xiii
cerebral palsy (CP) 87–91
   Darius 4–9
Characteristics Matrix xii, xvii, **xviii–xix**
Chaya
   assistive technology 9–13
   autism spectrum disorder (ASD) 9–13
   classroom management 10–11
   one-on-one aides 11, 13
   picture schedules 12
   teamwork by teachers 10–11
   transitions 13
   weighted vests 12–13
Check-In, Check-Out 48, **49**
choice boards 28
city life, visual impairment and 112
classroom management 10–11
cochlear implants 7–8, 95
cognitive impairments 5, 26–7, 37, 41, 65, 131, 143, 238
collaboration 199
   co-teaching 10–11, 246–54
   defined 245
   home-school 255–60
   transdisciplinary practice 233–6
communication
   assistive technology 88
   augmentative and alternative communication (AAC)
   multiple disabilities 76–8
   Proloquo2Go 27
community-based instruction 33, 59, 190, 201
confidentiality, FERPA and 142, 145–8
conflict resolution

due process 155-6, 163-8, **165**
mediation 155
consultation 10-11, 251-2
co-teaching 10-11, 245-54
  models 251, 252-3
Crosswalk Table xii, xxi, **xxii-xxiii**
culturally and linguistically diverse
    exceptional learners (CLDE)
  disabilities, learners with 31
  diversity of cultures 31
  early childhood 32-3
  Mateo 32-5, 270-3
  school 33-5
culturally responsive teaching (CRT)
  270-3

D
daily living skills 3, 5-6, 7, 59, 194, 218, 239
Darius
  assistive technology 4-9
  least restrictive environment (LRE) 173
  school 5-6
  strengths and challenges 6
  support needs 7
deaf-blindness 93, 98-104
deafness 93-8
delayed development *see* developmental delay
developmental delay
  defined 37
  diagnosis 41
  early intervention (EI) 41-2
  Hao 38-42
  subtle differences noticed 39-41
  symptoms 37
  types of 37
diagnosis
  Aaron 18
  attention deficit hyperactivity
    disorder (ADHD) 18

cerebral palsy (CP) 4-5
Darius 4-5
developmental delay 41
families, responses to disability
  diagnosis 237-43
process for 223, 224-31
disability
  families, responses to disability
    diagnosis 237-43
  multiple disabilities (MD)
dispute resolution
  due process 155-6, 163-8, **165**
  mediation 155, 157-62
diversity
  culturally and linguistically diverse
    exceptional learners (CLDE) 31
  culturally responsive teaching (CRT)
    270-3
drift 252
due process 155-6
  complaint filing 163-4
  decision 166-7
  hearing 164-6, **165**
  impact of 168
  implementation and follow-up
    167-8
  unsuccessful mediation leading to
    162-3
  waiting for decision 166

E
early childhood
  Alex (epilepsy) 82
  Anna (learning disabilities) 67-8
  attention deficit hyperactivity
    disorder (ADHD) 16-17
  autism spectrum disorder (ASD) 10,
    22-3, 26
  culturally and linguistically diverse
    exceptional learners (CLDE)
    32-3
  deafness 95-6

developmental delay 38–42
emotional disturbance (ED) 46–8
Eva (trauma-informed practice) 127–9
gifted and talented students 55–6
Lauren (traumatic brain injury) 132–3
Mahsumah (multiple disabilities) 76
Sara (speech and language impairment) 116–17
special education service delivery 231–7
early intervention (EI)
autism spectrum disorder (ASD) 10, 26
cerebral palsy (CP) 90–1
deaf-blindness 101–3
deafness 95–6
developmental delay 41–2
diagnostic process 225–6
evaluation 240–1
educational advocates 197, 199
electives 268, 269, 272, 273
elementary school
Aaron (ADHD) 17
Alex (epilepsy) 82, 84
case management **186–7**, 186–90, **188–9**
Chaya (ASD) 10
confidentiality of students' information 145–8
Darius (ASD) 7
Eva (trauma-informed practice) 128–9
Gabriella (gifted and talented) 54, 56–7
gifted and talented students 56–7
home-school collaboration 256
IEP meetings 191–7
Jackson (deafness) 96
Jonathan (trauma-informed practice) 123–6

manifestation determination 151–4
Mateo (CLDE) 33–4
Sarah (ED) 51
Trevor (ASD) 151–4
eligibility
504 plans/agreements 176–7
special education services 71–2, 117, 129
emotional disturbance (ED)
behaviors displayed 45–6
characteristics of 45
Check-In, Check-Out 48, **49**
defined 45
early childhood 46–8
Eva 129
Matthew 46–50, **49**
Sarah 50–2
school 51–2
emotional regulation 129
emotional support teachers 129
enrichment for gifted and talented students 54, 56, 57, 129
epilepsy 82–5
Eva
early childhood 127–9
school 128–9
trauma-informed practice 127–30
evaluation
in diagnostic process 225
early intervention 240–1
Every Student Succeeds Act (ESSA) 141–2
state testing requirements 143–4
executive function 131, 272
expressive language 11
externalizing behaviors 45, 247–8

F
families
dynamics of 123–6
responses to disability diagnosis 237–43

Family Educational Privacy Rights and Education Act (FERPA) 142, 145–8
fetal alcohol syndrome (FAS) 72, 98, 191
fine motor skills 5, 6, 8, 24, 37, 195, 235
First-Then boards 194
504 plans/agreements
   accommodations 106–7, 177–8
   components of 178
   eligibility 176–7
   explanation of to parents 174–9
   role and purpose 173–4, 176
free and appropriate public education (FAPE) 150
functional living skills 7, 11, 59, 195
funding for assistive technology 3

G
Gabriella, gifted and talented student 53–7
general education teachers 135
   caseload and teamwork 10–11
   collaboration with 186, 187, **188, 189**
   co-teaching with 245–55
   504 plans/agreements 176
   IEPs and 181, 182, 193
   knowledge of special education 139
Gia
   504 plans/agreements 106–7, 179
   hearing impairment 104–7
gifted and talented students
   characteristics of 53
   early childhood 54, 55–6
   Eva 129
   Gabriella 53–7
   reading comprehension 56
gross motor skills 37, 235

H
Hao
   developmental delay 38–42

early intervention (EI) 41–2
   subtle differences noticed 39–41
hearing, assistive technology and 7–8
hearing impairment 93, 104–7
hearing screening 5, 95, 230
high school
   Alex (epilepsy) 84–5
   IEP meeting 197–202
   transition planning 216–22
home-school collaboration 255–60
hyperactivity 128
   see also attention deficit hyperactivity disorder (ADHD)

I
identification
   of gifted and talented students 57
   letter 69
   for special education 268–9
IEP meetings *see* individualized education programs (IEPs)
impulsivity 19, 134
inattention 15
   see also attention deficit hyperactivity disorder (ADHD)
inclusion
   concept of 169
   full 170, 172
   lack of leading to conflict 157
inclusive practice
   consultation 10–11, 251–2
   co-teaching 10–11, 245–54
   culturally responsive teaching (CRT) 270–3
   defined 245
   home-school collaboration 255–60
   paraprofessionals 232, 261–7
individualized education programs (IEPs)
   Aaron (ADHD) 18–19
   Alex (epilepsy) 84
   annual goals 183–6, 193–4

assistive technology 4
attention deficit hyperactivity
  disorder (ADHD) 18–19
cerebral palsy (CP) 90, 91
deaf-blindness 102
due process, meetings after 167
general education teachers 182
importance of 182
least restrictive environment (LRE)
  discussion 169–73
mandatory components 182
manifestation determination 153
Markeith (multiple disabilities)
  191–7
meetings 167, 169, 191–202
preparing for meetings 169,
  191–2
Rahul (ASD) 197–202
Sara (speech and language
  impairment) 117–18
special education teachers 182
specially designed instruction (SDI)
  205–9
teams for 181
transdisciplinary practice 235
transition planning 216–22
traumatic brain injury 135–7
individualized family service plans
  (IFSPs) 101, 241–2
Individuals with Disabilities Education
  Act (IDEA) 9, 18, 71, 87, 117,
  142, 149–54, 156, 175–6, 216
instructional assistants 200
intellectual disability 59–63
intelligence quotient (IQ) 23, 27, 59,
  129, 143
internalizing behaviors 45–6, 247–8
interpreters 97, 197, 198
interventions
  Check-In, Check-Out 48
  Darius (ASD) 5–6
  delayed development 37

Mateo, reading and writing 34
Trevor (ASD) 27–8
see also early intervention (EI)

J
Jackson, deafness 94–8
Jalen, mediation 157–62
Jonathan
  Family Educational Privacy Rights
    and Education Act (FERPA)
    148
  schedules 123–5
  school 125–6
  trauma informed practice 121–30

K
Kerry 143–5

L
language
  disorders 115–19
  gifted and talented students 55–6
  learning disabilities and 67
  receptive/expressive skills 11
  written 19, 65, 67, 68–9, 117
Lauren
  least restrictive environment (LRE)
    173
  traumatic brain injury 132–7
learning disabilities 65–70
learning support
  Aaron 19
  Alex 84, 220
  Anna 67, 69
  attention deficit hyperactivity
    disorder (ADHD) 19
  case management **186–7,** 186–90,
    188–9
  culturally responsive teaching (CRT)
    270–3
  Sam 171–2
  Tyrese 61

least restrictive environment (LRE) 99, 150, 169–73
legislation
   Every Student Succeeds Act (ESSA) 141–2, 143–4
   Family Educational Privacy Rights and Education Act (FERPA) 142, 145–8
   Individuals with Disabilities Education Act (IDEA) 71, 87, 117, 142, 149–54
   Section 504 of the Rehabilitation Act of 1973 173–80
   state testing requirements 143–4
Los Lunas, New Mexico 36

M

Mahsumah
   alternative assessment and 145
   Every Student Succeeds Act (ESSA) 145
   multiple disabilities 75–9
manifestation determination 150, 151–4
Markeith
   assessment 195
   individualized education program (IEP) meeting 191–7
   multiple disabilities 72–5
Mateo
   culturally and linguistically diverse exceptional learners (CLDE) 32–5
   electives 268, 269, 272, 273
   transition to middle school 268–73
Matthew
   Check-In, Check-Out 48, **49**
   emotional disturbance (ED) 46–50, **49**
   point cards 211, **212,** 213
   school 47–8, **49**
   specially designed instruction (SDI) 210–15
Max
   athletics 111–12
   early years 108–10
   504 plans/agreements 110–11, 179
   school 110– 111
   visual impairment 108–13
mediation
   defined 155
   end of session agreement 160
   follow-up to session 160–1
   Jalen 157–62
   preparation for 158
   session 158–60
   unsuccessful example leading to due process 162
medication 18, 83, 84, 85, 90, 257
mental health 46, 121, 122, 264
Michael
   cerebral palsy (CP) 88–91
   early childhood special education service delivery 232
   transdisciplinary practice 236
middle school
   Aaron (ADHD) 17–18
   Alex (epilepsy) 84–5
   deafness 96–7
   Eva (trauma-informed practice) 129–30
   Jackson (deafness) 96–7
   Mateo (CLDE) 34–5
   Sarah (ED) 51
   transition to 96–7, 267–73
mobility
   assistive technology 8
   posterior walkers 8
modifications 10, 83, 110, 155, 157, 162, 163, 182, **188,** 192, 199, 200, 215
motor skills
   fine 6, 8, 24, 37, 195, 235
   gross 37, 235

multidisciplinary teams 18–19, 181, 225
multiple disabilities (MD) 71–9
multi-tiered system of supports (MTSS) 48

N
neurotypical children 26, 176

O
observation 18, 40, 178, 193, 194, 195, 239
occupational therapists 195
   diagnostic process 227–8, 229
   individualized family service plans (IFSPs) 242
   transdisciplinary practice 235
occupational therapy 195
   cerebral palsy 90
Office of Vocational Rehabilitation (OVR) 201, 202
one-on-one aides 11, 13
One Teach, One Assist 252
One Teach, One Observe 252
organization 17, 18, 19, 131, 178
orthopedic impairment (OI) 87–91
other health impairment (OHI)
   Alex 81–5
   attention deficit hyperactivity disorder (ADHD) 18
   defined 81
   epilepsy 82–5

P
parallel teaching 253
paraprofessionals 232, 261–7
parents
   dynamics between 123–6
   home-school collaboration 255–60
   support groups for 102
pencil grips 8
perception 65, 68–9, 108, 110, 112, 204, 207

person-centered planning 218
physical therapists 195
   diagnostic process 228–9
   transdisciplinary practice 235
physical therapy 195
   cerebral palsy 91
Picture Exchange Communication System (PECS) 11, 14
picture schedules 12
placement 46, 59, 94, 156, 170–1
point cards/sheets 48, **49**, 211, **212**, 213
positive reinforcement 10, 263
posterior walkers 8
post-secondary goals 219–21
preschool
   Allie (deaf-blindess) 102–3
   Michael (cerebral palsy) 90
present levels 184, 185
problem-solving 5, 53
procedural safeguards 150–4
processing deficits 65
progress monitoring 195
Proloquo2Go 27

Q
questionnaires 192

R
Rahul
   autism spectrum disorder (ASD) 22–5
   home-school collaboration 257–8
   individualized education program (IEP) meeting 197–202
   student advocacy 199–200
   transition planning 200–1
reading
   Anna (learning disabilities) 67–9
   gifted and talented students 56
   strategy/ies 69, 207, 208–9
receptive language 11
regression 21, 26, 163, 215

Rehabilitation Act of 1973, Section 504 142
504 plans/agreements 173–80
reinforcement
    Check-In, Check-Out 48, **49**
    First-Then boards 194
    of good behavior 28–9, 48, **49,** 194
related services 90, 101, 155, 173, 181, 182
repetitive behavior 21
residential schools/facilities 21, 94, 99, 170
routines 10, 25, 73, 85, 124, 152, 232, 234, 235, 264

S
Sara
    alternative assessment and 145
    Every Student Succeeds Act (ESSA) 145
    individualized education program (IEP) 117–18
    speech and language impairment 115–19
Sarah
    emotional disturbance (ED) 50–2
    paraprofessionals, working with 264–6
schedules 123–5
school
    Alex (epilepsy) 83–5
    autism spectrum disorder (ASD) 23–4
    culturally and linguistically diverse exceptional learners (CLDE) 33–5
    Darius 5–6
    emotional disturbance (ED) 51–2
    Gia 105–7
    gifted and talented students 54–7
    hearing impairment 105–7
    intellectual disability 61–2
    Jonathan 125–6
    learning disabilities 67–8
    Mahsumah (multiple disabilities) 76
    Matthew 47–8, **49**
    multiple disabilities 73–4
    Trevor 26–9
    Tyrese 61–2
    visual impairment 110–11
school psychologists 7, 18, 34, 117, 135, 158, 164, 168, 171, 181, 193, 225, 229
secondary transition planning 216–22
Section 504 of the Rehabilitation Act of 1973, 504 plans/agreements 142, 173–80
self-care skills 59
self-contained classrooms/schools 5, 21, 59, 90, 96, 99, 151, 191, 231, 262, 264
self-injurious behavior 129
sensory impairments
    deaf-blindness 93, 98–104
    deafness 93, 93, 93–8
    hearing impairment 93, 104–7
    visual impairment 107–13
    visual impairment including blindness 93
shadow days 269
sign language interpreters 97
slant boards 8
social life and skills
    autism spectrum disorder (ASD) 24
    traumatic brain injury 136
special education service delivery 231–7
special education services
    attention deficit hyperactivity disorder (ADHD) 18
    early childhood 231–7
    eligibility for 71–2, 117, 129
special education teachers 10–11
    IEPs and 182
specially designed instruction (SDI)

    Anna 203–9
    Matthew 210–15
    revising 210–15
speech and language pathologists 194–5
    individualized family service plans (IFSPs) 242
    transdisciplinary practice 235
speech and language therapy 194
speech and/or language impairment (SLI) 73, 115–19
speech disorders 115–19
speech-language pathologist in diagnostic process 226–7
speech-to-text 97
sports, visual impairment and 111–12
state testing requirements, ESSA and 143–4
station teaching 253
strabismus 108, 109
strategy/ies
    articulation, improving 118
    classroom management 10
    communication 236
    conflict resolution 221
    deaf-blindness 103
    home-based 18
    impulsivity, decreasing 19
    letter identification 69
    memory and concentration 84
    prewriting 19, 69
    reading and writing 69, 207, 208–9
    self-regulation 167–8
    speech and language impairment 118
    tactile learning 103
student, environment, tasks, tools (SETT) framework 7
student advocacy 199–200
summer transition days 269

T

tactile learning strategies 103
teacher preparation faculty, case studies, use of xiii
teachers
    co-teaching 10–11, 245–54
    deaf students 96–7
    emotional support 129
    team teaching 253
    see also general education teachers
team decision making 236
    see also collaboration; co-teaching
team teaching 253
teamwork 10–11
text-to-speech 27, 177, 208
timers, visual 13
token boards 28
token economy 28
transdisciplinary practice 233–6
transitions
    autism spectrum disorder (ASD) 13
    Chaya 13
    to middle school 96–7, 267–73
    planning 200–1, 216–22, 267–73
    secondary 216–22
trauma informed practice 121–30
traumatic brain injury 131–7
Trevor
    autism spectrum disorder (ASD) 25–9
    behavior, communication issues and 27
    manifestation determination 151–4
    Proloquo2Go communication app 27
    reinforcement of good behavior 28–9
    school 26–9
Tyrese
    diagnostic process 224–31
    intellectual disability 59–63

V

Vineland Adaptive Rating Scale 239, 242
visual aids
　point cards/sheets 48, **49,** 211, **212,** 213
　timers 13
　token boards 28
visual impairment 107–13
　including blindness 93
vocational programs/schools 24, 201
Voice 4U 8

W

walkers, posterior 8
weighted vests 12–13
writing
　adaptive 8
　Anna (learning disabilities) 67–9
　learning disabilities and 67
　pencil grips 8
　slant boards 8
written language 19, 65, 67, 68–9, 117

About the Authors

Dr. Mary A. Houser received a BFA in related arts from Kutztown University of Pennsylvania, an MAT in special education from the College of New Jersey, and an EdD in educational leadership from Fayetteville State University. She is currently a (full) professor of special education at West Chester University of Pennsylvania. She teaches both undergraduate and graduate courses in foundations of special education, behavior management, autism spectrum disorder (ASD), multiple disabilities, and family systems. Dr. Houser also provides special education professional development courses to Irish school teachers via the Cork Educational Support Center, Cork, Ireland. Further, she serves as an educational consultant for the American College of Financial Services (King of Prussia, PA) for the Chartered Special Needs Consultant designation program. She taught graduate special education courses for Walden University, where she served as a graduate special curriculum and assessor. In addition, she has taught graduate special education courses and supervised pre-service teachers for Campbell University (NC). Dr. Houser has worked as a learning disabilities specialist and has taught high school special education in both inclusive and self-contained settings to children with various disabilities. Her research interests include families of students with autism spectrum disorders, improving home-school relationships, and special education paraprofessionals.

Dr. Tara S. Guerriero received her PhD from Northwestern University in learning disabilities, with a concentration in cognitive neuroscience. She also received her master of arts degree in learning disabilities and her bachelor of science degree in communication sciences and disorders with a concentration in learning disabilities and a minor in psychology from Northwestern University. She is a (full) professor in the Department of Special Education at West Chester University of Pennsylvania. She teaches at the graduate and undergraduate levels in the areas of foundations of special education, assessment, curriculum and instruction/methodology, literacy, family systems, and communication/language development and assistive technology. Dr. Guerriero was previously a clinician and supervisor in a learning clinic that focused on both the assessment and diagnosis of learning disabilities as well as the remediation of learning disabilities. Her research interests include assessment practices in special education and both assessment and teaching within the areas of mathematics and reading in the field of learning disabilities.

Dr. Colleen E. Commisso is an associate professor in the Department of Special Education at West Chester University. She earned her BS in special education, MS in special education, and supervisory certificate at Bloomsburg University. Her PhD in special education is from Lehigh University. Dr. Commisso spent seven years as a high school special education teacher where she taught special education classes in reading and co-taught multiple subject areas in the general education classroom. Currently Dr. Commisso teaches graduate and undergraduate courses in behavior management, trauma informed practices, and teaching special education at the secondary level. Her research interests include effective instructional practices and hands-on experiences for pre-service teachers, behavior management strategies/interventions, and supporting teachers who have students who have experienced trauma.